# RED IS NOT THE ONLY COLOR

**ASIAN VOICES**
Series Editor: Mark Selden

*Tales of Tibet: Sky Burials, Prayer Wheels, and Wind Horses*
edited and translated by Herbert Batt, foreword by Tsering Shakya
*Comfort Woman: A Filipina's Story of Prostitution and Slavery under the Japanese Military*
by Maria Rosa Henson, introduction by Yuki Tanaka
*Growing Up Untouchable in India: A Dalit Autobiography*
by Vasant Moon, translated by Gail Omvedt, introduction by Eleanor Zelliot
*Japan's Past, Japan's Future: One Historian's Odyssey*
by Ienaga Saburo, translated and introduced by Richard H. Minear
*Rowing the Eternal Sea: The Life of a Minamata Fisherman*
by Oiwa Keibo, narrated by Ogata Masato, translated by Karen Colligan-Taylor
*Unbroken Spirits: Nineteen Years in South Korea's Gulag*
by Suh Sung, translated by Jean Inglis, foreword by James Palais
*Bitter Flowers, Sweet Flowers: East Timor, Indonesia, and the World Community*
edited by Richard Tanter, Mark Selden, and Stephen R. Shalom
*Voicing Concerns: Contemporary Chinese Critical Inquiry*
edited by Gloria Davies, conclusion by Geremie Barmé
*Dear General MacArthur: Letters from the Japanese during the American Occupation*
by Sodei Rinjiro, edited by John Junkerman, foreword by John W. Dower

# RED IS NOT THE ONLY COLOR

## Contemporary Chinese Fiction on Love and Sex between Women, Collected Stories

Edited by
Patricia Sieber

ROWMAN & LITTLEFIELD PUBLISHERS, INC.
*Lanham • Boulder • New York • Oxford*

ROWMAN & LITTLEFIELD PUBLISHERS, INC.

Published in the United States of America
by Rowman & Littlefield Publishers, Inc.
4720 Boston Way, Lanham, Maryland 20706
www.rowmanlittlefield.com

12 Hid's Copse Road, Cumnor Hill, Oxford OX2 9JJ, England



British Library Cataloguing in Publication Information Available

**Library of Congress Cataloging-in-Publication Data**

Red is not the only color : Contemporary Chinese fiction on love and sex between women, collected stories / edited by Patricia Sieber.
p. cm.
Includes bibliographical references and index.
ISBN 0-7425-1137-5 (alk. paper)—ISBN 0-7425-1138-3 (pbk.: alk. paper)
1. Chinese fiction—20th century—History and criticism. 2. Women in literature. I. Title: Contemporary Chinese fiction on love and sex between women, collected stories. II. Sieber, Patricia Angela.

PL2303 .R43 2001
895.1″3509352042—dc21 2001020458

Printed in the United States of America

∞ ™ The paper used in this publication meets the minimum requirements of American National Standard for Information Sciences—Permanence of Paper for Printed Library Materials, ANSI/NISO Z39.48–1992.

*To Rosemarie, Pascal, and Dee*

# Contents

# Acknowledgments

As all books, this one owes many debts to many people. First and foremost, I thank all the authors—Chen Ran, Chen Xue, He An, Hong Ling, Liang Hanyi, Wang Anyi, Wong Bikwan, and Zhang Mei—for agreeing to have their stories translated and published in this volume. Second, I thank all the translators—Kimberly Besio, Naifei Ding, Paola Zamperini, and Jingyuan Zhang—for their work.

Among the authors and the translators, I am particularly indebted to Naifei Ding, Hong Ling, Wong Bikwan, and Jingyuan Zhang. Naifei Ding, together with Wang Ping and Ni Jiazhen, provided the critical impetus for this project. In her own inimitable style, Hong Ling wrote a call for entries, which resulted in He An's submission. Wong Bikwan as well as Wong Nimyan generously shared books and reviews. Jingyuan Zhang brought stories and addresses to my attention, contributed to three of the biographies, solved translation puzzles, and above all, never lost faith in the project.

The enthusiasm of Ines Rieder and Frederique Delacoste helped get the project underway. Dee Elling's love and generosity nourished it in its gestation. Ho Chao-ti's hospitality nudged it along. The encouragement of several OSU colleagues, including Todd Kays, Bill Tyler, and Steven Yao, facilitated its transition into print.

Earlier drafts of the introduction benefited from the observations of a number of individuals, including Xiaomei Chen, Colleen Lye, Diane Furtney, Jeredith Merrin, and Mark Selden. Kirk Denton forwarded many useful bibliographic references. Leo Yip's expert research assistance and timely help with the completion of the manuscript was invaluable.

Leah L. Wong created the thoughtful and inspired cover image. Li Yu and Suhsing Lin graciously helped with its realization.

At Rowman and Littlefield, Mark Selden's critical acumen, attention, and enthusiasm not only shaped the final book in ways large and small but made the editorial process a pleasurable journey of discovery. Susan McEachern's unflagging support brought the project to conclusion.

I thank everyone and hope that the book itself will be a small token of my gratitude.

All stories are translated and printed with the permission of the authors.

Chen Ran. "Pokai." In her *Zhan zai wuren de fengkou*. Kunming: Yunnan renmin chubanshe, 1995.

Chen Xue. "Xunzhao tianshi yishi de chibang." In her *E'nü shu*. Taipei: Huangguang, 1995.

He An. "Ruge de xingban." Unpublished manuscript.

Hong Ling. "Fashao." In her *Yiduan xixuegui liezhuan*. Taipei: Huangguang, 1995.

Liang Hanyi. "Chun." *Lianhe wenxue* 2: 3 (1986): 102–4.

Wang Anyi. "Dixiongmen." *Shouhuo* 4 (1989): 4–30.

Wong Bikwan. "Ta shi nüzi, wo ye shi nüzi." In her *Ta shi nüzi, wo ye shi nüzi*. Taipei: Maitian, 1994.

Zhang Mei. "Jilu." In her *Jihou de aiqing guan*. Beijing: Zuojia chubanshe, 1995.

# 1

# INTRODUCTION

Patricia Sieber

What part does intimacy between women play in shaping Chinese social and political worlds? And what are the implications of such imaginings in a transnational setting? This anthology represents an attempt to imaginatively answer these questions and explore Chinese female same-sex relations and their broader significance in Chinese as well as English-speaking contexts. Bringing together contemporary literary works from the People's Republic of China (PRC), Hong Kong, and Taiwan, the anthology eschews singular national and ideological affiliations. Instead, the collection examines how various Chinese writers construe the place of female same-sex intimacy in relation to discourses of gender, sexuality, and nationhood.

## A BRIEF HISTORY OF FEMALE SAME-SEX ASSOCIATIONS

Until recently, the history of Chinese women prior to the twentieth century—in as far as they were thought to have a history at all—seemed unremittingly bleak. The shadows of deformed feet, neglected wives, competitive concubines, educationally deprived daughters, and widow suicides loomed so large that all inquiry into historical particulars seemed moot. Now, after two decades of feminist scholarship, the picture appears no longer quite as stark. We now know that history did not simply bypass women, but that women were an integral aspect of the economic, social, cultural, and political functioning of Chinese society.[1] We also know that women wrote admiringly about each other's bound feet;[2] that gentry and merchant wives entered into intimate friendships with each other and with courtesans;[3] that on occasion they encouraged their husbands to take concubines either because they were in love with a particular woman[4] or because they did not want to assume the risks of pregnancy;[5] that daughters were chosen to carry on the literary or medical patrimony;[6] and that, attended by one hundred thousand people, a teenage widow could ascend to heaven after having converted some of the most prominent literati of her day to her brand of mystical Taoism.[7] Further research will undoubtedly alter not just the history of Chinese women but perceptions of Chinese and world history alike.

Yet the twentieth century brought radical transformations in China. The first four decades, in particular, witnessed tremendous changes, most obviously in the realm of family, marriage, and sexuality. Beleaguered by a sense of national inadequacy in the face of Western imperialism, Manchu domination, and Japanese ascendance, Chinese reformers identified the traditional social structure, most notably the disempowered position of the female half of the population, as one of the primary causes for China's political predicament. In addition to other issues, the first generation of feminist reformers such as Qiu Jin (1875–1907) advocated free choice in marriage.[8] Such calls did not go unheeded. Educated urban elites began to form consensual unions rather than submitting to their parents' marital arrangements, creating a conflict often explored in contemporary fiction.[9] In the short-lived but radical revolutionary movement between 1924–1927, women and men in both major parties, the Nationalists (GMD) and the Communists (CCP), drafted language for the new-style marriage. The Nationalist government's new Family Law of 1931 and the Communist Party's 1934 Constitution of the Jiangxi Soviet began the legal consolidation of free-choice monogamous marriage.[10] Eventually, the PRC Marriage Law of 1950, quickly nicknamed "Divorce Law," made divorce available for women, especially in the early years of its promulgation, and particularly for rural women,[11] albeit at great cost.[12]

The increasing availability and normalcy of free-choice marriage and divorce certainly can be understood as a signifier of progress, yet the interaction between modern and traditional forces of history also underscored another set of social relations—namely, that between non-kin women. In other modernizing societies, such as the German-speaking world around the turn of the twentieth century, the legal, professional, and political emancipation of women produced both new discourses on heterosexual marriage and on same-sex intimacy, with modernizing male elites often delegitimating the latter.[13] In the case of China, scholars have studied nineteenth- and twentieth-century female networks and the intimate relations embedded within them primarily as a localized phenomenon. Yet as Cathy Silber has pointed out, "as an integral aspect of local society, [formalized non-kin arrangements] could be just as important to those who participated in them as family ties. . . . Furthermore, the fact that social arrangements such as sworn sisterhood . . . are already recognized for many and diverse times and places in China . . . indicate that it is time to stop looking at these as isolated exceptions."[14] In surveying these practices across region, class, and profession, it would appear that the new opportunities for women fostered, among other things, same-sex allegiances. Such ties could be of a social, professional, political, literary, religious, emotional, or sexual nature and were often nested within or overlapping with educational, cultural, professional, and political relations.

A new-style, single-sex education proved to be an important aspect of the socialization of the "New Woman" of the 1910s and 1920s. Of course, Chinese elite families had begun to educate their daughters in greater numbers after 1600; however, such instruction generally took place neither in collective settings nor in extrafamilial locations.[15] In contrast, after 1907, a system of public girls' schools offered educational opportunities in addition to missionary and private schools. Since the equivalent of girls' high schools (girls' middle schools and girls' normal schools) were located in large cities and provincial capitals, girls had to leave home in order to attend, thus removing them from the immediate surveillance of their families.[16] While early curricula were often still geared towards home economics and moral training,[17] gradually new subjects were added. In the early 1920s, girls represented 6 percent of all students in state-run primary schools; in the early 1930s, around 15 percent.[18] The exposure to a new environment had a formative influence on many of the women who gained public visibility in the Republican era (1912–1949).[19] In middle schools, young women learned to test limits with teachers, and formed ties with non-kin peers, which could be passionate and enduring. For instance, up through middle school, Ding Ling (1904–1990), the well-known writer, made friends with young women who, like Ding herself, would become active in Communist Party politics.[20]

Same-sex relations also underwrote many of the literary and cultural endeavors of Republican women intellectuals. Unlike their late imperial counterparts who had collected, edited, and printed the work of other women in the name of showcasing paragons of Confucian virtues, the modern women pursued these activities in the context of the professionalization and commercialization of all writing. In short, writing offered educated women a means of earning a living. The first generation of professional female writers such as Ding Ling, Lu Yin (1898–1934), Ling Shuhua (1900–1990), and Chen Xuezhao (1906–1991) portrayed same-sex intimacy with homoerotic overtones in their fiction.[21] Furthermore, some writers such as Lu Yin, Lu Jingqing (1907–1993), and Shi Pingmei (1902–1928) used the new media of the women's press and literary supplements to celebrate their intense friendships, publishing their epistolary exchanges with each other. By the 1930s, when the New Woman, donning the newly invented *qipao* dress and bobbed hair, had become a fashionable commodity, a group of women intellectuals capitalized on this trend and set up a Woman's Bookstore in Shanghai, which from 1933 to 1936 published and sold a wide range of books by and about women.[22]

Same-sex relations that fostered social and economic interests among women were not confined to urban intellectuals. For instance, in Shanghai, so-called sisterhoods (*jiemei hui*) formed an important professional and social resource for many urban dwellers, including courtesans,[23] concubines, dance hostesses, silk workers, and policewomen.[24] The sisterhoods in Shanghai Cotton Mills started out as mutual aid societies in the 1920s. In addition to helping each other on the factory floor and protecting one another against harassment from male workers, bosses, and hoodlums, the women set up lending societies to aid sisters in need. The "sisters" also socialized with each other, sometimes frequenting Buddhist temples. In the 1940s, after the YWCA had done educational outreach among these women, the CCP adopted the social practices of the sisterhoods to further the politicization of the women involved, transforming the sisterhoods from small-scale to large-scale political organizations in the late 1940s. Such mobilization efforts culminated in at least partially successful strikes.[25]

However, sisterhoods were not limited to Shanghai and other cities. Various rural regions produced their own adaptations. In the early twentieth century in Chuansha, near Shanghai, young widows affiliated with lay Buddhist sects refused to remarry and instead formed sisterhoods while earning a living in cotton spinning and weaving.[26] In the nineteenth and early twentieth century, women in rural Hunan used a particular form of writing, the so-called women's script (*nüshu*), as one means to articulate intimate ties between two young women (*laotong*) and among women more generally (*jiebai zimei*).[27] The best-studied case of sisterhood concerns silk workers in the rural areas of Guangdong, and is the subject of Zhang Mei's story (chapter 4). A major phenomenon in the nineteenth and early twentieth century, so-called self-wedded women (*zishunü*) refused to get married altogether in an area where delayed marriage transfer was standard practice. In that latter pattern, "absentee wives" (*buluojia*) declined to live with husbands for at least three years, and on occasion postponed consummation indefinitely, especially if the wives could afford to bring in a concubine whose child would continue the family line.

Modern scholarly explanations for the *zishunü* have variously emphasized economic, religious, demographic, sexual, and ethnic factors.[28] As early as the eighteenth century, upwardly mobile families adopted delayed marriage as a means to socially distinguish themselves among the ethnically diverse inhabitants of the Pearl River Delta. In the nineteenth century, the mechanization of the silk industry displaced male labor, spurring men to immigrate to Southeast Asia. A preference for unmarried women in the silk reeling factories created new economic opportunities for young women, a pattern that was to be repeated in the post–World War II industrialization of Taiwan. Drawing upon non-Han marriage strategies of delayed cohabitation, Buddhist and folk beliefs in the karmic pollution of childbirth, as well as certain single-sex settlement patterns related to agricultural practices, young women transformed those traditions into lifelong communal living with other women. Often acting with the approval and support of her natal family, the "self-wedded woman" performed the equivalent of a wedding ceremony. She was committed to her vow in perpetuity. Like the factory women in the Shanghai, these self-wedded women would pool financial resources for family emergencies, funerals, festivals, and retirement. Some women forged practical, emotional, and sexual bonds with other women. Female couples as well as single women adopted daughters to carry on the tradition and care for their ancestral tablets. When interviewed in their old age in the 1960s, these women expressed a distinct preference for their relatively unencumbered lifestyle. However, after 1949, if *zishunü* had a natal family or were not too old, the CCP forcibly reincorporated them into their families of origin or arranged heterosexual marriages for them, thereby accelerating the demise of such practices in the local repertoire.

Upon the founding of the PRC in 1949, the new government made the procreative nuclear family the bedrock of socialist renewal. Implicitly building on Republican "sexual discourses [that] constructed a conceptual link between individual, conjugal couple, population and state,"[29] the state not only regulated familial and sexual institutions but, imbued with a spirit of utopian fervor and empowered by a dense distribution of local functionaries, envisioned nothing less than the total elimination of all nonprocreative, nonmarital arrangements. Different practices elicited different mechanisms of eradication. In the case of prostitution, a high profile campaign in the media coupled with the arrest of the brothel owners and the "reeducation" of the sex workers put an end to a once flourishing sex industry in Shanghai.[30] In the case of homosexuality, the preferred state tactic, at least through the early 1980s, was silence. Rather than criminalizing female or male homosexual behavior outright,[31] the government acted as though it did not exist in China. Neither the sex education literature nor the official journals of the women's and youth organizations made mention of male or female homosexuality from 1950 to the 1970s.[32] However, as new archival research about the early 1950s shows, such official rhetoric did not necessarily represent reality, especially among the working class who had more liberal attitudes toward sexuality than their intellectual counterparts.

> Take as an example the case of a woman surnamed Bao, deputy director of the party's Women Workers Committee (and a member of the factory committee as well) at a Shanghai rubber factory. Bao took advantage of her access to surplus rubber to fashion a dildo, which she used in her relationship with a woman surnamed Lin, also a party member. Bao and Lin slept together the report noted, "just like husband and wife." Bao, however, was unhappy with the fact that Lin was married, and tried to convince Lin to divorce her husband by yelling at and insulting him in front of other workers. This dispute was well known both to fellow workers and to cadres in the neighborhood. In the factory, when workers saw Bao, they would yell out, "Hey, Bao! Is the dildo as good as the real thing?!" Coworkers were not, however, pleased with her attempt to induce Lin to divorce her husband, since they considered him a decent fellow; they were also dissatisfied that Lin was a party member but was nonetheless "taking the lead in divorcing." Lin, however, was unrepentant, and

> accused the union members who were interfering with her relationship of having affairs themselves.[33]

In addition to the interesting interweaving of class, gender, and sexuality, the men's misgivings about Bao on political grounds as well as Bao's retaliatory accusations also illustrate the use of sexual conduct as an ad hominem political weapon. Such a practice gained its power not just by incriminating the moral character of the person in question but his or her ability to represent the interests of the state. Nationalists had used sexual innuendo to discredit the Communists after the fracturing of their joint alliance in 1927, and Red Guards made it an integral part of their struggle sessions against particular individuals.[34] Such denunciatory uses of sexuality contributed to a conservative climate wherein a sex drive, especially masculine sex drive, was constructed as normal and natural, but allowed only one legitimate form of expression: monogamous marriage. All other forms of sexual inactivity or activity such as extramarital sex, celibacy, masturbation, sex for pay, or same-sex liaisons could be construed as refusing to play one's part as a responsible citizen of the state, amounting to a form of dissidence punishable by social, economic, medical, or criminal sanctions.

Although the parameters of sexual conduct were narrowed after 1949, the realm of same-sex friendship encompassed nonsexual physical affection as a matter of course. Public display of physical affection among members of the same sex was exceedingly commonplace. In fact, same-sex affection was the most conspicuous and most casual form of public physical contact until the 1980s. In a thoughtful travelogue first published in 1982, Dutch feminist Anja Meulenbelt remarked not only on the casual and pervasive tenderness among Chinese women, but also tried to situate the phenomenon in a comparative framework.

> As far as normal, everyday, affectionate ties between women are concerned, we in the West are much more impoverished. We have to make efforts in this regard and have to fight through layers of [modern] prejudice. In contrast, women in China are rich: there a woman can put her arm around your shoulders without any sexual implications. Nobody looks askance at you when you say that you are very fond of another woman. So you could say that in this regard, Chinese women are more lesbian than their Western counterparts, even if sexual relations between women are clearly taboo, even if marriage is practically compulsory, and even if Chinese women are bewildered by the term "lesbianism."[35]

The 1980s and 1990s witnessed massive real and ideological dislocations in the PRC, which were to affect the reality and representation of same-sex intimacy in tangible ways. Clearly, the CCP apparatus was still in place. At the same time, economic liberalization and political disillusionment in the wake of 1989 have resulted in what has been variously called the post-Dengist or a post-Socialist era. Examining the cultural production in new media during the 1990s, Lisa Rofel observed that an allegory of post-Socialism claims that Maoism repressed innate "human nature," thus delaying China's entry into modernity. Forming an intrinsic part of this newly discovered "human nature," gender and sexuality have been at the heart of an emergent public realm, which the post-Socialist state can no longer completely control.[36] The fate of the word "comrade" (*tongzhi*) in the Chinese-speaking world is instructive in mapping the change from a political discourse of a class-based to a gender-based narrative of difference and emancipation.

Drawing upon the long-standing connotation of *zhi* with political aspiration, the neologism *tongzhi* was popularized by one of the retroactively enshrined father figures of the Chinese Republic, Sun Yat-sen.[37] As the standard form of address in the PRC that superseded gendered, hierarchical, and familial forms of appellation, the daily usage of the term "comrade" subtly invoked a utopian ideal in everyday practice only to be replaced in turn by a host of particularizing forms of address in the 1990s.[38] Reacting against the ostensibly desexed socialist comrade (*tongzhi*) of Maoist China, leading PRC women's studies scholars, such as Li Xiaojiang, invoked female subjectivity through new terms. Li, for instance, conceived of "woman" (*nüxing*) and of "women" (*nüren*) as a biologically and psychologically determined and materially oppressed social category, thereby defying the already liberated woman of state-sponsored feminism (*funü*), the humanist Man (*ren*) of masculinist Chinese intellectuals or the modern Western woman.[39] Official feminism, academic women's studies, and commercial distribution of women's work were all amplified through the hosting of the United Nations Fourth World Conference on Women held in Beijing in the fall of 1995,[40] exemplifying the complex interaction between competing constructions of post-Socialist women.

Increasingly, the idea of post-Socialist "woman" also accommodated sexual variation. The first major sexological survey of 20,000 men and women conducted in 1989/1990 touched explicitly and relatively nonjudgmentally on attitudes toward and experiences with homosexual behavior, revealing that 8.4 percent of the female college population had had some form of homoerotic contact.[41] In a series of interviews with forty-seven women after 1994, the prominent sociologist Li Yinhe included several lesbian and bisexual women from various backgrounds. The overall tenor of these women's comments about their lives was quite positive, pointing to the rewards and repercussions of greater sexual awareness among women friends used to casual physical affection.

> Once there was a young single woman playing cards at my place. We played so late that she ended up staying overnight. We slept in the same bed. I don't know how but I suddenly felt aroused. In the past whenever I was with my husband, I felt like a stone or a piece of wood, without any sensation whatsoever. But with this young woman it was completely different. She was not particularly pretty, but whenever our bodies bumped against each other so that my skin would touch hers, I felt aroused. She asked me to put my arms around her as she was falling asleep. She

perhaps just thought of it as a gesture of friendship, but my body responded very intensely. I was embarrassed. I thought of kissing her, but I did not dare. I was embarrassed. That night I did not sleep a wink. The next day when I told her how I had felt, she thought it was very strange. She said, "Are you sure you are not a hermaphrodite?" I said, "Yes, I am sure." For some time I thought of her quite a bit, but I knew there was no point. She wanted me to introduce a potential fiancé to her, which I did even though I did not like to. Later I asked her: "Is it possible that I am homosexual?" She was quite scared, and started to avoid me. My self-esteem is very healthy, if you don't like what I cherish, I will distance myself from you.[42]

At the same time, lesbian visibility in the broader public consciousness in the PRC owed something to the increased commodification of gender and sexuality in the mass media. For one thing, women writers became not only more numerous and highly visible, but as Jingyuan Zhang has pointed out, by the 1990s, women writers were happy and eager to describe themselves as "women writers" rather than aspiring to the implicitly male category of "writer."[43] What previously might have been a liability for women writers—namely the fictional exploration of the self—came to be regarded as an asset in the wake of broad interest in "human nature." In the mid-1980s, Wang Anyi (chapter 5) broke new ground with her portrayal of extramarital heterosexual relations. Her trilogy—known as the *Three Loves*—caused controversy, especially the final volume, *Love in Brocade Valley*, in which no one pays with their lives or in any other way for their erotic transgressions. By the 1990s, the popularization of the twin languages of psychology and sexology had paved the way for the fictional exploration of a range of new topics. In the wake of this psychological turn, lesbianism emerged as a novel, albeit contested, literary trope. On the one hand, Dai Jinhua, one of the leading feminist scholars in the PRC, singles out autobiographical and semi-autobiographical works that articulate the fear of and longing for sisterhood and lesbian relationships as the most noteworthy works produced in the 1990s.[44] On the other hand, echoing a recurrent accusation levied against women writers, conservative literary critics have continued to denigrate these works as self-indulgent and socially irresponsible.[45] The mixed critical evaluation notwithstanding, the works of this new generation of writers, among them Chen Ran (chapter 3), have enjoyed popularity among a diverse spectrum of readers.

In the 1990s, Hong Kong writers, hailing from what previously was often considered a "cultural wasteland" by Hong Kong and non–Hong Kong intellectuals alike, assumed greater visibility within Chinese literary circles. While leftist intellectuals had been quite active in post–World War II Hong Kong, it was difficult for Chinese writers to establish a reputation or gain a large audience, up until the 1970s, in a money-driven city of workers and managers where English was the sole official language. However, in the 1980s, after Britain legalized the official use of Chinese in the early 1970s and after Britain and Hong Kong agreed in 1984 to the return of Hong Kong in 1997, a new cosmopolitan Hong Kong culture began to flourish, thanks to private, commercial, and governmental initiatives. Film became the most visible and innovative medium of this hip urban culture, yet writers would also capitalize on the abundance of newspapers, magazines, and journals to create an audience for their writing. Some writers took advantage of Hong Kong's lack of a ready-made national affiliation and the absence of engrained literary traditions by globalizing the settings of their stories or by cross-fertilizing them with aesthetic techniques from other media, such as newspapers, TV, and film. Admixing a graphic lyricism and dispassionate objectification, Wong Bikwan (chapter 1) examines the dislocation attendant upon the global peregrinations of her Hong Kong protagonists.

It is perhaps not a coincidence that a new definition of the term "comrade" (*tongzhi*) came about in this city situated between cultures and countries. As the term was losing in the PRC as a form of everyday address, gay male activists in 1990s Hong Kong appropriated the idea of the kindred spirit encoded in the word "comrade" to sex comrades and used it to refer to same-sex lover. It was in Taiwan that the mutual imbrication of sexual identity with political citizenship latent in this new definition of "comrade" proved to be very enabling for increasing numbers of activists in the wake of the lifting of martial law in Taiwan in 1987.[46] Having brutally suppressed the progressive and ethnically Taiwanese uprising in 1947, the Taiwanese GMD found that with the success of its economic policies in the 1960s, local citizens, including feminist and pro-independence activists and now Taiwanese vice-president Lü Xiulian and current Taiwanese president Chen Shuibian (that is, of the Republic of China), began to organize once again for democratic reform in the 1970s, a movement that eventually resulted in the abolition of the repressive measures designed to limit power to the GMD.

In the 1990s, many Taiwanese social movements came into their own, including a "comrade" movement often divided along gender lines. Sexual preference thus was constituted as a primary axis of commonality with other women. Unlike the sisterhood practices described above, such sexually defined same-sex intimacy was not nested within familial or professional contexts. On the contrary, often leading closeted lives, lesbian women eked out their own social and cultural spaces to facilitate reflection, socializing, and activism with regard to their sexual identity, incorporating elements from Chinese, Taiwanese, and American discourses. A new generation of high school and university students, young professionals, and intellectuals returned from studies abroad created a visible lesbian presence in their own media, workshops, classes, mainstream and alternative press, and in electronic media. In important ways, such organizing overlapped with other social movements and academic activism, most notably the feminist movement. While relations within and between organizations could become strained, such overlap nonetheless suggests that the articulation of lesbian identity took place within a context of active citizenship, that is, in a broader practice of grassroots political movements working for democratization on a variety of fronts.[47]

Spurned on by feminist thought and activism, Taiwanese women writers have sought to intervene in the sexual politics of their own society. For instance, in the 1980s, Li Ang's writings on the sexual life of both intensely urban and shockingly rural characters made sex fashionable, with lesbianism hovering on the margins of representation.[48] In the 1990s, female authors carved out new spaces in a variety of genres, including realist fiction, science fiction, and cyberpunk, adding queer sexuality to the fictional repertoire. To a greater degree than in the PRC, young writers such as Hong Ling (chapter 7) not only wrote fiction but also contributed related columns and articles for newspapers and magazines as well as scholarly articles on the new avant-garde literature in established literary journals. At the same time, as in previous decades, the major dailies and publishing houses awarded first prizes to work with controversial sexual content, thereby launching the careers of new writers such as Chen Xue (chapter 8) and boosting sales. Intimate relations between women acquired not only currency "amongst ourselves" (*women zhi jian*), in the "circle" (*quanzi*), or in the "glass bowl" (*boli quan*)[49] but became fixtures in the broader cultural, social, economic, and political imagination.

## SOME OBSERVATIONS ON THE GLOBAL CIRCUITRY OF SAME-SEX INTIMACY

How does an anthology such as this one intersect with the above history? A possible short answer is: translation. Scholars of translation have noted that "it is impossible to separate the history of translation from the history of languages, of cultures, and of literatures—even of religions and nations."[50] Conversely, scholars of modern China have come to recognize that in addition to military, economic, political, and other forces, translation played a crucial role in mediating the encounter between China and Japan, Europe, and the United States.[51] In Hu Ying's apt formulation, in translation "different traditions meet and wrestle on the solid ground of language, and . . . the cultural implications of global and local politics manifest themselves in submerged, though no less intense, ways."[52] As Lydia Liu has noted, translation establishes a hypothetical equivalence between languages, but not necessarily reciprocity.[53] The emergence of "new women" in China illustrates the power, potential, and problems of translation between China and, for example, the United States.

Translation played a major role in the formation of the New Woman in China at the beginning of the twentieth century. Such new articulations of "woman" were no idle exercise in literary aptness. On the one hand, conceptions of the New Woman were mediated by translations from Japanese and European languages.[54] On the other hand, as real women experimented with "new womanhood," they not only provided real-life examples but they in turn produced their own literary versions of the New Woman. Insofar as the "woman question" was thought to reflect on China's standing as a nation both inside and outside China, the New Woman also was a touchstone for China's national progress. As Wendy Larson has pointed out, "the literary field and the modern woman thus became the site of a debate that revolved around the inclusion of women writers, feminine styles, and female topics in an arena [that is, world literature] . . . that . . . involved China in a worldwide power hierarchy."[55]

While the Chinese translated and read nineteenth-century and contemporary Western texts of all sorts in great numbers, some Europeans and Americans were interested in Chinese texts, but mostly of the classical variety.[56] Nevertheless, as Chinese women began to write in the 1920s and 1930s in the international forms of poetic free verse, novels, short stories,[57] and autobiography, some of their works—most notably versions of their autobiographies—were translated and circulated in the West. During the second burst of women's writing in the 1980s and 1990s, Chinese women's fiction was translated more extensively than ever before. At the same time, however, Chinese and Chinese-American women's autobiographies, especially those originally written in English, garnered the lion's share of popular attention. Among these, two widely read and reviewed memoirs, Xie Bingying's (1906–2000) *Yige nübing de zizhuan* [The Autobiography of a Female Soldier] (1936), alternatively titled *Girl Rebel* (1940) and *Autobiography of a Chinese Girl* (1943), and Anchee Min's (1957–) *Red Azalea* (1994) became best-sellers. Interestingly, to varying degrees, both texts touch upon intimacy between women in a narrative of political revolution.[58]

Far from providing unchanging essentials about Chinese women, these texts highlight the compelling historical contingencies of all acts of translation.[59] The Chinese text of Xie's 1936 *Yige nübing de zizhuan* grew out of the tremendous political fervor and subsequent disillusionment of the 1920s and 1930s. Between 1925 and 1927, women were mobilized in unprecedented numbers during the various political and military campaigns. To be sure, women's battalions had fought in the 1911 revolution, but during the heady mid-twenties, women carved new roles for themselves in the public arena—as party officials for both the GMD and the Communists, as union organizers, and as graduates of military training academies.[60] A graduate of the most famous military program in Wuhan, the author Xie Bingying became part of an all-female detachment. Describing her experience as a propagandist of the joint CCP/GMD expedition against the warlords in 1927, Xie's serialized *War Diary* (*Congjun riji* 1928) catapulted her to prominence in China.[61] Incorporating parts of the *War Diary*, Xie's 1936 *The Autobiography of a Female Soldier* traced her fight for an education, her growth as a writer, her military exploits, and her battle against an arranged marriage.

On both sides of the Pacific, Lin Yutang (1895–1975), one of the most influential cultural intermediaries between China and the United States, shaped the reception of Xie's works in significant ways. Guided by the notion that a nation's standing was partly judged by the status of its women, Lin presented Xie as an emblem of "Young China." Having written a preface for Xie's *War Diary*, he produced an English translation of that work entitled "Letters of a Chinese Amazon."[62] In 1939, Lin's two precocious daughters, Ador and Anet, translated parts of Xie's *Autobiography* as well as excerpts from Xie's *New War Diaries* (*Xin congjun riji*) on the Sino–Japanese war (1937–1945) and published it under the title *Girl Rebel* in 1940. As the preface by Lin and the two teenage translators suggests, the translation was meant to draw attention to the civil war in China. At the same time, the inclusion of the chapters on the Sino–Japanese war also had geopolitical ramifications, speaking to a desire to align the Chinese with the United States against the Japanese.[63]

However, while reviewers thought that *Girl Rebel* gave "a feeling of what is happening in China in its essence"[64] and was written "with a beautiful straightforwardness,"[65] they were oblivious to the fact that the Lins had truncated and expanded the 1936 text, essentially creating a new story. At the same time, the new English text was legitimated by the appearance of a bilingual edition in Taiwan in 1940. Even more abbreviated than the English translation, the bilingual edition nevertheless adopted the new English title as its new Chinese title (*Nüpantu*). Lin Yutang's preface declared it a suitable text for youngsters studying English.[66] Catering to American and Chinese sensibilities at once, the Lins' text provided a rousing yet inoffensive text designed to foster rapprochement between Chinese and American cultures. In this way, a number of chapters, including one on same-sex intimacy in Xie's middle school, appear to have become a casualty of the cross-cultural dialogue.

The 1943 British translation by Tsui Chi, the author of a then widely reviewed *Short History of Chinese Civilization* (1940), presented a fuller picture of Xie's *Autobiography*. Entitled *Autobiography of a Chinese Girl*, the translation limited itself to the 1936 work. However, Tsui too fudged the text, often tampering with the self-reflexive elements of Xie's narration. In the chapter entitled "The Trials and Tribulations of Same-Sex Love" (*tongxing'ai de jiufen*), Xie's original narrative begins:

> The word "same-sex love" (*tongxing'ai*) was unfamiliar to us at the time. However, it was very strange that everyone began to pair off in couples, never leaving each other walking or sitting down. From knowing each other, mutual love developed and from mutual love, marriage. (Once the girls slept in the same bed, it was called "marriage.")[67]

Tsui glosses the relevant chapter as "platonic love" and translates the identical passage in the following way: "It seemed very strange to me when I first perceived that many of my schoolmates began to become inseparable pairs. They would never leave each other, whether walking or sitting down, and that was something very new to me."[68] Subsequently, Tsui's text systematically elides details of physical intimacy throughout the chapter. Instead, his rendering highlights the unnaturalness of such attractions.[69]

As Xie's self-conscious opening indicates, the chapter on "same-sex love" spoke to a lively discussion in the 1920s and 1930s among Chinese intellectuals about the merits and demerits of same-sex intimacy among young educated women. Situated at the crossroads between traditional same-sex sociability and Western-style sexualization of romance, opinion about same-sex love among schoolgirls was by no means uniform. Interestingly, translations from a variety of European and Japanese writings on the subject fueled the debate. Ranging from Edward Carpenter's emphasis on the educational value of same-sex love to Havelock Ellis' dismissal of same-sex love as a rehearsal for marriage, such translations did not, by and large, posit same-sex attraction as an innate sexual disposition. Instead, as the choice of the word "love" (*ai*) to render "homosexuality" (*tongxing' ai*) suggests, the translators posited it as a form of relation rather than as an essential aspect of personhood.[70] However, as time wore on, the conservative spectrum of Western sexology held sway, disseminating its pathological conception of "homosexuality" through manuals on sexual hygiene and medical texts.[71]

Xie's narration reflects an ambivalence between old-style approbation and modern unease. The long-standing practice of same-sex interaction in China may explain the relatively relaxed atmosphere at Xie's school. In some instances, Xie's couples engage in actions similar to those noted for the sisterhoods: mutual care in times of need, joint activities such as travel and shopping, and poetic declarations of love. In other instances, their actions are more overtly physically intimate: they sleep in the same bed and talk lovers' talk. In the climax of the chapter, a group of girls forces Xie and one of her admirers to spend a tense night in the same bed, suggesting that refusal "to get married" resulted in punitive reprisals by one's peers. However, Xie's description notes that such passionate crushes among young women were not only considered normal by her schoolmates but sanctioned by some authority figures.

> Every day at the crack of dawn or after supper, especially in the deepening shades of mist at dusk, there were always countless couples sauntering on the sports ground. They were strolling about, talking lovers' talk, or reading books while leaning against each other. However, I often read a novel by myself, at times I stood at the pond or sat on the grass. I was always by my lonesome self. "Why are you all alone? Don't you have a friend?" [The principal nicknamed] Grandmother came walking past with a broad smile. So unexpectedly it turned out that he was aware of the secret amongst ourselves.[72]

Even if Xie's narrator is at pains to distance herself from overt passionate interests, she seems to be the exception rather than the rule. Such social ease and approbation contrasts rather remarkably with the tortured atmosphere of other contemporary international best-sellers on same-sex schools, such as the German-language *Girl in Uniform*.[73] Yet Xie's persistent emphasis on her singularity signals that the translated neologism of "tongxing'ai" gradually made common modes of intimacy between young Chinese women salient, exceptional, and ultimately suspect. With the exception of a 1954 Hong Kong edition, subsequent Chinese editions of Xie's autobiography, including those expressly reissued by the author herself, omit the chapter on same-sex love.[74]

If Xie's text has been destabilized by translations of both the text itself and of the cultural concepts informing it, what about a work originally written in English? In recent years, many English-language memoirs by first-generation immigrant intellectuals have made the United States' and other best-seller lists. Many of these focus on one of the most turbulent and poorly understood periods of recent Chinese history, the Cultural Revolution (1966–1976). Among recent female-authored Cultural Revolution memoirs and fiction, Anchee Min's *Red Azalea* garnered attention, partly because of its evocative style, and partly because of what appears as an unprecedented portrayal of lesbian or bisexual eroticism.[75]

The memoir focuses on the narrator's Cultural Revolution experiences on a collective farm and in a film studio in the 1970s. At the heart of Min's memoir is the emotionally and erotically charged relationship between the narrator and the female commandant, Yan, her superior at the farm. The narrator's subsequent involvement with a male and unnamed supervisor at the film studio occupies a secondary place, if only because that relationship is mediated through her feelings for Yan. It may be valid to read Min's work factually, especially in light of other recent Cultural Revolution recollections of same-sex eroticism. As a heterosexual woman noted in a recent interview with the prominent Chinese sociologist Lin Yinhe,

> The first time I had first-hand exposure to homosexuality was when I had been sent down to a collective farm. There were two women, one of whom was feminine, dainty and a high school graduate. The other one was masculine, her build was rather coarse and tall and she was a junior high graduate. They were very close and spent all their time together. At one point, a tall, big, and ugly woman told me: "The two of them are a pair." I said, "What nonsense is that?" She said, "They are a pair just like a man and a woman." In the summertime, we all slept in tiny mosquito nets, but the two of them insisted on sleeping inside the same net, covering themselves with a towel and refusing to come out. . . . I did not think there was anything wrong with their behavior. After all, it is not easy to find someone with whom you are both sexually and emotionally compatible, so if people like each other, why not?[76]

Tempting though it may be to read Min's *Red Azalea* as a "lesbian" or "bisexual" memoir, especially since the text features similar scenes of intimacy in a mosquito net, upon closer examination, the text's representation of the twin narratives of revolution and love is significantly mediated by Maoist political and theatrical conventions. If single-sex schools offered one of the modern institutional settings for fiction and autobiography dealing with same-sex intimacy in the Republican era, traditional theater not infrequently forms the backdrop for contemporary works on the subject.[77] Traditional opera had long provided an arena for the exploration of same-sex intimacy both in terms of content and context, with cross-gender performance forming part of many Chinese theatrical forms. The model operas of the Cultural Revolution fused both traditional and modern elements, while prominently featuring revolutionary heroines. In Min's memoir, the narrator is infatuated with model heroines, their visible and invisible incarnations (Yan and Jiang Qing respectively) and herself insofar as she can become one with her role of Red Azalea after having left Red Fire Farm and Yan behind.

> The story of Red Azalea was a story of a passion in the midst of gunfire. It was about how a woman should live, about a proletarian love unto death. To me, it was not only about the past wartime, about history, but it was also about the essence of Yan, the essence of how I must continue to live my life.

Contrary to Meng Yue's claim that model theater used women exclusively as a signifier for a given class, a sociopolitical group, or the Communist Party itself,[78] and contrary to Bai Di's assertion that model theater placed women in a desexualized realm of androgyny,[79] Min's account offers a sexualized perspective on political theater. Corroborated by other memoirs or fictionalized autobiographies of the period, the erotic charge might in part explain the effectiveness of political movements.[80] In the rhetoric of fusion between two people—one herself, the other a state representative—Min simulates a unity between subject and state. Whereas other English-language Cultural Revolution memoirs often disavow revolutionary passion,[81] Min's captures the abolition of boundaries between self, representation, and state power. Her representation of same-sex desire blends acceptable affection between women and the political symbolism of Woman with what in a Western context can be construed as "lesbian" sex.

Thus, Min's public wavering when it comes to defining Yan and the narrator's relation in lesbian terms in American contexts might point to a question of cultural translatability. Nowhere does the incongruity of erotic categories become more obvious than in the ending of a recent feature on Min in the *New York Times Magazine* entitled "The Re-education of Anchee Min." When Min compares the ballet teacher of her eight-year-old daughter to Madame Mao, the interviewer observes: "Surprised to hear a dance teacher compared with a genocidal dictator, I mutter something about how severe she [Madame Mao] seems. 'No,' Anchee says quietly. 'Her face, that pale skin. So beautiful, don't you think?' "[82]

So what do these two autobiographies tell us? First, perhaps, same-sex intimacy has been part and parcel of the "new Chinese woman's" representation in the West. Perhaps not so surprisingly, such same-sex intimacy is in each case filtered through the dominant paradigm current at the time, that is, a largely platonic conception in the first fifty years, and an explicitly sexual one in the second half. Second, such same-sex intimacy is neither strictly "Chinese" nor categorically "Western." In Xie's story, her girlhood memories draw on the trope of same-sex schools, but infuse it with the ritual exchanges common among sworn sisters. In Min's story, her reconstruction of her days on the farm invokes a form of situational lesbianism but mediates it through the literary and political vocabulary of Maoist China. Third, best-sellers thrive on particular political and cultural constellations. It is difficult to imagine that Xie's military exploits would arouse much interest now, just as it is barely conceivable that Xie could have represented amatory adventures with a female commandant of her all-woman brigade. In the end, Xie's and Min's stories caution us against assuming that an "other" is either radically different or quintessentially the same. At the same time, they call on us to historicize the terms of translation.

## A BRIEF ACCOUNT OF HOW THIS ANTHOLOGY CAME ABOUT

Suspended between the unintelligibly exotic and the falsely universal, all translations make more or less visible interventions, intertwining the global and the intimate in both obvious and unpredictable ways. In 1994, I spent a few summer weeks in Taiwan, my first extended stay there. As I wandered around the streets of Taipei, I marveled at the palimpsestic nature of the city's architecture. Objects from the various countries I had lived in—Japan, Switzerland, the PRC, and the United States—assembled into an unfamiliar and yet recognizable array of patterns, making the odd ebb and flow of historical processes—colonialism, imperialism, acculturation, globalization—tangible and tenuous at the same time. The smell of basted soy and the nasal sound of megaphoned voices wafting through the alleys did not unleash remembrances of times past, but made me feel strangely at home. In talking to intellectual urbanites, I relished the sense that literature mattered in a way that it did not in the United States. I also heard echoes of a Swiss sense of willful smallness in relation to a Big Brother to the North.

One afternoon, I was—as usual—spending time with my Taiwanese Berkeley-educated friends at offices of the feminist organization Awakening (Funü xinzhi). I bought an issue of the avant-garde magazine *Isle Margin* (*Daoyu bianyuan*) next door at Fembooks (Nüshudian), the newly opened and then only women's bookstore in Asia. I went downstairs to the coffee shop called Nüwudian (Witches Den) to read Chen Xue's "In Search of the Wings of the Angels." My friend, colleague, and activist Ding Naifei had told me about the prepublication uproar—how Chen's story had been selected for first prize in the annual new fiction contest sponsored by the prestigious daily *China Times*, how the sole female judge threatened to resign, how Chen was awarded the prize in the end, but how the paper decided not to print the story as was customary with the winning entry, resulting in its appearance in this independent venue. As I read, I was stunned—not simply because the story defied Chinese conventions but also because it resonated uncannily with my own literary experiments in German.[83] Dealing with the difficulties of reconciling a passion for words with the legacy of a socially taboo mother figure, Chen's narrative compelled me to entertain the possibility of finding other related texts, the hazards attendant upon cross-cultural translation notwithstanding.

If indeed all cross-cultural translation participates in conflicting discourses with emphases on what's modern,[84] then in its choice of title, *Red Is Not the Only Color* seeks to get out from under the heroics of the grand narratives, the sort that pit the "either" of the political against the "or" of the personal. As so many English-language books about the PRC, in particular, feature "red" in the title, they not only foreground the political, they also—even if inadvertently—perpetuate the stereotype of cultural and political uniformity. At the same time, as many Chinese films produced for an international market present the Chinese past in visually spectacular terms, they reinforce the association between China and the color red, not so much in political as in familial terms, given all the traditional marriages featuring brides in red veils. "Red" appears to reduce China to two stories, one dealing with political revolution and the other with women's roles. While obviously tapping into the two dominant connotations of red—marriage and revolution—this anthology seeks to tease out what's located between the interstices of such epic, and often sensationally bloody, rhetoric.

When Deng Xiaoping opted for economic liberalization and Jiang Jingguo lifted martial law in the 1980s, they hardly anticipated that such reforms might lead to the creation of the Women's Hotline (*Funü rexian*) in Beijing[85] or Fembooks (*Nüshudian*) in Taipei. To a significant degree, the stories in this anthology grew out of, and speak to, the new cultural cachet of same-sex intimacy in urban China and Taiwan. With the commodification of culture and entertainment, new public spaces have emerged, ranging from cafes and bookstores to nonprofit organizations and electronic bulletin boards. Newly independent media have proliferated, both in print and electronic realm. In short, a range of new social possibilities calls into question the exclusionary normativity of procreative marriage. However contradictory in their assessment of these alternatives that mainstream media and publishers may be, they have nonetheless seized upon the private trials and tribulations of "a generation of new beings" (*xinxin renlei*) to cater to a voyeuristic mass market.[86]

Portraying passionate friendship, intellectual and emotional companionship, sexual liaisons, and long-term partnership, the stories in this anthology, at least in part, derive from these new political, social, and cultural spaces. Yet being neither personal autobiographies nor political manifestos, they also engage with a literary tradition that fetishizes female suffering. Classical poetry, biography, and vernacular fiction had all dwelt on the emotional and physical pathos of maltreated women, often figuring the woman as a stand-in for the politically underappreciated male literatus. During the Republican era, generations of male writers explored the national political crisis as well as their own alienation from the political status quo through the portrayal of lower-class women.[87] After 1949, the Communist Party assumed the self-proclaimed role of guarantor of women's liberation. The Party's legitimating power depended in some measure upon its ability to evoke both actual and fictional memories of a horrendously oppressive past, of which the oppression of women constituted an important aspect. Not only did the new literature feature obligatory moments of past bitterness[88] but literary scholarship recast large numbers of traditional texts in that light. In post-1980 male-authored fiction, films, and TV series, the suffering woman has resurfaced either to distract from political failure or to assume responsibility for the political malaise, whether as the self-sacrificing mother or as the beset and vindictive concubine.[89]

Male authors have not had a monopoly on the suffering woman. Female suffering has figured prominently in the writings of Chinese women of all periods. The representations of suffering not only reflect women's actual lives but may also constitute a necessary prerequisite for literary recognition. Perhaps not so surprisingly, abject elements of female existence—illness, madness, self-loathing, suicide, and death—occur regularly in female-authored novels and films from both the PRC and Taiwan,[90] especially in the context of same-sex intimacy. The most sensational example concerns the life and fiction of Taiwanese author Qiu Miaojin (1969–1995). Becoming known with the publication of the lesbian coming-of-age novel *The Crocodile's Diary* (*E'yu riji*) in 1994, Qiu went on to study in Paris after working as a counselor and journalist in Taipei. After Qiu's lover left her because Qiu battered her, Qiu wrote *Testament from Montmartre* (*Mengmate yishu*) (1996) only to kill herself after its completion. Projecting the persona of the mad artist,[91] the posthumously published and thinly disguised description of events leading up to the suicide appeared to corroborate the lurid scandals that the Taiwanese tabloid and mainstream press like to fabricate about lesbian women and gay men.[92]

Weary of and skeptical about playing up violence and suffering as the sole element of cross-cultural representation, I selected stories that explore alternatives to the familiar plot of female doom and destruction, while at the same time avoiding a programmatic cheerfulness. At its simplest, then, this anthology claims that the intersubjective space between women matters. As the subtitle suggests, this anthology does not define this space in the singular. In Chinese, a similarly wide range of terms could be invoked, each with its own nuances and history, including the idealistic coinages of May Fourth parlance (*lian'ai, aiqing, nüquan*), the ambiguous neologisms of Republican translators (*tongxing'ai, tongxing lian*), the harsh labels of quasi-scientific sexology (*biantai, diandao*), the neotraditional and feminist rhetoric of sisterhood (*jiemei hui, jiemei qing*), and the creative appropriations of the transnationally Chinese gay and lesbian movement (*tongzhi, nüpengyou, ku'er, nannan nünü*).[93] In choosing "same-sex intimacy" as the overarching figure in my discussion, rather than being vague or evasive, I am seeking to do justice to the complex interweaving of different discourses, past and present, Chinese and other, in particular contexts.

As my discussion of the background of the individual stories will show, the stories use same-sex intimacy to explore a variety of contemporary issues—local and global commercialization, utopian social aspirations, the problems and possibilities of historical memory, the lure of sexual desire, and the question of self-realization—in short, questions that have surfaced in specific, but not unrecognizable, ways across different cultural contexts. So rather than proposing to replicate Fredric Jameson's guilt-ridden angst over the "already-read," "nationally allegorical," and yet absolute alterity of non-Western texts,[94] I suggest we pay attention to the mutually "overwritten" (crisscrossed), "underwritten" (imbricated), and "counterread" (queer) quality of all cultural terrains. In short, the anthology invites readers to consider that the transnational forces of flux that conspire to pull the proverbial rug out from under everyone's political, social, and sexual certainties may also enable authors and readers to be oddly and obliquely at home in places they have never been before.

## A BRIEF DISCUSSION OF THE STORIES

### New Media, New Markets, Old Values

Perhaps precisely because the greater visibility of same-sex intimacy coincided with economic liberalization, recent Chinese fiction avails itself of such subject matter to reflect upon the price of modernization. Interestingly, such stories often rely on another trope much used to explore issues of modernization—namely the performing arts, broadly defined. Fictional characters assume the roles of fashion model, pop singer, and film star, all professions that authorize the conscious display of female beauty, charm, and sexual allure.[95] New media encourage different forms of audience participation from traditional theater, casting viewers in the roles of consumers rather than participants or patrons. Accordingly, such stories appear to use the trope of same-sex intimacy as a way to show unease over the alienation attendant not just upon the commodification of a woman's body but of all objects, people, and values. Set in regions known for their fast-paced economic developments, such stories map the undoing of a friendship between women onto the professional success of a woman without genuine intellectual aspirations. As the protagonists infatuated with the performers tend to be more intellectually inclined and from a more solid middle-class background than their eroticized counterparts, one wonders to what extent such stories express intellectuals' anxieties over their own irrelevance in a consumer culture, in which less-educated but street-smart figures begin to define the terms of success. Contrary to Anchee Min's fantasy of theatrically engineered oneness, these stories deploy the performing arts and same-sex intimacy to reveal something of the relentless fragmentation, alienation, and stratification between and within people that consumerism brings about.

Perhaps not coincidentally, one such story is set in Hong Kong. In Bikwan Wong's "She Is a Young Woman and So Am I," the narrator, Yip Saisai, tries to create a social space for a passionate intimacy between herself and Hui Jihang, a possibility that exists only precariously during their college years and seems to recede into impossibility thereafter. With her neotraditionalist *qipao* and embroidered slippers, Jihang sets herself up as the object of a sexualized gaze, intent on using her allure to become a publicly circulated icon of femininity. In her quest to become another Isabella Rossellini, Jihang willingly commodifies herself and her relations with others. By contrast, Saisai seeks to establish a domestic ideal of jointly owned cats and rugs, a utopian space freed from the trappings of sexual desire of any kind, including lesbian desire. Saisai figures lesbian passion as yet another instance of a sexualized male gaze. Throughout the story, the narrator seeks to distance herself from this gaze, since it appears to reduce every woman to the incidentals of her appearance. As she wonders whether she has in fact a position from which to view Jihang as something other than femininity incarnate, she invents a language of sensuous details to register her physical appreciation of Jihang, which simultaneously conveys her own difference as a female observer. The two women share an idiolect of stenographic scripts, lost bras, shared shawls, and painted toenails that borrows from the dominant vocabulary of femininity, but registers a difference in its nonsexual and domestic uses. However, the question of whether it is possible to establish a self independent of a hegemonic gaze insistently haunts the narrative.

As Jihang succeeds in her modeling career and disappears from Saisai's life, Saisai closes the narrative with her remembrance of a Jihang who no longer exists, a Jihang who did not make distinctions between success and failure. This nostalgic gesture points to an interpersonal space that perhaps exists only hypothetically, not even within the grounds of the narrative itself—after all, Jihang sees herself in competition with Saisai throughout most of the story. Still, in Saisai's vision of certain shared moments, the story uses a sensuous, deliberately desexualized idea of female bonding to interrogate more generally the effects of commodification. Perhaps it is no coincidence that Saisai and Jihang first bond over the latter's decipherment of Jihang's class notes on the Marxian notion of surplus value. In locating female intimacy in the interstices beyond irrelevance and pathology, the story appears to hint at an unself-conscious pleasurable abandon freed from the need to turn people or things into objects, a brief moment when economies of calculation are suspended, and the last money can be willfully spent on half a dozen oysters on the half shell.

**Time, Place, and the Possibilities of History**

In Wong's story, the site of the narrative, presumably the city of Hong Kong, does not overtly mediate the relation between the two protagonists. The city in some sense is taken for granted. In PRC fiction, due to the ambivalence surrounding both city and country in modern and classical discourses, fictional narratives often waver as to what places facilitate individual or collective redemption and renewal. Since at least the Republican period, the countryside has been both innocent and benighted, the city decadent and modern, thus offering contradictory resources for fiction. Whereas male writers in the 1980s and 1990s polarized city and country in conceptual terms, often opting for an idealization of the latter, female writers embraced the urban environment more readily, partly because it appeared to offer greater possibilities for same-sex interaction.[96]

Chen Ran's "Breaking Open" grapples with the question of constructing a social space for female companionship in an urban environment. En route from the rural hometown of one of the protagonists to the other's city home, two thirty-something women wait in an airport lounge, then board the plane, and finally arrive in the bustling city of N. In each of those spaces, they discuss the possibilities of being female, a discussion that is obviously informed by a broader contestation over the meaning of "woman." While the emergent discipline of women's studies in China might attempt to consolidate the particulars of female experience,[97] Chen Ran's narrative does not make an essentialist case of gender difference. Instead, as one of the protagonists puts it, just as God is unsexed, so can two women attain that state of grace in their interaction with each other. Contrary to the trope of two mates falling in love with each other as part of their dedication to the party,[98] Yunnan and the narrator bond over the formation of an art organization for women, thus hinting at the creation of the sort of women's cultural space that PRC women, caught between the hegemonic discourses of state feminism and male elite intellectuals, have found difficult to establish.[99] Thus, the story paradoxically maneuvers between a desire to transcend gender difference and a desire to imprint that transcendence with female specificity.

The figure that mediates this tension is a semi-divine, semi-human mother. As Xiaomei Chen has observed, through the articulation of an intellectual bond with a mother, daughters in post-Mao Chinese feminist narratives can think through their relation to history and furthermore, are able to authorize themselves to make socially unorthodox choices.[100] However, Chen Ran's narrative takes the idea of female self-determination even further, both in her critique of the past and in her vision of the future. Contrary to Republican era female narratives where a woman's love for a partner of her choice often cements or precipitates the loss of the mother,[101] Chen Ran's narrative combines the injunction to honor one's mother's wishes with the new social possibility of a partnership with a woman. Such a reconciliation of filial and intimate desires takes place at the heart of the city, a vast and empty city square. Once animated by the drama of

parades and rallies, the square, bathed in the overpowering light of the sun once associated with Mao Zedong, propels the narrator into the recognition of the artificiality of both the commercial present and the political past. Through reference to a series of symbols of Western modernity (feminist and spiritual writers, music, space travel, theories of gender and sexuality) and of Chinese tradition (fate, reclusion, filiality), the story creates its own vision of maternally sanctioned, urban sisterhood. In its final sequence of images, the story not only points to the invention of alternate forms of adult womanhood but also connotes some of the difficulties, fears, and uncertainties associated with this process.

Zhang Mei's "Record" also explores contrasts between the city and the country, but in a reverse spatial trajectory. The narrator joins a filmmaker on an exploratory mission to the countryside. Incidentally, such an inverse movement between city and countryside also signals a different temporal progression: instead of creating a new future for women in the city, Zhang's story examines the past, specifically the Guangdong phenomenon of the self-wedded wives and absentee wives discussed above. Such a reconsideration of historical Chinese women for current literature raises interesting issues. Although often conceived within an intensely antiforeign climate, post-1949 PRC literature more often than not made nineteenth-century foreign its primary, if hidden, intertext, rather than earlier twentieth-century Chinese literature. Only in the late 1980s and 1990s did Republican era women's literature reenter the imaginative arena,[102] thus creating an enabling sense of stylistic and thematic continuity among contemporary women writers.[103] With the return of pre-Revolutionary history as something other than sheer oppression, the past becomes a contested site. Zhang's narrative confronts this issue head-on in the context of filmmaking.

As Rey Chow has suggested, filmmakers such as Chen Kaige and Zhang Yimou use film in order to translate a culture onto film and to transcribe it from text to image, all the while deconstructing the division between viewing subject and viewed object.[104] Situating the story in the context of the global filmic commodification of the Chinese past, Zhang's "Record" meditates on the construction of

viewing objects and subjects in relation to these self-wedded women and absentee wives.[105] Zhang's story resists any ready-made explanations. Instead, as a young female reporter accompanies a scriptwriter and a film director during their interviews of a handful of self-wedded women, the story suggests that such women—and the past as a whole—can only be assimilated into present categories at the price of distortion. Zhang celebrates the virtues of skepticism: instead of writing an ethnographic account sure of its object, the story interrogates the standardizing forces of both revolutionary historiography and capitalist romanticism, suggesting that the bonds between historical and contemporary women are more tenuous and discontinuous than various forms of historiography would have us believe. Rather than offering an ethnographic account sure of its object—the oppressed or the embellished woman—Zhang offers a critique of unambiguous female "to-be-looked-at-ness," regardless of whether the appropriative gaze belongs to Chinese male intellectuals or to a Western film audience.

### Families, Sisterhoods, and Other Such Fictions

While Wong's, Chen's, and Zhang's stories seek to imagine "woman/women" as something besides "man's other," Wang Anyi's "Brothers" situates the quest for "woman" and "self" in the rhetoric of kinship. Exploring competing loyalties between different sets of kinship ties, Wang's story explicitly brings the two relationally and temporally disparate dimensions of Zhang's story, namely the "sisterhood" of the past and the "marriage" of the present, into conflict with each other. Insofar as ritual obligations rather than blood ties define Chinese family structures, such chosen familial relations as sworn sisterhood or brotherhood could and can have considerable social weight. Sworn sisters and women swearing brotherhood populate the pages of traditional literature, women's poetry, and local gazetteers. As noted above, they form important axes of social organization in modern settings. They also appear in contemporary literary production. For instance, Zhang Jie's influential feminist novel *Ark* (*Fangzhou* 1978) did not expressly make its three female protagonists sworn sisters, but the middle-aged intellectuals think of their unusual and congenial cohabitation as a "widows' club."[106] The three women make their shared apartment a space of bad language and bad housekeeping, lending the space an aura of sisterhood as well as brotherhood. As Chen Yu-shi observes, "we must see a basic difference between the dirty dishes that pile up in the kitchen sink of *Ark* and other piles of dirty dishes elsewhere. The dishes in *Ark*, one may note, exist outside of a language system that controls who is thought of as the natural person to wash them."[107]

As Lydia Liu has noted, Wang's "Brothers" does not situate itself against a discourse of lesbian manipulation of gender identity.[108] Instead, the story examines how the ties of assumed kinship between three female sworn "brothers" fare against ties within their respective nuclear family unit. Two major confrontations take place, one revolving around the idea of "wife," the other around the notion of "mother."[109] The "brotherly" bonds between the women do not offer an alternative sexualized identity; rather, they offer relief from the sexualized identity of wife and the subordinated category of woman. The assumption of quasi-male kinship ties allows not only for the enjoyment of certain male privileges such as unwashed dishes,[110] but also draws on gender to form a basis for joint action without sexualizing identity.[111] When the husband of the youngest tries to (re)assert his authority—significantly through sexual intercourse—the youngest of the three women sacrifices her own aspirations and subsumes her identity under the label of dedicated wife (*xianqi*). The remaining two women rename themselves "Old Li" and "Old Wang," a somewhat unusual form of address that suggests a bond characterized by independent thinking and emotional intimacy among women intellectuals.

In the second part of the narrative, two families are pitted against each other, one consisting of the father, the mother (Old Li), and the child, and the other of the mother (Old Li), the child, and a godmother (Old Wang). The first family is a material entity, grounded in sex, a patrilineal and shared daily drudgery. The second family is a spiritual unit, revolving around deep feelings, endless conversations, joint art projects, and shared vacations. The first kind of family is unproblematically Chinese, the other precariously foreign by virtue of an acknowledged borrowing from a Western context, namely the idea of a godmother derived from reading foreign novels. Just as the friend submits to the role of the selfless wife (*xianqi*), after a minor mishap with the child, Old Li sacrifices both the possibility of her own and her friend's engagement in that alternative family for the sake of living up to the expectation of the ideal mother (*liangmu*). The friend leaves of her own accord, never to return, pursuing her quest for fulfillment in her professional assignments, but to no avail. The power of material

forces buttressed by a restrictive mothering ideology proves too much for the spiritual but nameless family unit between the two women.

## The Complications of Sexual Desire

Although Wong's, Chen's, and Zhang's narratives all touch in passing upon the question of sexual intimacy between women, some of the stories in this volume make same-sex eroticism a main concern. In each narrative, such an exploration is mediated through figures of ghosts and spirits. In traditional Chinese fiction, ghosts and spirits were often portrayed as lustful and seductive creatures, intent on absorbing human humors, especially semen, in order to perpetuate or transcend their liminal state.[112] While early stories stressed the predatory nature of such beings, later ones focused on the ghost's capacity to evoke such passion that the human partner would disregard the social taboos.[113] Thus, ghosts were suspended between being symbols of death and destruction and agents of social transformation. While the most common scenario involved a female ghost and a male scholar, other variations included, albeit rarely, female same-sex passion. In the Western fictional tradition, lesbian desire has consistently been associated with ghostly presences.[114] As a result, the associations of the ghostly with lesbian desire in these contemporary Chinese stories may well constitute creative adaptations of intersecting cultural codes, with varying emphases on the destructive and the liberating aspects of ghosthood.

First published in 1986, Liang Hanyi's "Lips" constructs lesbian desire as a polluting force that kills the subject of the desire and turns its object into a ghost of sorts, an anemic young woman whose sexual and emotional development have been arrested by a single passionate kiss of her closest high school friend. Haunted in nightmares by ghostly replays of this kiss, the young woman, Shuiping, struggles in vain to remove her sense of pollution with obsessive cleaning and grooming habits. The power of that deathbed kiss is such that no man, let

alone another woman, can come close without her reviling them for their revolting and disgusting behavior. In contrast to Wong's "ghosting" of a censorious dorm instructor, Liang's story depicts the inverse phenomenon: rather than asserting her own subjectivity in the face of her classmates' obscene gossip about Shuiping and her friend, Shuiping comes to view herself as nothing but an embodiment of precisely those rumors. Overpowered by a social sanction at once omnipresent and intangible, she severs all ties with her dying friend after the fateful and innocent kiss, only to be reduced to a diminished, ghostly existence. Ultimately, the narrative need not be read as a psychologically accurate account of a young woman's trauma, but can be interpreted as a symbolic retelling of the difficulty of carving out a private meaning for a gesture—in this case, a kiss between women—that is socially overdetermined.

In Hong Ling's story "Fever," the main protagonist is a vampire, whose extravagant flights of fancy clearly underscore the ghost's capacity to transgress taboos of all kinds. In its imagery, "Fever" mirrors the problematic of same-sex desire articulated in "Lips." Both stories make contrasting use of the colors red and white, focus on lips as a site of same-sex desire, take place in confined and marginal interior spaces such as hospital rooms and seedy motel rooms, and center on protagonists afflicted by lethal wasting diseases. In its outlook, however, "Fever" proceeds from a different premise than "Lips," pointing to the impact of feminist thinking and queer theory in 1990s Taiwan. Contrary to "Lips," where both protagonists assume the status of ghosts on account of their socially problematic desire for each other, in "Fever" such ghostliness is ascribed to the debilitating effects of the official protocols of sexuality.

"Fever" pits two systems of desire against each other, both of which kill the objects of desire, albeit for different reasons: in the case of unspecified heterosexual relations, the woman whom the vampire loved dies as a result of a botched abortion. Since abortion has been legal in Taiwan since the 1970s, abortion here serves more as a symbolic shorthand for the consequences of mandatory heterosexuality rather than as a local historical critique. In the case of the lesbian vampire, the vampire's marginal status leads to the destruction of the lives of the women she loves. It is not the vampire's sexual excess per se that kills the women, but the lack of desire induced by her inability to realize her affections in a socially sanctioned environment. Interestingly, even when the vampire wants to transcend her ghostly nature in an orchestrated, consuming, and explosive encounter with social legitimacy (symbolized by the "sun"), she remains trapped within a universe that offers no respite from social regulation. In the image of the artificially regulated sunrise, individual acts of redemptive heroism are led ad absurdum by the encompassing control of all social and natural processes.

Whereas "Fever's" vampire operates in a dystopic space, Chen Xue's "In Search of the Wings of the Angels," while hovering on the edges of the fantastic, attempts, as Fran Martin has compellingly argued, to reclaim a social space for its marginal protagonist.[115] The story conjoins two narrative strands, one centering on the erotic and literary explorations between the narrator and her female lover, the other focusing on her tormented yet unarticulable relation with her mother. In contrast to the two preceding stories, Chen Xue's narrative proposes that sexual love for a woman does not disembody her, but on the contrary, reembodies her fully. This reembodiment is figured in three different ways: through the erotic discovery of the female body, through the writing of the first complete story after the lover's sudden disappearance, and, finally, through a reconciliation with her mother at the site of her parents' grave. In a move very similar to the ending in Chen Ran's story, Chen Xue's protagonist finds a mystical object with which her mother blesses her daughter's love for women—for herself, for her mother, and for her imaginary lover, A-Su. What Sally Lieberman noted in the context of Republican writer Xiao Hong's conception of mothers resonates with Chen Xue's take on motherhood: "If we resist the temptation to flee the familiar text of maternal grief and madness, we may be tempted to discover between its lines a subtext that reads "Survive! Survive! Survive!"[116] Because control over language and filiality figured prominently in GMD conceptions of citizenship,[117] Chen's maternal mythology not only empowers the narrator as a cultural, familial, and sexual entity but also opens a space for political resistance.[118]

In He An's "Andante," the figure of the ghost is invoked in yet another fashion, symbolizing the narrator's fear that her lover might leave her for someone else. In this narrative, two love stories—one set in Taiwan, the other in the United States—are intertwined. In the Taiwan segment, love with a school friend is pitted against the social imperative of marriage. In the U.S. segment, love is contrasted with the vagaries and impermanence of individual choice. The narrator envisions her new lover, Chunliang Wang, as a translucent, ghostlike figure on a vast plain, roaming freely among many tents, uncertain as to whether she could ever be sufficiently attached to anyone in particular. The tension indicates that a lack as well as an abundance of choices can evoke images of "ghosting." Unmoored from the singular, fateful relations of most of the previous stories, He An's narrative allows for the everyday intimacy that Wong's narrator was hoping for, but even in this instance, the union is precarious, perhaps not so much because of social strictures as the precarious nature of love itself. Accordingly, "Andante" still does not anticipate a permanent "happily ever after," merely a temporary materiality and conditional commitment, which may or may not last into old age.

## Bodies, Texts, and Endings

"Andante's" Wang Chunliang offers something of a fictional rarity, a Chinese woman who comfortably reconciles artistic talent, lesbian desire, physical robustness, and social respectability. The Ming/Qing opposition between virtue (*de*) and talent (*cai*) continued to affect the social and literary conception of female intellectuals in the twentieth century. Virtue was first and foremost a bodily regime, centering on the maintenance of chastity, whereas talent circumscribed a male sphere of self-cultivation. Reconfiguring the relation between the two has been an ongoing negotiation between conflicting imperatives of literary productivity and sexual self-restraint.[119] Throughout the twentieth century, women writers discovered that a feminine identity was a public liability, especially if a writer's private life did not conform to the norms of propriety. For instance, one well-known Republican writer, Lu Yin, who—much to the dismay of her contemporaries—married a man nine years her junior, omitted virtually all references to her private life in her autobiography, emphasizing only her literary accomplishments.[120] In the 1990s, writers (including Zhang Jie) found that they could explore questions of love and desire in their fiction, but not without having their own personal lives subjected to moralizing scrutiny.[121] Laboring under a presumed autobiographical imperative, the price of women's admittance into the literary field appears to hinge upon gestures of renunciation of one kind or another.

Yet Wang Chunliang is only the most obvious example of a "new" New Woman. Even a cursory reading of the stories reviewed above reveals a disproportionate number of artists, musicians, journalists, and the like. Rather than simply construing this abundance of intellectuals as a reflection of the backgrounds of the authors, it may point to another dimension of same-sex intimacy in the 1990s. Fictional protagonists are allowed to have their creative cake and eat it with someone, too. In Wang Anyi's story, the two married women subordinate their creative and professional impulses to their roles of wife and mother. In Zhang Mei's story, the journalist is unattached and reveals little about her private aspirations. Although such disclosures about her romantic life are hardly mandatory, she might nonetheless typify the literary trope of the professionally successful, but unmarried, woman. By contrast, in Chen Xue's narrative, the writer writes herself into respectability through her exploration of sexuality. In so doing, the story proffers sexual alternatives other than marriage and prostitution, both of which placed the protagonist's mother out of the realms of literary creativity and social respectability. In He An's story, Wang Chunliang exists ready-made, albeit only in the diaspora, presenting a portrait of the happy (woman) artist in love (with another woman). No textual sacrifices—no suicide, illness, madness, loss—expiate any transgression, offering a fictional entity that, given the perennial popularity of the suffering woman, is banal and scandalous at once: the happy ending.

In the end, the unrepentant protagonists of Chen Ran's, Chen Xue's, and He An's narratives disrupt certain local and global circuits of vicarious empowerment. In a Chinese context, such independent women highlight the paternalistic presumptions inherent in much state-sponsored rhetoric of emancipation. A female sexuality most obviously unbounded by marriage and/or procreation creates a subjectivity that exceeds and thus delineates the interpolation of women into a nationalist enterprise. In short, together with other alternative modalities, such a dimension may yet foreground another horizon of liberation, namely the female body not in its productive and reproductive capacities, but in its ability to experience pleasure, that is, a superfluous *jouissance* not assimilable to any statist agenda. In a Western context, the possibility of such protagonists should give pause to anyone too keen on reifying the West as the sole site of sexual modernity. At the same time, in their peculiarly hybridized state, such representations also remind us not to fall prey to facile universals, which more often than not prepare the ground for relations of domination either between or within cultures. Hence, it is the particulars that matter, matter above and beyond the categorical. If the stories in this volume have something in common, it is this insistence on the opening up of interstices between what is either too easily trivialized or too readily pathologized. While other anthologies of Chinese fiction may focus on aesthetic experimentation, these stories look at forms of social contestation that challenge both dominant Chinese and Western conceptions of gender, sexuality, and the political. Rather than having to speculate on what might happen to politics if women's love for each other mattered, we can see what has happened—if only we start reading.

## NOTES

1. No single work synthesizes these new findings yet. For ancient China, see Lisa Raphals, *Sharing the Light: Representations of Women and Virtue in Early China* (Albany: SUNY Press, 1998); for the Tang period, see Jowen R. Tung, *Fables for the Patriarchs: Gender Politics in Tang Discourse* (Lanham, Md.: Rowman & Littlefield, 2000). For the Song, see Patricia Ebrey, *The Inner Quarters* (Berkeley: University of California Press, 1993). For the Ming, see Victoria Cass, *Dangerous Women: Warriors, Grannies and Geishas of the Ming* (Lanham, Md.: Rowman & Littlefield, 1999). For the Qing, see Ko (1994), Bray (1997), and Mann (1997) quoted below.

2. Dorothy Ko, *Teachers of the Inner Chambers: Women and Culture in Seventeenth-Century China* (Stanford, Calif.: Stanford University Press, 1994), 169–71.

3. See, for example, the writings of Lu Qingzi (fl. 1590), Xu Yuan (fl. 1590), and Wu Zao's (1799–1863) in *Women Writers of Traditional China: An Anthology of Poetry and Criticism*, ed. Kang-i Sun Chang and Haun Saussy (Stanford, Calif.: Stanford University Press, 1999), 239–65 and 601–16.

4. Shen Fu, *Six Chapters of a Floating Life* (Harmondsworth: Penguin, 1983), 51.

5. Francesca Bray, *Technology and Gender: Fabrics of Power in Late Imperial China* (Berkeley: University of California Press, 1997), 335–68.

6. On the former, see Dorothy Ko, *Teachers of the Inner Chambers*, 129–36. On the latter, see the discussion of the sixteenth-century female physician Tan Yunxian in Charlotte Furth, *A Flourishing Yin: Gender in China's Medical History, 960–1665* (Berkeley: University of California Press, 1999), 285–95.

7. Ann Waltner, "Visionary and Bureaucrat in the Late Ming: T'an-yang-tzu and Wang Shih-chen," *Late Imperial China* 8 (1987): 105–33.

8. See Amy D. Dooling and Kristina M. Torgeson, eds., *Writing Women in Modern China: An Anthology of Women's Literature from the Early Twentieth Century* (New York: Columbia University Press, 1999), 7. For a collection of Republican era writings on marriage reform and women's emancipation more generally, see *Women in Republican China: A Sourcebook*, ed. Hua R. Lan and Vanessa L. Fong (Armonk, N.Y.: M. E. Sharpe, 1999).

9. See, for example, Feng Yuanjun, "Separation," in Torgeson and Dooling, *Writing Women in Modern China*, 105–13.

10. Christina K. Gilmartin, "Gender, Political Culture, and Women's Mobilization in the Chinese Nationalist Revolution, 1924–1927," in *Engendering China: Women, Culture, and the State*, ed. Christina K. Gilmartin, et al. (Cambridge, Mass.: Harvard University Press, 1994), 225.

11. Neil J. Diamant, *Revolutionizing the Family: Politics, Love, and Divorce in Urban and Rural China, 1949–1968* (Berkeley: University of California Press, 2000).

12. Ono Kazuko, *Chinese Women in a Century of Revolution, 1850–1950* (Stanford, Calif.: Stanford University Press), 181.

13. See, for instance, Hanna Hacker, *Frauen und Freundinnen: Studien zur "weiblichen Homosexualität" am Beispiel Österreich 1870–1938* (Weinheim und Basel: Beltz, 1987).

14. Cathy Silber, "From Daughter to Daughter-in-Law in the Women's Script of Southern Hunan," in *Engendering China*, 48.

15. Susan Mann, *Precious Records: Women in China's Long Eighteenth Century* (Stanford, Calif.: Stanford University Press, 1997), 54–62.

16. Sally Taylor Liebermann, *The Mother and Narrative Politics in Modern China* (Charlottesville: University of Virginia Press, 1998), 105–06.

17. Wendy Larson, *Women and Writing in Modern China* (Stanford, Calif.: Stanford University Press, 1998), 55–56 and 68–69; Weikun Cheng, "Going Public through Education: Female Reformers and Girls' Schools in Late Qing Beijing," *Late Imperial China* 21 (2000): 118.

18. Dooling and Torgeson, *Writing Women in Modern China*, 12.

19. Christina K. Gilmartin, *Engendering the Chinese Revolution: Radical Women, Communist Politics, and Mass Movements in the 1920s* (Berkeley: University of California Press, 1995), 98–99.

20. Tani E. Barlow, introduction to *I Myself Am a Woman: Selected Writings of Ding Ling*, ed. Tani E. Barlow with Gary J. Bjorge (Boston: Beacon Press, 1989), 19.

21. For Republican fiction on passionate friendships with other women, see Lu Yin, "After Victory," and Ling Shuhua, "Once Upon a Time," in Dooling and Torgeson, *Writing Women in Modern China*, 143–56 and 185–95.

22. Dooling and Torgeson, *Writing Women in Modern China*, 19, 27–29.

23. Gail Hershatter, *Dangerous Pleasures: Prostitution and Modernity in Twentieth-Century Shanghai* (Berkeley: University of California Press, 1997), 169; Emily Honig, *Sisters and Strangers: Women in the Shanghai Cotton Mills, 1919–1949* (Stanford, Calif.: Stanford University Press, 1986), 212–13.

24. Honig, *Sisters and Strangers*, 215.

25. Honig, *Sisters and Strangers*, 209–43. See also Elizabeth J. Perry, *Shanghai on Strike: The Politics of Chinese Labor* (Stanford, Calif.: Stanford University Press), *passim*.

26. Honig, *Sisters and Strangers*, 214.

27. Silber, "From Daughter to Daughter-in-Law," 47–68.

28. Marjorie Topley, "Marriage Resistance in Rural Kwangtung," in *Women in Chinese Society*, ed. Margery Wolf and Roxanne Witke (Stanford, Calif.: Stanford University Press, 1975), 67–88; Janice Stockard, *Daughters of the Canton Delta: Marriage Patterns and Economic Strategies in South China* (Berkeley: University of California Press, 1989); Andrea Sankar, "Sisters and Brothers, Lovers and Enemies: Marriage Resistance in Southern Kwangtung," *Journal of Homosexuality* 11 (1985): 69–81; Helen Siu, "Where Were the Women? Rethinking Marriage Resistance and Regional Culture in South China," *Late Imperial China* 11:2 (1990): 32–62; Ono, *Chinese Women in a Century of Revolution*, 121–24.

29. Frank Dikötter, *Sex, Culture, and Modernity in China: Medical Science and the Construction of Sexual Identities in the Early Republican Period* (Honolulu: University of Hawaii Press, 1995), 180.

30. Hershatter, *Dangerous Pleasures*, 304–24. See also Gail Hershatter, "Modernizing Sex, Sexing Modernity," in *Engendering China*, 146–74.

31. For the possibility of using other vague criminal categories to prosecute gay men and women, see Dikötter, *Sex, Culture, and Modernity*, 183–84.

32. Harriet Evans, *Women and Sexuality in China* (New York: Continuum, 1997), 202–6. Interestingly, despite the pervasive rhetoric of Communist camaraderie, mainland short fiction published in the early 1960s did not treat close friendship. See Ai-li S. Chin, "Family Relations in Modern Chinese Fiction," in *Family and Kinship in Chinese Society*, ed. Maurice Freedman (Stanford, Calif.: Stanford University Press, 1970), 119.

33. Diamant, *Revolutionizing the Family*, 193–94. Diamant does not divulge the outcome of the story.

34. Gilmartin, *Engendering the Revolution*, 9; Diamant, *Revolutionizing the Family*, 285–307.

35. Anja Meulenbelt, *Kleine Füsse, grosse Füsse* (Munich: Knaur, 1984), 189.

36. Lisa Rofel, "Museum as Women's Space: Displays of Gender in Post-Mao China," in *Spaces of Their Own: Women's Public Sphere in Transnational China*, ed. Mayfair Mei-hui Yang (Minneapolis: University of Minnesota, 1999), 117; Mayfair Mei-hui Yang, "Introduction," *Spaces of Their Own*, 1–31.

37. On Sun Yat-sen's elevation to the status of the father figure at the expense of possible mother figures, see Gilmartin, "Gender, Political Culture, and Women's Mobilization," 199–206.

38. For a series of new and demeaning terms highlighting the sexual and economic dependence of women on men, see Jingyuan Zhang, "Breaking Open: Chinese Women's Writing in the Late 1980s and 1990s," in *Chinese Literature in the Second Half of a Modern Century: A Critical Survey*, ed. Pang-yuan Chi and David Der-wei Wang (Bloomington: Indiana University Press, 2000), 174.

39. See Li Xiaojiang, "Economic Reform and the Awakening of Chinese Women's Collective Consciousness," in *Engendering China*, 360–82. On the complexities of Li Xiaojiang's position, see Lisa Rofel, "Museum As Women's Space," 129. For a genealogy of the terms involved, see Tani E. Barlow, "Politics and Protocol of *Funü*: (Un)making National Woman," in *Engendering China*, 339–59.

40. Zhang, "Breaking Open," 162.

41. Dalian Liu et al., *Sexual Behavior in Modern China* (New York: Continuum, 1997), 162.

42. Li Yinhe, *Zhongguo nüxing de ganqing yu xing* (Beijing: Xinri Zhongguo, 1998), 207–8. Interestingly, the heterosexual women commenting on lesbian or bisexual women also are generally supportive, a picture that contrasts with the disgust often informing heterosexual reactions towards lesbianism in fictional writings of the 1990s. For the latter point, see Zhang, "Breaking Open," 167.

43. Zhang, "Breaking Open," 162. For an example of three PRC women writers distancing themselves from the label of "woman writer," see Wang Zheng, "Three Interviews: Wang Anyi, Zhu Lin, Dai Qing," in *Gender Politics in Modern China*, 159–208; for a Taiwanese example, see Sheung-Yuen Daisy Ng, "Feminism in the Chinese Context: Li Ang's *The Butcher's Wife*," in *Gender Politics in Modern China*, 270–71.

44. Dai Jinhua, "Rewriting Chinese Women: Gender Production and Cultural Space in the Eighties and Nineties," in *Spaces of Their Own*, 203.

45. See Zhang, "Breaking Open," 178, n. 5.

46. See also Fran Martin, "Hybrid Citations: Chen Xue's Queer Tactics," *Positions* 7 (1999): 93, n. 12.

47. For an account of the feminist organizing in Taiwan from the 1970s to 1990s by one of the leading early feminists, see Lee Yuan-chen, "How the Feminist Movement Won Media Space in Taiwan: Observation by a Feminist Activist," in *Spaces of Their Own*, 95–115. For a discussion of the tensions between feminist and/or lesbian activists in the mid-1990s, see Tze-lan Deborah Sang, "Feminism's Double: Lesbian Activism in the Mediated Public Sphere of Taiwan," in *Spaces of Their Own*, 143–49. For a provocative articulation of real and imagined relations between sexuality and political formations, see the papers gathered in the special issue "Queer Theory and Politics" of *Xing/bie yanjiu* 3&4 (1998).

48. Best known for her novels *The Butcher's Wife* (*Shafu*) (1983) and *Dark Night* (*Anye*) (1985), Li raised and rejected the possibility of lesbianism in her short fiction collection *Their Tears* (*Tamen de yanlei*) (1983). For a discussion of sexuality in 1980s Taiwanese women's fiction in general, see Sung Mei-hwa, "Feminist Consciousness in the Contemporary Fiction of Taiwan," in *Cultural Change in Postwar Taiwan*, ed. Stevan Harrell and Huang Chün-chieh (Boulder, Colo.: Westview Press, 1994), 275–93; on Li Ang, see Howard Goldblatt, "Sex and Society: The Fiction of Li Ang," in *Worlds Apart: Recent Chinese Writings and Its Audiences*, ed. Howard Goldblatt (Armonk, N.Y.: M. E. Sharpe, 1990), 150–65.

49. The first term refers to the first lesbian group founded in Taiwan in 1990, the other two designate the Taiwanese lesbian and gay subculture more generally. See Zhuang Huiqiu, ed., *Zhongguo ren de tongxing lian* (Taipei: Zhang Laoshi, 1991).

50. Antoine Berman, *The Experience of the Foreign: Culture and Translation in Romantic Germany* (Albany: SUNY Press, 1984), 2.

51. Lydia H. Liu, *Translingual Practice: Literature, National Culture, and Translated Modernity—China, 1900–1937* (Stanford, Calif.: Stanford University Press, 1995).

52. Hu Ying, *Tales of Translation: Composing the New Woman in China, 1899–1918* (Stanford, Calif.: Stanford University Press, 2000), 12. In the original, the verbs are in past tense, since Hu is referring to the late Qing in particular.

53. Lydia H. Liu, "The Question of Meaning-Value in the Political Economy of the

Sign," in *Tokens of Exchange*, ed. Lydia H. Liu (Chapel Hill, N.C.: Duke University Press, 1999), 34–37.

54. Hu, *Tales of Translation*.

55. Larson, *Women and Writing*, 34–35, 43.

56. See, for example, Xiaomei Chen, *Occidentalism: A Theory Of Counter-Discourse in Post-Mao China* (Oxford: Oxford University Press, 1994).

57. Larson, *Women and Writing*, 43. Sophia Chen (Chen Hengzhe) wrote the very first story in vernacular form in 1917, a feat with which conventional histories credit Lu Xun. See Dooling and Torgeson, *Writing Women in Modern China*, 10, 91–99.

58. Xie Bingying, *Yige nübing de zizhuan* (Shanghai: Liangyou, 1936). The first English-language translation appeared in the United States: Hsieh Pingying, *Girl Rebel: The Autobiography of Hsieh Pingying, with Extracts from Her New War Diaries*, trans. Adet and Anor Lin (New York: John Day, 1940). An alternate translation appeared in England: Hsieh Bing-ying, *Autobiography of a Chinese Girl: A Genuine Autobiography*, trans. Tsui Chi (London: Allen & Unwin, 1943). Both translations were given a new lease on circulation through reprints, the first by DaCapo Press in 1975, the other by Pandora in 1986. For a new translation, see Xie Bingying, *A Woman Soldier's Own Story*, trans. Lily Chia Brissman and Barry Brissman (New York: Columbia University Press, 2001). For Min's text see, Anchee Min, *Red Azalea: Life and Love in China* (New York: Pantheon, 1994).

59. I am indebted to Jing Wang for bringing Xie's memoir to my attention. For a discussion of Xie's memoir in the context of Orientalism, see Jing Wang, "Strategies of Modern Chinese Women Writers Autobiography," Ph.D. diss., The Ohio State University, 2000, 157–65, 180.

60. Gilmartin, *Engendering the Revolution*, 115–99.

61. See the four essays on "Bing Ying" gathered in Huang Renying, ed., *Dangdai Zhongguo nüzuojia lun* (Shanghai: Shanghai guanghua, 1933), 79–118. On Xie Bingying's biography and for an excerpt from the *War Diary*, see Dooling and Torgeson, *Writing Women*, 253–62. For a discussion of the gender politics of the Northern Expedition and Xie's role, see Gilmartin, *Engendering the Revolution*, 174–99.

62. Lin Yutang, ed., "Letters of a Chinese Amazon," in *Letters of a Chinese Amazon and War-Time Essays* (Shanghai: The Commercial Press, 1930), 3–47. The diary was translated into other languages as well. Other writers reinforced such portrayals of "revolutionary female fighters"; see, for example, Agnes Smedley, *Portraits of Chinese Women in Revolution* (New York: The Feminist Press, 1976).

63. On Lin Yutang's and his three daughters' activities on behalf of such a U.S./Chinese alliance, see John Diran Sohigian, "The Life and Times of Lin Yutang," Ph.D. diss., Columbia University, 1991, 589–94.

64. Isidor Schneider, "Both Sides of the China Sea," *New Republic* 103 (1940), 391.

65. *The New York Times Review*, 28 July 1940.

66. Xie Bingying, *Nüpantu/Girl Rebel* (Taipei: Minguang, 1940).

67. Xie, *Yige nübing de zizhuan*, 95.

68. Hsieh, *Autobiography*, 76.

69. Xie, *Yige nübing de zizhuan*, 95–107; Hsieh, *Autobiography*, 76–81.

70. Tze-lan Deborah Sang, "Translating Homosexuality: The Discourse of *Tongxing'ai* in Republican China (1912–1949)," in *Tokens of Exchange*, 276–304.

71. Dikötter, *Sex, Culture, and Modernity*, 137–45; Sang, "Translating Homosexuality," 301, n. 2 and 303, n. 47.

72. Xie, *Yige nübing de zizhuan*, 97.

73. Christa Winsloe, *Mädchen in Uniform* (München: Frauenoffensive, 1983).

74. Luo Sha (pseudonym), *Yige nüxing de zishu* (Hong Kong: Qunle tushu, 1954); Xie Bingying, *Nübing zizhuan* (Taipei: Lixing, 1976) contains a preface by Xie dated 1955, in which she presents that (substantially revised) version as the legitimate one; Xie Bingying, *Xie Bingying wenji*, ed. by Ai Yi and Cao Du (n.p: Anhui wenyi, 1999) includes another preface by Xie touching upon the complicated translation and publication history of the text. Jing Wang observes that the "lesbian" episode was omitted in a 1980 Taiwanese edition. See her "Strategies of Modern Chinese Women Writers' Autobiography," 157, n. 1.

75. See, for example, the review by Judith Shapiro, "Counterrevolutionary Sex," *New York Times*, 27 February 1994, 11 (Section 7).

76. Lin, *Zhongguo nüxing de ganqing yu xing*, 218.

77. For a similar observation in the context of contemporary Chinese film, see Chris Berry, "Sexual Disorientations: Homosexual Rights, East Asian Films, and Postmodern Postnationalism," in *In Pursuit of Contemporary East Asian Culture*, ed. Xiaobing Tang and Stephen Snyder (Boulder, Colo.: Westview Press, 1996), 171.

78. Min, *Red Azalea*, 174.

79. Meng Yue, "Female Images and National Myth," in *Gender Politics in Modern China*, 118; Bai Di, "A Feminist Brave New World: The Cultural Revolution Model Theater Revisited," Ph.D. diss., The Ohio State University, 1997, 166–85.

80. For similar narratives of erotic projection onto figures of model performances, see Xiaomei Chen, "Growing Up with Cultural Revolution Posters," in *Picturing Power in the People's Republic of China*, ed. Harriet Evans and Stephanie Donald (Lanham, Md.: Rowman & Littlefield, 1999), 110–12; Lin Bai, *Yige ren de zhanzheng* [One Person's War], in *Lin Bai wenji* (Nanjing: Jiangsu wenyi, 1997), 2:35–36. For a critique of Meng Yue's argument, see Xiaomei Chen, *Acting the Right Part: Political Theater and Popular Drama in Contemporary China* (Honolulu: University of Hawaii Press, forthcoming 2002).

81. See, for example, Jung Chang who writes primarily from a point of view of disaffection, with the occasional acknowledgment of the tremendous hold of the political imagery and practices on her emotional life at the time. See her *Wild Swans: Three Daughters of China* (New York: Bantam Doubleday, 1991).

82. A. O. Scott, "The Re-Education of Anchee Min," *New York Times Magazine*, 18 June 2000, 44–47.

83. For one story with obvious resonance, see Patricia Sieber, "Eine unmögliche Geschichte," *Script* 7 (1995): 60–64.

84. Rey Chow, *Primitive Passions: Visuality, Sexuality, Ethnography, and Contemporary Chinese Cinema* (New York: Columbia University Press, 1995), 192.

85. Virginia Cornue, "Practicing NGOness and Relating Women's Space Publicly: The Women's Hotline and the State," in *Spaces of Their Own*, 68–90, esp. 80. On the sexual conservatism of the counselors at the hotline, see Zhou Huashan, *Beijing tongzhi gushi* (Hong Kong: Xianggang tongzhi yanjiu she, 1996), 102–07.

86. For Taiwan, see Sang, "Feminism's Double," 150–53; for the PRC, see Dai, "Rewriting Chinese Women," 204.

87. For an analysis of this process of representation and its attendant silencing of women, see Yue Ming-Bao, "Gendering the Origins of Modern Chinese Fiction," in *Gender and Sexuality in Twentieth-Century Chinese Literature and Society*, ed. Tonglin Lü (Albany: SUNY Press, 1993), 47–65. See also Lieberman, *The Mother and Narrative Politics in Modern China*, 193–202.

88. The best-known example is undoubtedly the story of the *White-Haired Girl* (*Baimao nü*). See Meng, "Female Images and National Myth," 119–24.

89. Dai, "Rewriting Chinese Women," 191–202.

90. See for example Zhu Hong, "Women, Illness, and Hospitalization: Images of Women in Contemporary Chinese Fiction," in *Engendering China*, 318–38.

91. Liu Liangya, "Aiyu, xingbie yu shuxie: Qiu Miaojin de nü tongxinglian xiaoshuo," *Zhongwai wenxue* 303 (1997): 24.

92. On the latter practice in the Hong Kong and Taiwanese press, see Bret Hinsch, *Passions of the Cut Sleeve*, 169–70 and Sang, "Feminism's Double," 150–53.

93. For a discussion of the terms surrounding "feminism," see Wang Zheng, *Women in the Chinese Enlightenment: Oral and Textual Histories* (Berkeley: University of California Press, 1999), 7–9. For a discussion of the origins and uses of the terms surrounding "lesbianism," see Sang, "Feminism's Double," in *Spaces of Their Own*, 137–40.

94. Fredric Jameson, "Third-World Literature in the Era of Multinational Capitalism," *Social Text* 15 (1986): 65–88. For an excellent critique of Jameson's position in the context of modern Chinese women's literature, see Lieberman, *The Mother and Narrative Politics*, 189–90.

95. Other examples not included in this anthology include: Liu Xihong, "You Can't Make Me Change," in *I Wish I Were a Wolf: The New Voice in Chinese Women's Literature*, trans. Diana B. Kingsbury (Beijing: New World Press, 1994), 213–34; Liu Suola, "Blue Sky, Green Sea," in *Blue Sky, Green Sea and Other Stories*, trans. Martha Cheung (Hong Kong: Renditions, 1993), 19–56.

96. Dai Jinhua, Lecture, The Ohio State University, 20 August 1999.

97. Li, "Economic Reform and the Awakening of Chinese Women's Collective Consciousness," 360–82.

98. Kam Louie, "Love Stories: The Meaning of Love and Marriage in China," in *After Mao: Chinese Literature and Society, 1978–1981*, ed. Jeffrey C. Kinkley (Cambridge, Mass.: Harvard University Press, 1985), 61–87.

99. Dai, "Rewriting Chinese Women," 202–05.

100. Xiaomei Chen, "Reading Mother's Tale—Reconstructing Women's Space in Amy Tan and Zhang Jie," *Chinese Literature, Essays, Articles, Reviews* 16 (1994): 119–24.

101. Lieberman, *The Mother and Narrative Politics*, 104–33.

102. Dai, "Rewriting Chinese Women," 204; Dai, Lecture, The Ohio State University, 23 July 1999.

103. Previously, such continuity was primarily a strategic scholarly construct. Lydia Liu had argued that it mattered less whether such a tradition in fact existed, but that the conception of such a tradition enables female critics to contest both the exclusionary authority of the male critical establishment that trivializes women writers and of the official Women's Federation that represents them only as already liberated comrades. See Lydia H. Liu, "Invention and Intervention: The Female Tradition in Modern Chinese Literature," in *Gender Politics in Modern China*, 56–57.

104. Chow, *Primitive Passions*, 180–82.

105. For a compelling interpretation of this story, see Zhang, "Breaking Open," 169–71.

106. Ravni Thakur, *Rewriting Gender: Reading Contemporary Chinese Women* (London: Zed Books, 1997), 164.

107. Chen Yu-shih, "Harmony and Equality: Notes on 'Mimosa' and 'Ark,' " in *Gender Politics in Modern China*, 157–58.

108. Zhong Xueping wondered whether the ambivalence between the women was related to a tension between heterosexism and lesbianism or to a tension between gender norms and woman's desire to challenge them. See her "Sisterhood? Representations of Women's Relationships in Two Contemporary Chinese Texts," in *Gender and Sexuality in Twentieth-Century Chinese Literature and Society*, 172–73. Lydia Liu dismissed the question as irrelevant, since the text was not written within a context where sexual orientation was a meaningful category. See her "Invention and Intervention," 53.

109. Zhang Jingyuan, "Jiegou shenhua: ping Wang Anyi de 'Dixiongmen,' " *Dangdai zuojia pinglun* (1992:2): 33; Zhang, "Breaking Open," 168.

110. Liu, "Invention and Intervention," 54.

111. Tani E. Barlow, "Gender and Identity in Ding Ling's 'Mother,' " in *Modern Chinese Women Writers: Critical Appraisals*, ed. Michael S. Duke (Armonk, N.Y.: M. E. Sharpe, 1989), 16.

112. Judith T. Zeitlin, "Embodying the Disembodied: Representations of Ghosts and the Feminine," in *Writing Women in Late Imperial China*, ed. Ellen Widmer and Kang-i Sun Chang (Stanford, Calif.: Stanford University Press, 1997), 242–63.

113. The most famous and influential of these stories is the 1598 drama *The Peony Pavilion*, a play that struck a major cord with female audiences in the seventeenth century. See Ko, *Teachers of the Inner Chambers*, 68–112.

114. Terry Castle, *The Apparitional Lesbian* (New York: Columbia University Press, 1994).

115. Martin, "Hybrid Citations," 71–94.

116. Lieberman, *The Mother and Narrative Politics*, 217.

117. Hans Huang, "Be(com)ing Gay: Sexual Dissidence and Cultural Change in Contemporary Taiwan" (M.A. Thesis, University of Sussex, 1996).

118. Ding Naifei, "Feichang tiejin yinfu ji enü: Ruhe yuedu *Jinpingmei* (1695) he *E'nü shu* (1995)" *Zhongwai wenxue*, 26: 303 (1997): 48–67.

119. Larson, *Women and Writing*, 2–4, 72.

120. Wang, "Strategies of Modern Chinese Women Writers' Autobiography," 145–56.

121. Dai, Lecture, The Ohio State University, 23 July 1999.

# 2

# SHE'S A YOUNG WOMAN AND SO AM I

Wong Bikwan

*Translated by Naifei Ding*

I thought I could spend the rest of my life with Jihang.

Her name is Hui Jihang. When I met her for the first time, we were still college freshmen. Our paths first crossed when we were both taking "The Art of Critical Thinking," a required course for all new students.

Among my peers, she was the only one I knew of who would wear a tightly fitting *qipao* dress and dainty embroidered slippers to class. What nerve! How fake! Yet how very eye-catching! I remember that pair of bright red, embroidered slippers. Her hair was trimmed evenly to just beneath the earlobes. Often, with her eyes cast downward and her head lowered, she would take notes, as if she were one of those exemplary students. However, she painted her nails peach-red. Only bad women would wear nail polish. The kind who would quietly flaunt their seductive wiles through such minutiae were especially bad. I didn't know that I might like a bad woman.

Not surprisingly, she was talked about everywhere. The boys in my class told me that her name was Hui Jihang, that she was a Chinese major, that she had graduated from the famous Sojit public school, and that her family lived on Laamtong Street, an affluent neighborhood. They would be talking about her in small groups in their dorms when we were in class studying Plato. I would girlishly laugh at them, but I began thinking of them with increasing contempt. They continued to talk about her, and among themselves called her "Little Phoenix Goddess."

Jihang consistently skipped class. Once I bumped into her at the train station.

With her head bent down, she walked straight ahead, an obedient male student in tow.

The following year we met again in the "Introduction to Sociology" class. The lecturer disliked roll call and therefore he wanted us to sit in the same seat throughout the semester, so he could tell at a glance who was absent. I grabbed the chance to sit down next to Jihang. I remember that day she was wearing a loosely fitting, white and dark mauve cotton *qipao*. The hair on her arms was very fine. In addition, she exuded a certain smell, a mixture of make-up, perfume, milk, and ink. I called that odor the "Phoenix Goddess Smell" ever after. Her hands were so smooth and cold that I felt like touching them. But I didn't, since she took no notice of my existence.

She had skipped class again. Only when we came to the Marxist notion of surplus value did she reappear. She asked to borrow my lecture notes. "Even if I were to let you have them, they would be useless—only I can read these scrawls!" She lifted an eyebrow. "Not necessarily." Because I was lazy, I had written the notes in shorthand. My classmates all called them the "telegraphic notes." Hence nobody ever asked to borrow them. But she was copying them over just as rapidly as I had taken them down, and there was my "secret code" translated into legible, orderly script—I suppose if one doesn't attend class for a month, one still needs a knack for something in order to pass. I like people who are clever and don't follow the rules, maybe that is the reason why I asked Jihang out.

I said, "Let me take you out for coffee." She said, "Okay." We also shared a telegraphic mode of talking.

We sat in the slanting sun without saying a word. I looked at her intently. She looked at me and said, "I have seen you around. You are Yip Saisai. You practice the Shakuhachi flute all by yourself at night in the classroom. I have heard you play." She was wearing several thin silver bracelets, which glistened and clinked as she moved. She said, "I know that you lost a pink Maidenform bra last week, I read about it in the main hall of the dorm, on the events wall. It was yours, wasn't it?" She added, laughing, "The whole dorm knows about it, even the guys do! How silly of you to lose a 32B Maidenform bra!" I said: "No, 32A! I am thin you know!" I saw that her breasts were rather ample. "I bet you are at least a 34B and after you get married, you will become a 38." Jihang softly put her hand to her chest: "Ayah, that's what I am afraid of as well." Thus our rapport began somewhat unexpectedly over a Maidenform bra.

She suddenly started coming to class regularly and we would talk. "The old instructor is such an old fogy, his flesh-colored nylon socks are showing." I asked her where she bought her *qipaos*. She said that that was a trade secret. I arranged for us to go see a film shown on campus, Lau Shing-hou's *The House of the Lute*. We laughed really hard. I dragged her to a showing of Eisenstein's *October*. We both fell asleep, and did not wake up until everyone had left. We then went out for a midnight snack. Jihang would sometimes wear jeans too, as on that day when she went for stir-fried mussels with me, but she always insisted on those embroidered slippers.

The second semester of our junior year, her roommate moved out of the dorm. Jihang did not tell the dorm matron, and I moved in with her. Actually, that was when it all really started between me and Jihang.

To tell the truth, I simply felt that Jihang was femininely seductive, clever in a petty sort of way, and even-tempered, yet I didn't really understand her conduct. That's probably where our relationship most resembled the love between men and women. Our respective initial attraction derived largely from the other's ability to show off her looks. Even though I was neither a beauty nor did I possess Jihang's allure, I knew very well how to subtly sell myself. I think Jihang liked my kind, it's a, ah well, understated, worldly, sort of charm. Not unlike her *qipao* and her embroidered slippers.

In our dorm room, we created our own "smoke and flower alley," punning on the name for the traditional haunts of courtesans. We both smoked. She smoked Red Double Happiness, I smoked Menthol Dunhills, both irredeemably wild and wicked brands. We both liked Tom Waits. We would dance in our room, her body soft and pliant. We were both girls. On occasion I would translate some de Beauvoir, but after a while she did not seem up to snuff, and so I switched to Kristeva. Jihang liked to read Yi Shu, the popular romance novelist, to which I objected, thus she changed to Sagan, to which I objected again, so she read Angela Carter. We both gradually made progress. I got a scholarship. Jihang had applied for one as well, but did not get it. She had lost out to me.

The day I received the scholarship, my picture appeared in the school newspaper. I remembered that once when I'd gone shopping with her, she had had her eye on a fire red cashmere sweater, but since it cost an extravagant sum, she could not bring herself to get it. I bought it for her now, planning to give it to her at dinnertime. However, she did not come back for dinner. I waited until it began to get dark. I was alone in the room and did not turn on the lights. It was already late autumn. Outside the window, the sea was alight with scattered fishing boats. I suddenly felt as though she were one of those proverbially heartless men. I had had boyfriends before, but never once had I felt this anxious. Jihang had not made her bed that morning. Jihang was not wearing her embroidered slippers that day. Jihang's toothpaste was almost used up. I made a mental note to buy some for her. Jihang's Phoenix Goddess Smell filled the room. Her makeup and powder. Her tears. I motionlessly leaned against the side of the window. Two teardrops streamed quietly down my cheeks. Just two drops, then the tears dried up. Jihang, Jihang.

I woke up, ate some bread, suddenly finding that the bread had the stale smell of flour, a smell very similar to that of animal feed. I had been eating bread for more than ten years, and only now had I become aware of the smell and taste of bread. It was as if I had understood the truth about bread and could only feel a certain wistfulness. Wistfulness! What a commonplace! Yet at this moment I truly felt very wistful, mixed with a sense of seeing things afresh, as though for the first time. Ah, the feeling of tasting reality is difficult to describe.

An hour past midnight, as I stood by the window, I heard the sound of a car. Jihang alighted from a taxi. She was wearing a black skirt and top and black pumps. Poor woman! Even at this point I was still paying attention to what she was wearing. I realized I noticed her clothing and her smell much more than her character or her breeding—perhaps she did not have much character or breeding. I felt suddenly ashamed. How was I different then from those men? Just like the men, I set store by her looks, although I had never touched her. Perhaps because neither of us had wanted to broach the subject, we had neither done anything like kissing or caressing nor had we ever felt the need for it. Those so-called lesbian intimacies accompanied by moans and mutterings are merely a fantastic scenario men have imagined for the sake of feasting their eyes. Jihang and I had never done anything like that. I had never even said "I love you" to her. However, at that moment I knew that I loved her very much, to the point of wanting to find out if she had any character or breeding.

I leaned against the window, my heart afire and beating hard. Jihang was coming! Jihang was coming!

The door opened slowly and she dropped onto the bed. Her whole face was flushed and her entire body exuded the sour smell of alcohol. Strangely enough, Jihang's face had been heavily made up, but now it was all smeared. I suddenly recalled the stale smell of bread. I remained silent, the words frozen on my lips.

She laughed, "You must be happy today. I am very happy today." Suddenly, a handful of coins came flying in my direction. "Yip Saisai, I am merely an ordinary person." I covered my face without speaking. The coins hit the back of my hands, causing a sharp pain. When Jihang tired of throwing coins, she leaned back against the bed. For a time, there was dead silence. The light hurt my eyes.

"Jihang."

She didn't answer me. She had fallen asleep. I wiped her face with a washcloth, took off her clothes and her shoes, and kissed her feet.

I perfunctorily straightened the room, then left a note on her desk. "Jihang, if one day we find ourselves drowning in a sea of people just living our lives in busy commonsense, that will have been because we did not try hard enough to live life to the fullest." At the time, I had no ambitions, but Jihang did.

That same night, I went and knocked on the door of a guy. This guy had had a crush on me for a long time. His whole face was filled with impatient lust. Of course, I knew it would be like that. I had gone to his room on the spur of the moment. Quite possibly this was a way of taking revenge on myself and on Jihang and on this person, because I have no heart. And my body does not belong to me. The whole next day, I was very absentminded. I had the guy rent a room for me off-campus. When he was gone, I didn't care. I continued to go to classes; in fact, contrary to my usual habits, I became more mindful of my schoolwork.

When I walked past the dorm, I would always look up. Was Jihang there? Was she combing her hair? Was she doing her homework? Was she reading a newspaper? Could she be thinking about me? Jihang had suddenly disappeared from my life. How calm I appeared, yet no one knew my heart's ups and downs. Jihang, Jihang.

One late autumn night, I was having dinner with the guy. The man's conversation was bland. I just kept drinking wine. At the end of the meal, my whole body had turned red. Walking out into the evening chill, I vomited, my face soaked with tears. The man gave me his handkerchief and I held on to him tightly. At that moment, any man with a handkerchief would have been a good man. I could not help despising him a little less. Really, if at that moment I could have had some feeling for him and forever thence severed ties with Jihang, that would not have been a bad thing. The man drove a little Japanese car. As soon as he got into it, he grabbed hold of me and pressed his face against mine. I laughed, "You could have been a good man, but since you are willing to kiss a woman who stinks of stale wine, I am beginning to strongly doubt your taste." Visibly annoyed, he started the car to take me back to the flat. I said, "Not so fast! I want to return to the dorm to get some things."

It was three o'clock in the morning. Jihang had turned on the desk lamp, but did not appear to be in. I stood in the night, craning my neck as I was looking up toward the window. There she was underneath the light! Jihang, I had never  meant to take away your luster, I am merely an ordinary girl who wants a simple emotional bond with another human being. Why won't the world grant me even that?

Suddenly, Jihang's shadow flitted past the window, and the light was turned off. In the space of that movement, had Jihang's hair grown? Was there anyone to cut her toenails? Anyone to paint her nails? After I'd left, who was there to button her dresses in the back? At night, who would come to see her or who would think of her? Who would know if she were happy or sad? Who would compete with her for that little bit of notoriety? Whom did she love and whom did she worry about?

I wanted to see her badly. Just one glance.

I rushed up the stairs. Jihang had locked the door, but I had a key. She was asleep, her chest moving up and down. Her breasts were as ample as they used to be. After a few weeks' separation, no telltale signs of being lovelorn: she had neither lost weight nor did she look haggard. I inspected her toenails—they were still well manicured and well painted, brilliantly red as usual. On her bed, there were a few more dolls. She was cuddling with a stuffed toy rabbit, sleeping soundly like an infant. What a peaceful sight! The sun was still rising, night was still falling, and at three in the morning, there were still those who are sound asleep and those who are wide awake. Who was still typing away next door, busy with homework in search of success? My eyes suddenly overflowed with tears. My throat made a gurgling sound, as if someone were throttling me. Who was that?

I was strangling myself as I thought to myself that tonight the stars were certain to fall like the rain. Jihang had betrayed my feelings for her.

My tears fell on Jihang's face. I had clutched my throat so tightly that my face was all red and I could breathe only with difficulty. Jihang suddenly awoke, and held tightly onto my hand, saying, "Why do this?"

Jihang held me in her arms, and suffused in her Phoenix Goddess Smell, I quietly fell asleep. I vaguely heard the sound of a car's horn downstairs. So what? That man had already outlived his usefulness in my life, and from here on out I would have nothing to do with him. For now, there was only Jihang.

Jihang held my face in her hands and said, "You're so stupid."

I didn't respond, wanting only to sleep. Tomorrow there would be sunshine.

After that, things with Jihang seemed a little better. When we studied until late at night, she would always boil a cup of ginseng tea for me. Jihang had always been too lazy to study hard. Why this sudden change of heart? I vaguely sensed that Jihang was different now, even her perfume, Opium, was a famous brand. I felt as though I was choking.

Jihang was going out again at night. At midnight, she always wore that large fire red sweater and black boots. She roamed like a leopard. There was always a bright blue sports car waiting for her downstairs. She always returned with flushed cheeks, bringing me warm, sweet rice balls that I could not swallow even if I felt like eating them. Once hardened, the rice balls were inedible. The next morning, faced with the hardened balls of glutinous rice, I was at a complete loss. Jihang was never there. We were now in our senior year; in all this time, she had only earned eleven credit hours.

Over Christmas break, I prepared to return to my family for one night. Jihang was packing, and I asked her how long she would be staying with her family. She shook her head, and said with a smile, "I am going to Beijing."

I silently stood there for a long time. We had been to Japan together, and had promised each that next time it would be Beijing. That was last Christmas. I covered my face, saying, "Jihang, Jihang, do you remember . . ."

She pried open my hands, and looked me in the eye. "I remember, but that was before. This time I have this chance. You too might have to make plans for your future. I don't have to live a commonplace life." She kissed me on the forehead and left.

I collapsed into a chair, alone in the half-empty room. I thought I might as well sit here for the rest of my life. Then I laid down on the floor, and found that the carpet had gotten dirty. Jihang and I had looked for a whole afternoon in the upscale Central neighborhood before finding and buying this carpet. She had insisted on an Iranian carpet, but I thought that was too unrealistic, and proposed that we get an Indian carpet instead. As a compromise, we settled on a Belgian carpet. We ate Dutch food while holding on to our new carpet. Jihang asked for a dozen oysters on the half shell. We spent all our money. . . . When did all that happen?

That Christmas, I spent every single, long day at the library feeling sickly and barely holding up. I leafed through a weekly magazine and came upon a big callow-faced fatso with a pair of flashy sunglasses. I flinched. I was struck by the sudden realization that the person standing next to him in all likelihood was Jihang. After closing the magazine, I went to the cafeteria as if nothing had happened. I found myself seated where Jihang and I had sat when we first met. A fit of nausea overcame me and I almost started to cry. I gritted my teeth and returned to the library. This time I finished my homework without a stray thought.

When Jihang returned, I was asleep with my head in my arms on the desk, and with the magazine opened to the page with Jihang's picture. I neither looked at Jihang nor did she move. She just sat there, smoking. Then she quoted the old adage describing a desperate situation, "The general has not only lost his wife, but also his army."

I went and made her a cup of hot green tea. She held tightly onto my hand, while I tenderly stroked her hair.

I did not press her further, and thereafter she never brought up the subject. Until now, I still don't know what exactly happened. She would no longer go out at night. Instead, she would stay in the dorm and assiduously practice all sorts of postures and expressions, holding her face this way and that, as though she were proud to look more and more sophisticated.

Graduation was drawing near. I too began to tone down what I considered my so-called understated, worldly charm. I was after all neither a society hostess nor a dance-hall girl, thus I could not make a living off of my charm. I applied for graduate school, hoping to get a position in academia in the future. Frankly, in order to get a job as an intellectual one does not need much wisdom or courage; someone as useless as me will do just as well so long as one is suitably packaged. So I went ahead and immersed myself in the study of contemporary Western philosophy. It was the easiest subject, since neither the teacher nor myself understood any of it. When I finished my thesis, everybody could read it and feel smug. At least it was done. Everybody truly heaved a sigh of relief, as if a heavy load had been taken from us, and was very happy.

My relations with Jihang gradually cooled off. She was even more seductively beautiful than before. She would dress up to the nines even for the exams. I heard from my classmates that she was having an affair with a teacher. Then someone else told me that she had become a model for some fashion magazine. Why did all these people know more about Jihang than I? Jihang and I did not have many days left. I wanted to rent an apartment with her. She could continue her public career, while I would continue my studies. I wanted to raise a cat together with Jihang, and to own an Iranian handwoven carpet. Then, at midnight, Jihang and I could eat those warm, soft glutinous rice balls together. What I wanted from life was very simple.

As I was thinking about this, I bought a bouquet of flowers and returned to the dorms to spend some time with Jihang. The girls' dorm was very quiet in the afternoon.

On our doorknob hung a man's tie. With the bouquet of gerberas in hand, I stood outside the door, not knowing whether to stay or to leave. Jihang's was an old English habit, which indicated that we had male company in our room. How could this be possible? This was mine and Jihang's place! They might even be making love on my bed, which meant that I would have to wash the sheets. If that were the case, I would never be able to sleep in that bed again. I often think that men's semen is the messiest thing there is, even more disgusting than dishwashing liquid, snot, or phlegm. Jihang, how could you do this?

The dorm committee chair who lived just across the hall came back just then and asked me, "What's the matter? Have you forgotten your keys? Do you want me to open the door for you?"

"No," I said quickly, and got out my own key.

And they really were on my bed, Jihang and a man, their frenzied passion approaching a climax. I felt the gerberas in my hand trembling so hard they nearly dropped to the floor. I was afraid the petals would scatter all over. Jihang had her eyes half closed, as if she did not care at all, but the man had stopped moving, without having the sense to cover himself. The man had pockmarks all over his face and his hair was disheveled. He was about thirty or so. I looked at him, "Mister, this is a girls' dorm, please put on your clothes." Jihang glanced at him sideways and said, "Don't listen to her." I picked up the clothes from the floor and threw them at this pair, shouting, "Get into your clothes! I refuse to speak to animals."

The man quickly put on his clothes, while Jihang turned over and started to smoke. She let out a breath of smoke. She did not say anything. I picked up the condoms that were strewn all over the floor and said to him, "Mister, here take these back, and please behave yourself."

". . . I'm sorry." He hurriedly stuffed the condoms in the pocket of his pants while I opened the door for him. I said, "Mister, my relations with Jihang are special, so please respect us and never again do what you did." At first, his face was expressionless, then after a long pause, it registered panic. He hissed, "You two! Perverts!"

I slapped his face and slammed the door shut behind him. Jihang glared at me, her eyes burning, her face flushed, and her cigarette about to singe her fingertips. She stared at me without moving in the slightest. I leaned against the door, entirely still. What does time matter when all has been destroyed and nothing is left? Why bother keeping track of time? I don't know how long we held out like that, but her cigarette went out. A feeling of midwinter.

Night fell upon us, heavy and dark. Jihang suddenly laughed lightly, then two tears rolled down her face.

I said, "Regardless of what has happened, we can still go on as before."

She said, "It's not the same. Really. You're too naive. In the future, you will be no match for me."

I covered my face, "I don't want to compete with you, why do you want to take advantage of everyone, everywhere?"

She said, "He can help me get into a magazine or even become a famous actress like Isabella Rossellini. Can you help me do that?"

I said, "Why should you want to take advantage of men? We are, after all, not prostitutes."

She said, "Have you never taken advantage of men? In this regard, it does not matter whether or not a woman is educated."

I slowly sank into a chair. I thought of some of the men with whom I had had breakfast, dinner, a drink. I thought of that man who, just because he had a handkerchief when I was drunk, I had almost committed the rest of my life to him.

Everybody had their weaknesses.

"I'm hungry." Jihang got up. She was naked. She randomly grabbed some clothes and said to me, "Excuse me, I have to go out." I let her go, listening to her footsteps determinedly move off into the distance. The gerberas silently wilted in the dark. I closed my eyes, and I suddenly understood what was meant by "external trappings of success." From here on, all things would be "external trappings."

That night I went to sleep early, and woke up the next morning to find Jihang with her toy rabbit in her arms, sleeping soundly like a baby. I left a note saying that I would wait for her in the cafeteria for dinner that night, and went off to classes. I didn't think she would be there.

I sat near the sliding doors waiting for her. The wintry day was nearing its end, the dusk hanging heavy like death. Jihang walked over, her long hair half tied up, dressed in a sweater and pants, a scarf draped over her shoulders, and blue, precious stone earrings dangling in her ears. When she saw me, she smiled lightly, and I realized that she had grown into a woman. Even her smile was quite distinguished. She had not been a student in vain.

We put in our order for food and had some beer. Jihang had very little to eat but drank a lot, and before we had finished our meal, her cheeks had turned bright red. We talked about the sociology instructor. He had finally been persuaded by the school administration to accept early retirement. We felt victorious and drank to his early retirement. She said she had gotten a modeling contract. We both said that that was a fine thing. I told her I had finished writing a thesis proposal, had applied for a scholarship to go to England, and had already been interviewed. We were happy and kept laughing. Once outside, I was shaking from having had too much to drink. Jihang put her scarf around my shoulders. It was windy and I said, "I'm cold," and walked close against Jihang. She put her arm around me as we crossed campus. The night was beautiful, the sky a deep dark blue. I said, "Let us move somewhere like this after we graduate. You could go out and work, I will stay home and study." She was silent for a moment, then said, "I'm afraid you would not quietly stay at home." I laughed, "I would. Look at how thin I am, do I have what it takes not to stay at home?" She pressed her bosom once again, and said, "Well then, I'm afraid I wouldn't be good and stay at home." We were both quiet for a long time. Jihang suddenly hugged me tightly. I was shocked by the passion of her unexpected embrace. She let me go, then said, "It's late, go to the library and get your stuff. I'm going back to the dorm."

I waved my hand, turned, and left. She was waving at me, saying good-bye. I scolded her saying she was crazy, after all, this wasn't some final farewell like that of lovers parted by circumstance or death, and I left without turning my head.

When I returned to the dorm, I met the dorm committee chair in the lobby. She immediately pulled me aside and said, visibly relieved, "The dorm matron is looking for you." I said I had to put down my books and what was the hurry anyway. She said it was urgent and shoved and pushed me to go.

I waited on the sofa of the dorm matron's room. I was bored and browsed through a copy of the magazine *Breakthrough*. One reader asked, "Mingsum, I am very frustrated, I don't know what to do, he has left me . . ." The dorm matron had prepared a cup of hot oolong tea for me. She was from Taiwan, and her Cantonese had a thick nasal accent to it. I waited for her to speak with both of my hands clasped around the mug.

The television was on, with only muted pictures flickering past the screen. The dorm matron's face went bright and dark, blue and white. It was frightening. Amidst the play of light and shadows she held back for a while, then spoke slowly, emphasizing each word, "I have received a letter reporting on the abnormal relationship between you and Jihang."

The oolong tea was scalding and burned the tip of my tongue. I lifted my head to look at her, and without knowing why, I had a smile on my face.

"University students not only have to have knowledge, they must also have high moral standards . . ."

"I don't think this is anything degraded. Many men and women behave in a much more degraded way than we do." I looked straight into her eyes. She did not try to avoid my glance, but looked straight back at me.

"It is abnormal, what you two are doing; it obstructs the development of human civilization. The reason society is a whole and can remain an orderly system is entirely dependent upon natural human relationships . . ." I no longer heard her clearly, I just picked up bits and pieces. I was no longer looking at her; instead, I began to flip through the pages of *Breakthrough*. Mingsum replies,

"Ling, that you should destroy another's relationship is not right, but the Almighty God will forgive you . . ." I was so frightened I hurriedly put the magazine away. I stared absentmindedly at the soundless images on the television screen. After a long time, I said very softly, "Why impose your moral standards on us? We haven't harmed anyone." I don't know if she heard; at the same time, my voice was so soft it seemed as if someone was whispering these words into my ears. I looked around in alarm, but there was no one beside me.

"Dorm matron." I put down my teacup and said, "As long as Jihang won't leave me, I will certainly not leave her." Having said this, I abruptly got up and opened the door.

"But this afternoon she already promised that she would move out of the dorm. I in turn promised that I would not make this matter public. My asking you here is merely a formality." Her words came from far away. As I stood at the door, I pushed the doorknob. My hand felt cold. "Thank you," I said. I did not make another sound as I softly shut the door and left.

I don't know how I made it back to my room. That staircase seemed simply endless. Was this perhaps Jacob's ladder leading all the way to heaven, which would ultimately lead to the truth? Every step was painful. It was as though my limbs had been ripped apart. Every single movement sent a searing pain through my eyes. I covered my eyes. Let it be. From here on out, I would go blind, unable to see the light of day.

The room was not locked. Someone was coming down the hall. I straightened my back, gritted my teeth, and slipped into the room. The good Jihang. In one afternoon, she had packed up everything and put everything back in order. The only things left were a pair of brand new, bright red embroidered slippers and a pink Maidenform bra on my bed. As I looked the bra over, I found that she had bought the wrong size—32B. I laughed, and said to myself: "It's 32A, Jihang, 32A. I am skinny!"

After she had left, I also moved out of the dorm and instead rented a dark and quiet little room near campus. My life was especially dark and quiet. I became increasingly nearsighted but I kept wearing my old rimmed glasses, so I would stumble from the classroom to the library day in and day out. I began to only wear blue, purple, and black. I quit smoking. I stuck to boiled water and vegetarian fare. When other people are heartbroken, they implore heaven and earth in their despair. I, on the other hand, found myself in a state so utterly calm that I could not imagine being any calmer. My heart was as placid and expansive as the landscape paintings from earlier periods, such as the Song and the Ming. At night, I would listen to the traditional, refined *kunqu* opera tunes, often retracing my own light and hurried footsteps, lonely as a shadow. I would hug myself and say, "I still have this." I would bite my lips and say, "Don't cry! Don't complain!" I was hoping that I would become someone who would understand the reasons of things—everything had a reason. She too had her difficulties.

Later on, I saw her on the cover of a magazine. Her luscious lips. The smile.

However, I did not open the magazine. She was merely one among many thousands of beautiful women, entirely different from the Jihang I had known. Afterwards, I saw her again at the commencement ceremony. With her gown flying, she smiled in the sunlight, looking at me from afar, her hand blocking the glare. I realized that she was too far away and I had no way of determining whether or not her smile had changed. I just stood there without moving, holding, embracing myself. Next to her stood a man. It seemed as though I had seen him before, and after a moment's thought, it turned out to be the guy I had seen in the magazine. Jihang had made her choice. She had left me because I was not good enough for her. But the Jihang I remember . . . we had never made distinctions between good and bad.

I remember her *qipao* and her embroidered slippers. I remember her self-contained confidence when she was copying from my notes. I remember her smile when she softly pressed her bosom with her hand. I remember her lazy demeanor when she used to lie in bed reading Yi Shu. I remember the time I was cold and she gave me her scarf to warm me up, and the time when I was proud and she had thrown coins at me. When I was cold and distant, she had held my hand tightly and said, "The general has lost his wife and his army." I remember. I remember, I tied up her hair, cut her toenails, bought her a bouquet of gerberas. I remember I had once attempted to strangle myself; my eyes filled with tears. She had pulled away my hands and said, "Why do this?"

Why do this. I thought I could spend the rest of my life with Jihang.

# 3

# BREAKING OPEN

Chen Ran

*Translated by Paola Zamperini*

Respectfully presented to women

*He tossed a woman toward the sky*
*To this day she floats in mid-air.*

—Alexander Eremenko

My friend Yunnan and I feel an acute sense of relief when the airport's waiting room suddenly empties out. Rising above the babble of accents in which they were drowning a moment ago, our voices seem instantaneously to become much louder. I can even hear her breath with which I am intimately familiar. Just now this lounge was thronged by a noisy crowd—their many arms dashed against the cavelike boarding gate like successive waves. Some people had looked as though they loved each other to death but were unable to marry, others as if they loathed each other with a vengeance but could not break up. They all had struggled forward to have their tickets inspected as though it were a matter of rushing to purchase a special amnesty certificate. As soon as they were allowed to pass through, they hurried to be the first to get on board, seemingly afraid of being left behind by the plane or of missing this historical moment.

Actually, the whole thing took no longer than a little over ten minutes.

We are not in a rush. On the contrary, we are even sort of calm.

Calm results from experience. Yunnan faces everything serenely and confronts change without ever being ruffled by anything. I am not as good at that as she is. Once she came up with all manner of metaphors to describe my timidity: a frightened little animal, a doe in a forest riddled with traps, a she-goat doomed to be slaughtered for a feast, a domesticated she-wolf who is howling her song of distress everywhere. Later, she pondered the matter again, and said that she did not like all those female qualifiers in front of all these words. The word "female" did not fit me, since that word had at times been associated with stupidity, weakness, passivity, and powerlessness. Instead, commenting on what she saw as my natural and unrestrained charm, she said that she liked my air of "little-brother-like kid sister" or "kid-sister-like little brother." She found it both strange and captivating.

She loved to talk about two of her family's dogs. She had named the female one Comma and the male one Period. She said that Comma really loved Period; in fact, she loved him to the point of distraction. Period loved Comma too, but the problem was that while he loved Comma, he also had feelings for the neighbors' female dog, which she had named Colon. She said that if an extremely audacious male dog that did not know any better dared to go near Colon, Period would jump out barking from the side of his beloved Comma and make them flee as he tyrannically snarled and growled at them. She said that Period's behavior made it impossible for Colon to ever have a mate. Colon always had an eagerly expectant but friendless and wretched look, as if there were a danger of provoking a fit at any time.

"Men, that's how they are," Yunnan said. "In my village, there was once a man and a woman who were in love, and because their marriage had met with opposition from their parents, they secretly swore to sacrifice their lives for love by jumping off the cliff of the highest peak in the area, Green Stone Mountain. At last, one evening, when the sun had not yet disappeared completely, the two of them, holding hands, climbed up along a path that coiled around the mountain like a twisting and turning intestine. Having arrived at the precipice at the mountaintop, they sat down, embracing each other. In the cold drizzle, below the desolate and rustling dead leaves, the two of them kept calling out each other's name, and made passionate vows. Gradually the evening wind sneaked up on them, and they were enveloped by darkness. The woman said, "Since we cannot go on living, we will be reunited in the other world. You jump first, and I will follow you." The man replied, "Well put, we will be together in the next world, but you must not prevent me from finding you. You jump first, and I will follow you." As a result, the woman clenched her teeth, stamped her feet, and jumped in the bottomless precipice. Just then the man came to his senses and leaned out to look down, trying hard to hear the sad sound of the woman hitting the ground. However, nothing could be heard from the fathomless precipice. All alone on the mountaintop, he began to be afraid and did not dare to jump, but he did not dare to return and face the parents of the woman either. All alone he mulled it all over, and under the cover of the darkness, he cried piteously through the night. The next morning, the first rosy rays of sunshine warmed the ground, and eventually, the golden globe of the sun glistened like an omelette. He felt hungry and got up from the root where he had sat all night. His vision blurred for an instant, and he felt tired. Then he went down the mountain and returned home. Oh, men!"

I said, "This sounds like the theater of the absurd."

"The problem is that men consider life a play, while women take plays to be life. In general, when two people compete with each other, the more ruthless one has the upper hand. This is especially true between a man and a woman."

My friend Yunnan—she utters strange conglomerates of words casually. Her intuitively artistic way of expressing herself often causes me to sigh in admiration—the innate beauty of her words sets me aflutter with emotion and makes me feel that my lips are merely a pretty but ultimately useless ravenous red insect.

When we are not together, I am fortunate to receive her long, exquisitely phrased letters. Once, she wrote, "Now I have sat down to write to you; it feels a little like an old man writing his memoirs. Distilling my life and my experiences, I attempt to relay things to you as clearly as possible. It is a little like arranging furniture. The only hard thing is my passion, which even at my advanced age has lost none of its youthful intensity. I have lived to where I am an old pedant, an old fuddy-duddy, I even have the appearance of old age." (Actually Yunnan is just over thirty, but she wanted to show off the vicissitudes of her life to me, four years her junior). "I have always wanted to buy a streamside log cabin in my mountain village. You would come, and gazing at the solitary peaks and the barren ridges in the distance, we would be free to listen to the deep and murky sounds of the water. Those would be days of immense peace." At the end of the letter, Yunnan, half in jest, half in earnest, grudgingly expressed her feelings for me, but immediately after those few lines, she added, unable to hold herself back: "Corny!" to dispel, to dilute, and to mock those last sentimental words. "Corny" made me laugh for a long time. I could almost see her long fingers sliding elegantly across the page as an unwavering artistic sensibility hovered around her fingertips.

We have not said a word for a long time: language can reach the interlocutor also through silence. The dialogue can still continue in ways that are difficult to fathom, but for people who have a tacit understanding, speech is not necessarily conveyed through sound.

I remember how Elie Wiesel pointed out in *Celebration Hassidique* that two people separated by time and space can have a conversation. One person raises a question, and after some time, another one, very far from her, asks something, which, without her intending to do so, turns out to be the answer to the question of the first person.

The people in the lounge are now slowly streaming into the jet way. As the waiting area empties further, the atmosphere gradually becomes more relaxed.

Yunnan turns around and stares at me, narrowing her eyes. Her face subtly fuses together mutually exclusive expressions: cold and severe but also warm and kind, experienced but also naive. Resembling a familiar stranger, she turns to look at me. Like a patch of wild and vigorous grass, her short, freshly washed, chestnut-colored hair flutters softly on her cheeks and surges from a head used to wild flights of fancy. Her brows are slightly knitted, a distinctive cold passion illuminating her fair face. Her lips, with no lipstick, reveal a slightly anemic pallor. Her long and indolent legs, tightly wrapped in a pair of light brown jeans, oppose the direction of her gaze. She raises her clean, long fingers to stroke her face, which, because of the customary absence of make-up, seems vast and solitary. It appears that she wants to wipe off a speck of dust. An imaginary speck of dust. A habitual gesture of hers.

My friend looks like a female chief I saw once somewhere in the Victoria Desert: this female chief's mien was handsome, martial, passionate, and cold-blooded. In her veins flowed a tender love for her fellow sisters, and there also burned an inveterate hatred, a hatred directed against other races as well as against the opposite sex.

Compared with the face of the female chief, Yunnan's bears the traces of life in a calm, advanced, and modern city. I am very familiar with that mannerism of hers, that is, bending over and narrowing her long eyes to stare at my face, but I can never grasp its significance, because it is one among many different words and feelings.

Not long ago, a certain official earnestly encouraged the women of the entire nation to wear the *qipao*. This emblem of China enwrapping the female body has indeed blinded the whole male population in China and abroad, wreaking havoc as it set the banners of men's hearts aflutter. But this kind of proposal turned the *qipao*s, which had been gaily flapping in the wind all over the streets, into a tool. On that day, Yunnan and I were standing by the river in the South, far away from the city of N, staring at the dirty and turbid water, the mud at our feet reaching all the way into our hearts: the gray sky, the gray earth, the gray water enveloped us in a particular melancholia. That day, Yunnan was looking at me this way, narrowing her eyes. After a long while, she turned her gaze to the river. It was dusk, and the setting sun colored the clear waters of the river in shades of turquoise and red. Yunnan's train of thought seemed to unconsciously float on the unexceptionally even surface of the river, but it also looked like it was hiding in the midst of some very serious matter.

She said softly, as if speaking to herself, "We must say that becoming indifferent to sexual difference is an advance in the culture of humankind. We are first of all persons, and only secondarily women. Some men always draw attention to our sexual difference, while they feign a deep respect; actually, behind this facade, they hide sinister intentions, namely to shelve, to lay aside, and to neglect us women, to leave us out in the cold, to not get to know us—it is a carefully disguised sexual hostility. This enmity, be it innate or acquired, is sometimes so well hidden that they themselves are not aware of it. In future generations, the greatest war will arise because of the divide between the sexes."

I said, "Don't you think that behind it all lies some fear of women?"

"Of course. Only the most outstanding men dare to befriend talented women. The average man only dares to look for a woman to be his wife or his lover," Yunnan answered.

"Oh, men!"

"It's the same even when men discuss the work of women writers or artists," Yunnan continued. "They only pay attention to the most feminine side of women's work. Without paying any attention to artistic quality, they simply establish the grounds to elaborate on sexual difference. A man, criticizing the work of the French writer Françoise Sagan, said, 'Poor old Francoise Sagan, today she is very old, and she is unable to be in sync with the latest trends of literature and its new prodigies. From the looks of it, her experience in the U.S. is comparable to the life of a Chinese beauty in the old days: At fourteen she blossoms, at fifteen she is plucked, at thirty she fades, at forty her face is full of wrinkles.' Later, a woman paid him back in kind, and made up a male writer Francois Sagan to return the compliment. She said, 'Poor old Francois Sagan . . . , from the looks of it, his experience in the U.S. is comparable to the life of a Chinese itinerant poet in the old days: At fourteen he masturbates, at fifteen he has intercourse for the first time, at thirty his male powers decline, at forty he suffers from an inflammation of the prostate.' This is the gap between male and female points of view."

Like invisible little daggers, her words darted over the piercingly cold riverside.

My friend Yunnan is an exceptionally acute art critic.

That day, leaning against the wet rocks by the river, we each lit a cigarette. Afterwards, some steel-colored storm clouds passed over our heads, and a single cold raindrop fell on the well-chiseled, white cheek of Yunnan. I raised my left hand, and wiped off that raindrop with the last joint of my index finger.

In general, it is necessary to keep a physical distance between women just as it is in the company of men: one must guard some territory for one's own private feelings. However, this separation is reduced according to the mutual degree of intimacy. Speaking just for myself, I believe that this, among the countless differences that exist between men and women, is one of the most distinctive. Women are a sex for whom it is relatively easy to develop physical intimacy.

I told Yunnan that in the thirty years of my life, I had only heard two beautiful forms of address: one came from an old lover of mine, a painter, who once called me in public "Brother Dai" (my name is Dai'Er); the other was in a letter of an ex-husband of mine, where he called me "my little wife," which I misread as "my little whore." I instantly called him on the phone to tell him how much I loved "my little whore," and he immediately said that he actually had called me "my little wife" and not "my little whore."

Yunnan chuckled. Tenderly, she brought the cigarette she held between her fingers to my lips. I took one deep drag, savoring our very precious friendship.

Later, I lifted my head to look at her. So I saw again that she had bent her head and narrowed her eyes to stare intently at my expression; her milky white neck and her chestnut-colored, wind-blown hair together with her gaze were all turned toward me.

That day, when we put out our cigarettes, it was almost dusk. The black rain clouds had interfered with our original plan of having a picnic by the riverside. As though speaking softly, light raindrops were already gliding down on our windswept clothes and on our glistening foreheads. Soon our big overcoats cheerfully screeched at each other.

Yunnan said, "You know, our foreheads look a lot alike."

I stroked my forehead with my hand, and said, "This place is the antechamber of our thoughts, the gateway to the hall of our jumbled minds, so I am afraid that, no matter if there is a gorgeous rainbow or just a tattered spiderweb on the inside, my and your structure will still look a lot alike."

Yunnan squeezed my shoulder in agreement.

Then she looked up toward the sky heavy with rain and said, "Very well, let's herewith end today's dinner party of this 'antechamber' and 'gateway,' which would never put any food in our bellies. How about going out to eat something irresistibly seductive?"

If we were to use one's love of food as a measure of one's love of life, then I could hardly be considered a person who deeply loves life. I cannot think of any kind of food that captivates me to the point of forgetting myself, where the desire for it is etched into one's bones and heart, as intense as the longing for a person.

Yunnan has much more of an appetite and is something of a gourmet. Her stomach is always very inspired. When she comes upon some food that suits her taste—noodles, for example—her words become long and elongated just like the noodles that she carefully chews and slowly swallows, one by one.

My friend Yunnan loves living and life more ardently than I.

Yunnan said, "How about going out for a hot pot? It's a specialty of the mountain village on this side of the river. It's as hot as a dream, and dark red like the deepest love."

Then Yunnan grasped my hand. Our hands interlocked quite naturally, and together they slid into her warm pocket.

We walked toward the faint lights of the fishermen's lanterns on the embankment.

Yunnan and I are now about to board the Southern Airlines Boeing 747 to return north to the stronghold of ancient culture where I live—the city of N. In less than half an hour, we will leave Yunnan's native place, a mountain town of lingering rain in the lower reaches of the Yangzi River.

In this gray, hazy, little town by the side of the river, even the sunshine is dripping wet, and the cobblestone alleys, winding and turning above and below, always lead my aimless footsteps toward the river, where the boats hoist black sails and the river steamers let out their drawn-out sirens. I would stand still for a long time next to the riverbank, as if I had come to this eastern capital of mists to wait for someone.

Truthfully, I do not know if I was waiting for someone's arrival. Looking back, I really have been waiting for all the thirty years of my life. Early on in my extravagant hopes, I was sure that this predestined person was a man—wise, gallant, and handsome. Later, I discarded the gender specification; I realized that the concept that a woman can or must only wait for a man is an age-old but coercive custom. To exist in this antagonistic world brimming with antagonism, a woman must choose a man in order to join the "majority," to be "normal." It is a choice that comes from not having any other choice. However, that is not how I feel. I am willing to disregard a person's gender identity in favor of their personal qualities. I do not care anymore about the difference between male and female, and I do not care about being part of a "minority" either; I do not even see it as "abnormal." I feel that an affinity between two people does not only appear between a man and a woman but that it is indeed also a kind of latent vital energy that has long been neglected among us women (my change of heart took place after I had systematically researched the many possible orientations of humankind's sexual identities as well as the complexity of the fundamentals of gender and visited Australia and some ancient and modern European countries). But such a person must, without a doubt, be predestined.

I know it is a matter of fate. One cannot consciously strive for it. Perhaps it will happen when you are not expecting anything.

Like it happened seven days ago, when, as I was flying toward this mountain town by the river, I formed a bond with former U.S. president Nixon on the plane in just one second.

Of course I had come to this southern town looking for a specific person—my friend Yunnan. During a long-distance phone call, we had conferred about establishing a women's association that would be truly free of gender discrimination. We would most certainly stay away from the rhetoric of Chinese-style "women's consciousness" or Western-style "feminism." Striving for real equality between the sexes, transcending any consciousness of sexual difference, we hoped to shatter the long-standing, well-established, and exclusively male rules and standards that pervade life, culture, and art. For a long time, we, faced with norms that men believe natural, have always passively accepted and conformed to them. We have never had our own women's norms. Our image is the simplified image of woman carved by the hard brush of male writers and artists. Our spiritual course and our intellectual history are what male specialists of the "woman's question" have fabricated. In order to stand out among other women, some women are diligently catering to the male concept of "woman's consciousness." When Yunnan and I had discussed this issue in the past, we felt sorry for our bosom sisters.

In the course of our long-distance phone call, Yunnan said that some female painter friends proposed to name this group "The Second Sex." But both Yunnan and I disliked this idea, since it acknowledged and confirmed men as the first sex. We talked and talked, and in the end we both agreed on naming this women's association "Breaking Open."

My relationship with Nixon had been established all of a sudden shortly after I had boarded the plane on my way to enlist Yunnan's help for the planning of "Breaking Open."

That day, I was already completely worn out when I found my seat, 17A; even when the plane was still gliding on the runway and had not yet taken off, I felt for some reason that the sun had already drawn closer. I felt a little bit dizzy. As I sat motionlessly in my seat, I thought about Yunnan, whom I was about to see. I pictured her sitting quietly in the little two-storied house next to the river, with her face turned toward the shutters. A sleepy river breeze enters through a slightly opened window and undulates between the low ceiling and the floorboards. An old clock hangs on the wall. She is reluctant as usual to wind it up, as if she did not believe in time and in the future. She likes to let the day pass in a lazy and relaxed manner. I imagined her sitting in her room, with her controlled and neat look as she quietly exhales the indigo-blue smoke. I pictured her pale face and the vicissitudes dwelling in the depths of her experienced and knowing pupils. Her calm and perfectly composed attitude has become an invincible strength; no matter where she is, it always enjoins all the men and women around her to obey her eagerly like joyful ponies.

Just then the flight attendant came by. Perhaps because I looked sick, she asked me if I was okay. I said I was all right. Then she gave me a newspaper, *The People's Daily*. Being an official organ, that paper generally concerns itself with serious matters. By contrast, every day I collect a big pile of marginal little newspapers to read. Their color is blackish like the whole-wheat bread I love to eat. They nourish my blank mind. These papers are a little like my life. I slowly walk alone in a quiet little side street, always beyond the hurly-burly of crowds. Solitude for me is the most congenial, the most profound emotional pattern; it courses indelibly in my veins. It is a natural part of living, and we peacefully keep each other company.

I put the newspaper the flight attendant had given me on the empty seat next to me. I relaxed my body and closed my eyes. The plane was gliding on the runway, shaking, screaming, so I let myself, from head to toe, sink into the tremors that hurried me toward a close and sincere friend. Then I opened my eyes and pushed the black button on my armrest with my right hand, trying to recline the seat. I wanted to relax my spine, which the long hours at work had made stiff, as much as possible.

When I dropped my gaze to my right, an eye-catching black headline, "Condolences on the death of the former U.S. president Nixon" in *The People's Daily* assailed my eyes.

My relationship with Nixon actually is only a relationship between me and his era. When the name "Nixon" flashed before me, what I actually saw was my naive, worried, sad, simple, and innocent childhood days when I sat in an old-fashioned big house with chestnut-colored window frames and rice paper window coverings. I sat in the hopeless, angry gaze of my father during the years awash in the red colors of perpetual revolution. His gaze stifled the fresh and unaffected childish voice in my mouth. I saw this little girl who, in her barren, delusional dreams, would hug her bony and shaky knees with both arms, her eyes wide with fear and her hair dried-up and yellowed like wild wheat in the wind. She was not able to comb her hair. She was waiting for Mom to come home. She stood waiting in the big antechamber outside the screen door. She stood waiting in front of the courtyard gate made of pitch black, damaged dead wood. As the pale brown clothesline swayed behind her, she strolled about in the empty courtyard, patient like a kitten at its wits' end. A breeze in the dusk of the summer day encircled her neck that was as thin as a hemp stalk. She looked like a little dog trying to cross the street, looking to the left, then to the right. Then, all of a sudden, she went across and climbed the tall white stone on the other side of the alley, where she stood very high, in order to sooner spot Mom, who might appear from an unexpected direction at any moment. A home without a mother was not a real home, a home without women was not a real home, and this little girl was not a woman after all.

Early on during Nixon's era, in my heart, woman had already established her splendor in this world. When a man was insufferably arrogant and vented his spleen, there was always a woman who would endure it silently like a draft-ox. In this regard, women resembled the pear tree in the courtyard of my childhood: dragged down by tightly strung clotheslines that in turn were weighed down by all manner of objects, the tree bore the humiliation and the burden day after day, but still invariably brought forth delicate and pervasively fragrant blossoms.

That day, when I picked up *The People's Daily*, the black-and-white propaganda pictures of my childhood stood out in my mind. Then I put the newspaper aside together with that distant past.

I turned my head to look out the window—the blue sky and white clouds were gradually getting closer. The clouds looked like huge rabbits leisurely playing. The sunlight was very bright, the color of gold, sending out rays that resembled the strings of a musical instrument. The wings of the plane trembled gently. Sounding like clusters of silver bells, a buzz filled the air.

"The Eastern wind is blowing, the war drums are booming, in today's world who's afraid of whom, the people are not afraid of the American imperialists, but the American imperialists are afraid of the people." I got lost in the choir of childish and delicate voices in the primary school's courtyard; some Yankees from Nixon's retinue happily listened to our song, without understanding its lyrics. Then they came forward to hug us. One by one they kissed us on the face.

The plane shook, and I turned my eyes away from the window.

I said in my heart, good-bye, Nixon, farewell!

It seemed that I had come especially on this journey to say good-bye to Nixon on the plane. At the entrance of heaven, high up in the sky.

Not having to engage in chitchat on a trip is extraordinarily pleasant. I had one hundred and some minutes of solitude to devote mostly to myself and also to the pleasant and precious memories of Yunnan. What a joy! If I could keep myself company, quietly, in solitude, then I would be willing to take a pill against motion sickness every two to three hours in order to hover forever in the sky.

I believe in coincidence and fated bonds. I believe that the sisterly feeling between me and my friend Yunnan is not in the least bit inferior to love.

Now my friend and I are sitting placidly in the waiting room. We will fly together from this low mountain basin toward my hometown—N. We are not in a rush, we do not want to flock aboard, we do not want to get lost in the dejected, tightly clustered, and prickly crowd. We do not want to have our relaxed ankles buried among piles of huge suitcases, among whimsically tossed beer cans, or among fallen-down Coca-Cola cups. We want to board the plane a few minutes before takeoff.

I say to Yunnan that I have to go to the restroom, that I am not used to using the restroom in the sky. Up there one is too close to God; earthly matters—regardless whether they concern us women or them men, especially everything connected to the sex organs—are best taken care of on the ground, because God has no sex, and we should not disturb such a being.

Yunnan laughs. Each peal of Yunnan's leisurely laughter resounds brightly. Her ivory teeth, spaced neatly and closely together, resemble a small shiny wall.

My friend Yunnan is a woman of a happy disposition, a quiet and solitary hedonist. She is not like me, always trapped by my thoughts, driven into distant corners of hopelessness and plagued by extremities of feeling. I always stubbornly push myself further without regard for anything. Even in a dead-end street, I bravely advance.

Not Yunnan. She often stands in a crowd without batting an eyelid. In a marketplace so dirty that even the sky has completely lost its blue color, she still can quietly use her two hands—those same hands that elicit sensitive music from a violin shake hands with the fat, big hands that count money or control the seals. She brushes aside the dryness in her throat. Then, standing in the sunlight, with complete ease and skill, she takes in the most cruel aspects of the human world.

But when she turns around, all you see is her relaxed and charming appearance.

She has mentioned it to me more than once. Both in her tender, tea-colored hometown and in my brutal N where even the sun seems to chase after success, she has told me, "We are really a perfect match."

But I know that when confronted with the harsh realities of life, I have nowhere near her resilience.

* * *

Now she is leaning against a chair in the waiting room painted in a spine-chilling blue hue. Her expression is more severe than before. Her soft, limpid, and unflinching gaze meets my eyes and tries to pierce them. In the net of my chaotic thoughts she has run into something noteworthy. At the same time, she seems to either grasp a fleeting thought in the deepest recesses of her own mind or attempt to get rid of some intractable problem that ought not exist.

I think that she is spacing out and has not heard me, so I turn and go toward the bathroom.

My two legs, which for many years have loved to walk without ever getting tired, are like two trunks of pliable and tough lilacs. They can walk about freely and they stand steadily and self-reliantly. At times I rely on them more than on my head, because they can supplant my brain's conclusions such as "There is no way forward" or "Retreat is another way to move forward; if you retreat one step, the sea is as vast as the sky." My foot has taken but one distinct yet careful step on the slippery floor, when Yunnan's deep voice catches up with my back and presses against my spine: "Hey . . ."

I turn around.

Quite possibly the eyes through which I see Yunnan are dazzled by the brilliance of the morning sun. Specks of dust pass through the big French windows like crystals floating in the air and cast limpid lines on her eyes. Her amber pupils send forth a light at once reflective and transparent.

"What?" I ask.

Her thin face has a cold intensity, "Don't you know that you are a kind of god?"

"What do you mean?" I do not immediately grasp the nuances of this abstruse and ambiguous remark.

"Don't you think that when we are together it is as if there were no sexes? That question . . ." She pauses for a second, "That question . . . it seems to retreat to a place of no importance. Don't you think this is a problem?"

"Well," I laugh, "Then hip hip hooray for our sexless roles!"

And, with those words, I turn as before and walk toward the restroom.

I come out of the bathroom behind a woman who is wearing a leather miniskirt so short that her thighs are almost completely bare. I look at them, white as snow in the glare of this winter where the cold wind cuts one to the quick. They are like two sturdy chopsticks standing on the ground and moving by themselves. They remind me of the very coquettish Hong Kong rock star Mei Yanfang, who wears miniskirts; during a benefit concert for disaster relief, her autoerotic (self-touching) and sensual dance captivated not only all the men present but charmed also many women. Ever since the shapely thighs of Miss Mei captured the audience, I have often seen thighs *à la* Mei of various ages in the streets of N—fat thighs, thin ones, all unlike one another, all competing to be the first to lay themselves bare. Summer or winter, thighs go unharmed by the assault of temperature; like a forest of tall and strong birches, they cross the street unhurriedly. Their allure is such that they make the heads of passers-by spin.

The woman wearing the miniskirt passes my and Yunnan's seats without a glance. I sit down, and then I laugh with Yunnan. "Woman at times is really a pitiful creature. On such a cold day, she first and foremost takes other people's aesthetic pleasure into consideration without even charging for it—one cannot help but think that she is altogether too interested in the public good," I say.

"People wear their own feelings."

"I just hope that's what they want."

At this time, we hear the voice of a member of the ground crew. "Immediate boarding for passengers traveling to N—the plane will take off in a few minutes."

We stand up, and we realize only now, all of a sudden, that nobody is around, that the whirling crowd has disappeared in the twinkling of an eye. Yunnan shoulders the two heaviest bags, leaving a light one lying on the floor. Then she points to that bag with the arrogant and ever-scheming slender tip of her foot and says, "Here, take this."

I do not have time to protest this unfair arrangement, as she is already walking toward the gate.

As she is heading forward with the heavy luggage on her shoulders, she turns around to tell me, "Which kind of man can possibly want mature and self-possessed women like us, who are also able to cope with the concrete realities of life? We can only make them feel inadequate or even depressed and inferior. What man would intentionally seek out this feeling?"

There is nobody in the empty waiting room except for me and Yunnan. The glass reflects the blinding morning light, making it seem as cold as though it were a wall of ice. Yunnan's words, like mist in the empty and vast hall, pour out as if animated by a strange hostility.

I add, "Most men with brains and talent are self-centered; they get a grip on life early on, and look for a woman to have a family which revolves around his career and life. Therefore, they are very clear about finding the kind of woman who is willing to put herself, or a big part of herself, aside. They will even seek out a woman who does not have a self to start with, who will then make her life revolve around them. Life! It is relatively easier with a shallow woman. Haven't you noticed, nowadays even all the new literary critics select the works of shallow women writers. Their motto is 'reject depth.' Actually, they are afraid of women like us; our brains have become a menace for them. Even if we look at them in a positive light, there is no way they can understand us. So they cannot look for women like us. But of the men who are willing to come and seek us out, and who are not too self-centered, the great majority are mediocre, and then we look down upon the others . . . so . . ."

Yunnan goes on, "So we can only spend our lives alone."

"Which is not bad at all."

"Of course." Yunnan's bony wrist pulls the luggage strap with some effort. "I cannot think what women need men for, aside from having babies. We can take care of almost everything by ourselves, can't we? As for having babies, as long as we women have our ovaries, things are fine; with the present scientific advances, it is enough for a woman to have ovaries to give birth to her own child."

"Ha!"

Hobbling along, Yunnan and I echo one another, and we are having a great time.

We accept reality.

The world wants us to accept reality calmly.

*She is the body, he is the brain; she is the foil, he the mainstay; she is the empty vessel, the mud basin in the corner, he is the pillar of the state; her legs are his legs, he is the rider who breaks in the horse; he puts chains on her neck, she ties freedom and dreams on his leather belt; she is like a little bird in the nest built with grass in his bosom, he piles chests on her ankles; her strength is a signal of danger, his strength is a wall to keep off the wind . . .*

When I and Yunnan fall down in our seats, we are out of breath, and covered with sweat.

Yunnan says, "It seems like I'll be gone from my hometown for quite a long time on this trip north." Clearly, the happiness that just now lit her eyes has disappeared.

The flight attendant has already started checking the passengers' seat belts. The plane will take off immediately. Yunnan looks out the window, as if her eyes were to say good-bye to this mountain town where the winter rain never stops.

My friend again brings up her hometown. She is a woman who has deep feelings for her native place.

That fills me with admiration and emotion. I have never felt anything for my hometown. I have always felt like a stranger, like a broken stalk floating about, regardless of whether I was in N, where I have lived most my life, or in any other place in the world; no road echoing memories under my feet, no old jujube tree or oak tree to awaken my past, no red room filled with a delicate fragrance to rekindle a dreamworld already gone cold. My hometown shifts to wherever my feelings take me. It is just an imaginary object for which I seek out a reason—an enormous delusion to fool myself and other people. It is a bottle of perfume, brand *Love*, stored away for the longest time, which, with increased age and experience, has completely lost its potency. It is a person waiting without hope.

Actually, these past few days, in that mountain town laden with mists, my gaze kept searching without pause for a wooden house or a stone house. For a fence enclosing vegetable beds and a garden, with white deck chairs lazily spread out in the front. For a house on the ochre slopes next to the river where the waters murmur softly.

In Yunnan's hometown, here and there I saw some lovely little houses; they stood, scattered like stars, halfway up the mountain in the thick forest or on the top of the mountain range; brown dirt paths came down, stretching toward each toylike window, which were left ajar wherever people lived. A slender and idle dog would slowly wander about in the wet grass, patiently admiring the sunset next to the branches of a twisted chestnut tree. I even heard music from a radio float out of those little houses and saw the swaying shadows of whirling leaves against a gray-white wall. It was as if that music were floating down to send a message to me from the confused shadows of the branches on the wall.

I have described this Pan's flute melody called "Beautiful Dream" countless times. That tune is as predestined as my lover. It stems from a two-storied small old house in another misty town, that one located in the western hemisphere—that's where I first came across this melody. I don't know why this music seems to exist just to exasperate me. At that moment in the past, all the endless rain of Europe surged into my eyes, flowing and flowing and flowing without cease. Now this music seems to have become an invisible singer sick at heart, treading on the moonlight, following an uninterrupted silklike thread, tiptoeing along, shuttling back to this misty town in the Eastern hemisphere.

In Yunnan's hometown, I imagined myself many times living in one of these solitary houses halfway up the mountain. In this unfamiliar little southern town, closing the door would be the same as opening it, since nobody knows me. I could pass myself off as an idle woman coming from far away to settle in the bosom of the mountains or as a quiet and idle young widow coming there to grow old. Of course, it would be best if my friend could be my neighbor and live on another mountain, not too close and not too far. We could often drink our morning tea together, and eat fresh organic fruit together. Most of the time, I could be by myself in my room, reading books, writing, far away from the humdrum of northern N where I live—N, which is but an emotional wasteland full of people chasing after fame and fortune.

> I gather chrysanthemums under the eastern fence,
> In the distance I see the southern mountains.

When I think of this famous couplet by the free-spirited recluse of old, Tao Qian, I feel completely at peace.

My friend Yunnan and I once went to a famous Buddhist mountain near the small town by the river, and there we unexpectedly had a very bizarre and yet pious idea. We would go and pay homage to the mausoleum for the wartime political prisoners held in Zhazidong Prison in Chongqing, and pay tribute to the remains of Sister Jiang—a staunch and devoted fighter for her idealism, who was executed along with other political prisoners when the Nationalists fled the country in 1949.

That day, as we traveled across the Gele Mountain where the Zhazidong Prison used to be, I recalled that this place was once described by a poet friend as having "cold clouds." I felt extremely melancholic and confused. Gu Cheng, the poet, is now dead, although his poems are still widely circulated. But as far as I am concerned, I don't even want to open his volumes of poetry anymore because they are still soaked in fresh blood. His hands, which held the ax with which he killed his wife, are like a banner; it serves not just as a call for debate on issues such as individual freedom and psychological trauma but also as a manifesto of engrained male chauvinism in the savage war between the sexes and as a call to arms for us women whose feminist consciousness has remained in a deep and silent slumber.

At the site of Zhazidong Prison, in a courtyard surrounded by towering walls, I saw ominous white lines written on the withered blue-gray wall: "Think carefully, once spring is gone it does not come back!" "Be aware of the here and now and don't harbor any delusion!" The sanctimonious slogans left behind by the Nationalist Party shocked me and Yunnan so much that we became almost speechless. All of a sudden we discovered that with all our acute intelligence, we could not grasp the dialectical relationship between human nature and justice. We could not understand how two words like "honorable" and "ridiculous," which by all rights were separated by an enormous chasm, could now come within an inch of each other. We were both upset. However, my friend Yunnan and I felt that revolutionaries such as Sister Jiang and Xu Yunfeng were lucky. People who can cherish something more than their lives (like faith) are, without a doubt, lucky. Nowadays people are so pitiful.

I remember that, just as we were coming out of the deserted Zhazidong Prison, Yunnan cast aside everything that was incomprehensibly weighing in on us and recovered her usual humor and mischievousness. Even her footsteps became subsequently lithe like a gazelle's. But I was still inextricably stymied by the impasse we had come to in our visit to the site. Yunnan said that she actually liked the story of Fu Zhigao: he had already been informed by his chief that the enemies had surrounded his home, and advised him not to go back in order to avoid the ambush. He, however, was anxious about his woman, for whom he had just bought dried beef with the money he had saved, and wanted to go back to give it to her. So heedless of the consequences, he went back to see her, and in the end he was captured.

Yunnan said laughing, "If I were a man, I would be for sure an insanely passionate man like Fu Zhigao, and would not have great prospects."

"Come on, do not be so hard on yourself. But if you were Fu Zhigao, don't even think about being seen with me in N."

My friend Yunnan often asks me, if she were a man, would I marry her?

"Of course," I say. "But you'd better bring along some money when you come looking for me. Matter is the foundation of spirit, otherwise how do you convey your feelings for me? Now, there is Fu Zhigao's bag of dried beef, but still . . ."

"And if I did not have a great deal of money?"

"Well . . . I would think of some way to make money. Love needs emotions to grow, and emotions need some money to grow, that is only logical. Some people think it is this way but don't dare to say it. Some have neither ways nor means, so they don't dare to say it, and then, as time passes, they don't think this way anymore."

"Ah—that's the way things are."

My friend makes a face as though she had just woken up from a dream.

The plane bound for N is already gliding on the runway like a huge clumsy bird. I and Yunnan are tired after a morning spent packing our luggage and getting to the airport, and we are now beginning to feel weary.

"God bless!" Yunnan pulls back her gaze from her hometown's rain-drenched airstrip. Her expressive brown eyes seem to grow calmer and assume a charming and hazy air.

"Bless what?" I ask.

"Our safety."

She pulls her hand back from the armrest and puts it on her shoulder next to me.

Yunnan says, "When I was very little, it must have been July 1969, the American astronaut Armstrong entered space aboard Apollo 11. He flew, and looked all around, carefully examining the scenery beyond the Earth. But he lost hope: there was nothing in that nebulous space. Emptiness stretched everywhere, boundless, limitless, like a huge curtain without awning, embellished with stars that looked like demons' eyes, now bright, now dim, ceaselessly twinkling. The sight would send a chill down one's spine. He could neither detect any living things nor any traces of life. There were only shooting stars, like fireworks, taking turns to cross each other's path, streaking across space, leaving behind silver-colored arcs of light that would glitter for few seconds and then vanish. Armstrong affectionately looked at Earth. As it floated in a corner of the sky, he appreciated watching that orange-colored football bobbing up and down and sparkling in the remote reaches of space. At the same time, he pitied the loneliness and the foolishness of human beings, who do not understand the value of their garden, but on the contrary, could only think of ways to destroy it. I remember that I was ten at the time. That event brought forth the first thought from a brain that was still steeped in primeval chaos. It made me realize for the first time that the human race is a lonely flock who could not look to anything or anyone for support, and that my future life lay in a lonely place, in a remote and uncharted corner of the universe."

Leaning on my shoulder, Yunnan's arm makes me feel sleepy, and I nod off. Her words are like celestial rain flowers blotting out the sky and covering the earth, blurring my vision.

"You are a virgin who has twice broken her chastity, who has broken two layers of meaning, a newly formed woman, so you are unique," I say.

"Isn't that the way a modern woman should be?" she says.

By now I cannot grasp anymore a clear train of thought to answer her. My mouth seems to have entered, along with my brain, an empty and deserted world. I can open my mouth, but I cannot make any sound. Next to me, I feel a flow of energy coming from the dim lamplight, exuding the refreshing and pleasurable aroma of ice cream. In a daze, I fall into a round, smooth whiteness. Oh, the sky is really big, so big that I have lost track of time and memory. My body is weightless, as if suspended by some invisible reins. All around me reigns a beautiful and quiet silence. Just when my fingers are about to touch that cool, hazy white color, a wall completely unexpectedly blocks my way. Following a remote and yet exceptionally close line, the wall enters my eardrums, then I realize that obstructive wall is Yunnan's voice on my shoulder. I hear her ask, "If there was only one minute left before our death, what would you do?"

I open my eyes, "But this is such a remote possibility, I refuse to speculate. I am about to fall asleep."

"Just answer this question, and then go to sleep."

I think about it for a bit, then I say, "I would tell you that I like you very much. I have never had the chance to tell you."

"Only this?"

"I would tell you that I love you."

"All the people about to die say 'I love you' to somebody else." Yunnan is still dissatisfied.

"Then what would you do?" I ask.

Yunnan pauses, searching through the jewel-box of words.

Then she says, "I would kiss you . . . we have been close for so long, why can't we . . ."

"Of course," I say.

"Why is it that only men can kiss women? Why can only they kiss you?"

". . . having lived until this historical moment, there really are no longer any restrictions. This is an era that seems to be made out of glass: many rules will be shattered for sure, one after the other, by the sound of steps leading forward."

Yunnan and I, having now arrived at this sensitive and taxing topic, stop and do not say anything anymore.

I close my eyes again.

Yunnan's words make me picture the beginning of the human race. Of course I don't imagine it according to the ancient legend about the dawn of the humankind in which Adam and Eve were the founders; this scenario, in which, birth after birth, they reproduced and mated without cease, is as old as humankind. Everybody knows that much.

The image I evoke in my mind is a different one: if multiplying were not humankind's only objective in coming together, perhaps Adam could have had a better rapport and tacit understanding with his brothers as Eve could have had a better understanding with her sisters.

If the dawn of humankind had begun without the drive for fame and fortune, then today's world would have been different too.

The plane has already left the runway. Like a lithe sun the color of silver steel, it rises upwards. I want to diligently meditate about some kind of a future time and a distant place. Just as one contemplates one's memories as though they were black-and-white photographs, one can in this fashion turn the future into a kind of past. But no matter how hard I try to follow that thread, now broken, now whole, in my mind, I have no way of flinging my sinking self out from under the increasingly numerous big white clouds that keep collapsing on me one after the other. I have been gradually submerged by that illusory white. Frightened, I climb on top of the clouds, stretching out both my arms, like the silhouette of an endangered mother hen perched on a white wall. I step on a layer of illusory white paper, precariously suspended over an abyss. As soon as I touch the paper, it breaks. Without coherence or order, objects emerge in riotous profusion. In the end, one of my feet strides through a novel and bizarre gate.

All of a sudden, the plane starts to shake. The pear juice and the sweets slide from the tray tables to the floor, where they bounce up and down automatically like balloons. Sounding as if possessed by demons, they seem to say: Run away from here, quick, run away from here, as fast as you can!

Yunnan and I simultaneously notice that all the doors of the plane, the hidden ones and the ones in plain view, open all at once. As though headed for a golden light source, the passengers surge toward the exits, staring down, panic-stricken, at the bottomless abyss below. Precariously sputtering in midair, the plane has become an isolated island, from which no path leads forward or backward.

The prospect of a crash transports my imagination to an unprecedented and unique place. It feels as though I am inside a gigantic symbol, a place with no trace of a past birthplace and with no other village in the remote future to send one's remains to.

Pulling the hair that has fallen into her face back behind her ears, Yunnan says very sadly, "Seems like today is our last day."

I look at her greenish shirt; in the windswept sky, the shirt rustles and flops in the air, shining like a diamond. Perhaps, in one minute, or even half a minute, we will miss the chance and be dead. . . . Nothing can be put off.

Yunnan forcefully grabs my shoulder and says with a stern face, "I have to tell you something I have been thinking about for a long time. If I still don't say, it will be too late: you are the finest, most congenial person I have met in my entire life. You make all the men at my side pale by comparison."

And with these words, Yunnan hugs me tightly.

I say loudly, "I too need to tell you something, otherwise it will be too late . . ."

Now there is a booming, crashing sound. The whole plane melts down among the clouds as it tumbles up and down amidst the collapsing rose-colored sun. Time is caving in, on the verge of disappearing altogether.

Then I hear all of a sudden my heart jumping out from my ribcage. I am all empty inside. I am leaving my physical body. I crash into a pitch-black tunnel, which leads toward a powerful source of light. Around me strange objects zoom by, gathering around me, urging me toward the irresistible white source. On the way, the air resounds with music from the movie *Somewhere in Time*.

At last I have reached that exquisite light source.

I know that since I am here, I am already dead.

I look around, and in front of me I see a pool glittering among dense greenery. The water is so limpid that one can see all the way to the ground. The surface is as shiny as a mirror. Seen from a distance the pool looks like a silver lamp. My feet are inexorably drawn toward it. I bend down and stare inside the mirror, to check who I am, and, much to my delight, I discover that I am still myself.

As this pool catches the light, I become aware that it is daybreak. With the demise of time as I had known it, this brand new, shadowless dawn seems extraordinarily strange. I did not know that death, conventionally portrayed as dark, scary, and horrifying, could turn out to be such an enchanting, luxuriant, and holy place.

A building emerges into my field of vision. I see it standing tall and upright in front of me, dark red, beautiful like a heavenly hall. I walk toward the arch-shaped, wooden door and discover that the walls are covered with cavities that look like eyes, big and wide open; the owner of this place can look outside from every angle and point of view. I open the wooden screen, and knock on the door. No answer. So I open a hidden door inside, and enter the vestibule of this residence. As expected, there is nobody inside to keep watch. This seems a very safe place. Then, I see a steep stairway; a muffled sound comes down from up there. I take the stairs and climb up, and I knock once more on the door of the room upstairs.

The sound of slow footsteps softly approaches, along with what sounds like murmuring water. The door opens all of a sudden. An old woman, who seems familiar and yet is a stranger, stands in front of me. Perhaps because the sun is too close to this place, her skin has assumed a golden color. It is as if the evening wind of autumn were lingering on her cheeks, reluctant to part, twirling around in the same spot. Against the foil of the turbid natural skin color, her dark brown pupils shine. The wrinkles on her face are illuminated like little pathways on a summer morning. Her gray hair looks like a sturdy steel helmet, standing stubbornly on her head. A pair of old white bifocal glasses greatly exaggerates the size of her eyes.

As the old woman sees me, she immediately comes forward to welcome me like an old friend. Unsure of her gait, she holds my hand and chats away with me about this and that. She looks at me warmly and kindly. She encourages me to return to my physical body, saying that I must not stay in this illusory realm but that I must return among the living to take care of my mother, and to keep my friend Yunnan company. She says, "You must work together, close as sisters, like mouth and teeth, like hair and brush, like socks and feet, barrel and bullet, because only women can really understand women—only they can really empathize with each other."

The voice of the old woman seems to come from far away, like an echo resounding in an empty valley. It's a little odd. I feel that I am not listening with my ears, but with my whole face, I am inhaling her voice. That voice is not muddled at all, I can hear it distinctly.

I say, "I want to find my friend Yunnan, only then will I go back. I want to find the morning when we were still together, a morning that instantly vanished without a trace. Just now we parted too hurriedly. There is still one very important thing that I haven't told her yet."

The old woman says, "You can wait till you get back to tell her what is on your mind."

I say, "I must tell her now, right now, otherwise there will not be another chance. Because even if I have the courage to tell her, my physical body could later lose it."

"And what are you in such a hurry about?" asks the old woman.

I say, "I want to tell her: If I cannot live with you, then I want you to be my closest neighbor, because I cannot stand anymore living alone, without a companion. We must bring together all the talented women of the world, we must bring together all the sisters."

The old woman says, "I just saw her, I have already persuaded her, and she is now on her way back to the human world."

"But how can I believe that you have already seen Yunnan, and that you have convinced her?" I ask.

The old woman says, "Your friend is wearing a greenish shirt that looks like light smoke, isn't she? Her short boyish hair shines in the sun like a brown bird taking flight. Her youthful teeth sparkle as though they were kindling her love of life. Her long fingers are sensitive and quick like her thinking. Her fingertips represent her independence of judgment. Her hometown is by a river darkened by rain. From the roof of her erect two-storied house, one sees a yard full of lead-colored rubble. Amidst the distant mountain ranges, there is one little road that comes down perfectly straight, as if stitched, from the curvaceous mountain top, dividing the densely textured hilly area into two halves, one fire red, the other dark green. She was born in September 1959, after a crazed year full of hyperbole, but she is very coolheaded. She likes the writings of Yourcenar, Borges, and Emerson. It is her habit to drink steamed green tea with chrysanthemum flowers added, which she lets slowly seep into her somewhat chronically inflamed throat. When she smokes, she always rubs a layer of cool tiger balsam on the snow-white long cigarette."

I am really surprised that the old woman has exposed so many secret characteristics of my friend. I say, "I really believe you, but now I cannot find my way back."

By now I have already understood that I still have a long way to go among the living. It is my duty.

The old woman adds, "If you follow your dream, you can go back to the first road and return to where you and your friend set out from."

The words of the old woman make me realize all of a sudden that I am having a dream, so I begin to struggle fiercely to come out of it. But it is as if the weariness of many years keeps me from waking up—it feels as though the weariness buries me beneath layers of dust or entangles me like an abstruse theory, making it impossible to break free. In my despair, I remember a sentence that I read in my youth in a rather strange book, so I start saying in a loud voice, "Waking up is useless, countless grains of sand can weigh down somebody and not let them breathe. . . . Waking up does not mean going back to a state of wakefulness, but returning to a previous dream. Countless dreams follow one another, like grains of sand. The path on which you will walk back is endless, and by the time you will really wake up, you will be dead."

The old woman says, "You must not lose heart. When you will open your eyes, the sky will lighten up and you will regain consciousness."

As she is talking, she puts a string of shiny, white stones in my pocket. She says, "This is a symbol of sorts: taken individually, these are not at all different from ordinary pebbles, but if you string them together, these precious stones can send forth a peculiar brilliance."

Then she taps lightly on my head, saying over and over again, "Go back, go back, go back."

When I come out of the dream at last, I discover that I am leaning on Yunnan's shoulder, a shoulder as soft as a pillow. Her hand is tapping on my head.

"Well, the plane has already arrived at N."

I straighten my body, moving my stiff neck left and right, and I say, "I was dreaming. Dreaming about you. If you had woken me up a moment later, I would have seen you. It was going to be a crucial meeting."

"Really, how come?"

"Because I wanted to tell you something."

"What a coincidence, I woke you up expressly to ask you something."

"Quick, what do you want to ask me?"

"First, you tell me about this dream you had about me. What do you want to tell me?"

I say, "I dreamt that our plane crashed. In heaven I saw an unknown old woman, who wanted me to return to my physical body, to return to take care of my mother and to keep you company. She said that we must not be like scattered grains of sand that cannot be together . . ."

Then I describe in detail the old woman's appearance, her wrinkled face, her relaxed posture, her peculiar skin color, her hair, and the timbre of her voice, remote like water flowing from a high mountain.

All of a sudden I notice tears glistening in my friend's eyes. Her lips have started to tremble, either because of surprise or pain.

I stop talking and look at her, not knowing what to do. Yunnan says that the old woman is her mother, who died thirteen years ago. She says that at the time she and I did not know each other.

While she talks, she pulls a black-and-white photograph from her wallet. As I look at the two-inch picture with yellowed margins, I am stunned. The woman in the picture is really the woman I saw in my dream.

When I and Yunnan climb down the stairs of the plane, N is just waking up from its hazy midday nap.

Keeping the rhythm of the riverside mountain town, we enter slowly, one step at a time, into this city's two o'clock sunlight. Now I hear, all of a sudden, that familiar and distant heartbeat that I haven't felt in ages. It meets me head-on, hard and cold. I take one step back, staggering, feeling instinctively that there is no way to harmonize this noise of quick success and instant gain with the sound of what is beating inside me. The former is a male rhythm that has become a public standard.

Yunnan shivers with cold. From her backpack she takes out a long black coat, puts it on, and pulls up the collar. Her whole body seems to have been covered by a dark shadow. "This city looks more and more surreal," she says. "It lacks any kind of authentic fragrance and feeling."

"It's obvious, isn't it? It is hard to imagine that I for so many years have been a wooden puppet on this huge stage."

We emerge from the terminal building. Under our steps, the slabs of the square in front of us unfold like the panels of a folding fan. The fierce sun pours down on us like a torrential white rain, making the stream of hurried passers-by look like a series of overexposed images.

At the periphery of my field of vision, I see the towering JG building. Its cold glass walls reflect a ghostly blue light. On many occasions, Yunnan has declared this building, shaped like a half arch that reaches the sky, to be the symbol of N. She says that that is an unstable and quite decadent leaden color that gives off the sensation of a whizzing refrigerator. She says that below its surface, in the unfathomable corridors that resemble a labyrinth, amidst the static doors and windows and the ceiling decorated with circling lines, one imagines dismal music seeping down, lingering in the air. A kind of contradictory feeling in which there is ambiguity and resistance at the same time.

Just then Yunnan says, "Right, you just said that you were looking for me in your dream. What were you going to tell me?"

She turns her head toward me, her brown eyes exposed under the moving sunlight. She squints, as if her long eyelashes wanted to block out everything in this city but me.

"Oh, that," I sigh. "You know that I have never felt at home anywhere, now

I have given up the idea of finding a home. I am tired, but no matter what I do, this city is the place where I was born, where I have gotten used to breathing, feeling, eating, and sleeping. My mother is always waiting for me with her door ajar. It is decreed by fate that I cannot sever my ties with this city. However . . . you know, a person's solitude does not depend on whether or not she has friends, but on whether she has close friends in the world, but if all her friends are far away . . ."

"What are you saying?"

I turn my head to look at the sun, following those eye-piercing rays of light. I see that the sun looks like a big solitary silver basin. The light moves to and fro among the branches and the leaves. The air is permeated with a sense of its own extraordinariness. All of a sudden I feel that that big chunk of dazzling light consists of nothing but artificially pasted together bits of sunshine.

Without turning my head to look at Yunnan, I say, "You . . . make me feel alone, in this city, I am always by myself . . ."

"But you make me feel the same way too . . ."

At last, I say very loudly (as if talking to the whole atmosphere), "I want you to go home with me! I need to feel at home, I need to have somebody to face the world with."

Yunnan turns around, narrowing her big, bright brown eyes to look at me, with the unique expression I know so well. Then she lifts one hand to brush off a speck of dust from her cheek, an imaginary speck of dust, as if she were wiping off something tangible or perhaps catching something abstracted.

Yunnan straightens her backpack, and then she raises one hand to grab me. "Very well," she says. "We are going."

With my practical right hand, I grasp the sleeve she is offering me as though it were a rice-straw drowning in water, while I put my dreamy left hand into my pocket.

My careless left hand unexpectedly knocks against a cold object, and some kind of premonition makes me think of the string of sparkling and crystal clear stones that the old woman in heaven put in my pocket. I hurriedly take the object out but because of my agitation, it falls to the ground: Stunned, Yunnan and I see a pile of milk teeth, rolling around on the ground.

My tongue deadlocks in my mouth, as though I had swallowed a tile in one bite.

# 4

# A RECORD

Zhang Mei

*Translated by Patricia Sieber*

Last night I slept rather fitfully. In my dreams I was harangued by all sorts of intimations about the course of my destiny. I dreamt that I was sitting on an ice-cold stone stool in a garden. Blackish green snakes were crawling all over the underside of the stone table in front of me. Later in the dream, I found myself standing next to a precipice. Below me an expanse of water extended as far as one could see.

The snakes and the waters woke me up at three thirty in the morning. After coming to, I smoked a cigarette on the sofa in the living room. When it got to be four o'clock, the stillness of the night was shattered by the ringing of the phone. Who could be calling at this hour? The voice at the other end of the line belonged to a man whom I did not seem to know. Only after he had talked for quite some time did I remember that I had recently made his acquaintance at a party. His surname was Li. He lived in Hong Kong where he worked as a businessman and as a writer. I had the impression that Hong Kong and other developed areas in Asia abounded with these kinds of cultural brokers. I asked whether he was currently in Guangzhou or in Hong Kong. It turned out that he was in Guangzhou and that he wanted to know whether I had any free time that day. He said that he was working on a movie script and since he still lacked some materials, he wanted to invite me for an outing to Shunde, a county in the Pearl River delta.

He mentioned that there was a certain film director who would come along as well. I had heard of that director, I had even seen his films. At one point, he had paid quite a bit of attention to the works of young authors. Later he had married a French woman and had gone off to France.

The prospect of the three of us traveling together excited me slightly. There was a feeling of action and accomplishment, as though a boat that had been sitting ashore for a long time was once again setting out for a journey. Of course, such a notion was a bit ridiculous.

## 1

On this spring morning, there was a slight chill in the air.

I was wearing a pair of light yellow Giordano jeans. On my back I sported a trendy black suede bag. I had put two packs of Kent in the outside zipper pocket.

Mr. Li and I had arranged to meet at six o'clock sharp at Triangle Market on Donghua West Road.

Triangle Market was an old part of town, full of ramshackle buildings and winding alleys. Raw sewage passed sluggishly beneath the derelict stone bridge, where I got off the bus, and filled the spring morning with a foul stench.

At six o'clock, it was still dark but light was coming out of one or two eateries. I gazed in every direction, but I did not see Mr. Li. There was a gust of wind on the bridge. I stiffened my collar and began walking toward the lit eatery.

In the distance, I saw a pair of white slacks loafing about. Because it was dark and because those slacks were exceptionally clean—in fact, so clean that there was not a speck of dust on them, it wasn't until I stood right in front of them that I realized that these slacks were worn by a short man.

The short man shot me a suspicious glance, which I returned. It was clear that we were both waiting, but he was even more impatient than I.

I took an abiding interest in those spotless slacks of his. Nobody could wear such white slacks in a city as grimy as Guangzhou. These slacks in this Guangzhou spring morning were as improbable as a martial arts action novel.

Full of indignation, we stood by the roadside and both craned our necks to survey the premises. We occasionally shot each other an exasperated glance since we were faced with the same predicament. Then we both turned around at the same time, and at the same moment marched into the lone eatery that was open on this chilly morning.

The diner was extremely dingy. To come upon such a dingy place on such a thriving stretch of the thoroughfare seemed as unreal as the green snakes and the vast waters I had encountered in my dreams that night. And the unreality of it all must have also struck the man in the white slacks. His face had the trance-like expression of a somnambulist, but upon entering the place, that look instantly disappeared.

We each took a rickety bench and sat down. Behind us a young waiter busied himself. We both pulled out our cigarettes. When he saw that I lit one, he was a bit stunned, but that too passed.

Three strangers meeting up in an establishment of this sort at the crack of dawn and not exchanging a word—it seemed like the opening scene from a martial arts novel. I thought that in all likelihood I must have read too many such novels, even to the point of being incurably poisoned by them.

Only when Mr. Li entered the diner and greeted both me and the white pants did I know that all of us were travel companions. When Mr. Li noticed the intense embarrassment on our faces, he quickly introduced us to each other. Then the three of us stepped into the chilly outdoors.

We flagged a taxi. In the car, I continued to obsess about the white slacks. Only film directors could wear slacks like these because they wanted to create something real out of unreality. In the car, the two men started to talk about the movie script.

The script dealt with self-wedded women.

When we got out of the car in a certain small town in Shunde County, it was already starting to dawn. The one open teahouse seethed with activity as scores of people streamed in and out. Because we had arrived too early, we would have to have some tea first.

We went up to the second floor of the teahouse and picked a spot. We were surrounded by brightly clad peasants. I looked at them; many people wore a kind of jacket made out of prewashed silk. Foreigners had first worn these jackets, then artsy circles, then city people, and now the peasants. Even though it was early, they drank a locally produced rice wine packaged in cup-sized containers. At 38 percent, the alcohol content was not very high.

Once they had had some wine, were the peasants likely to break into a song about self-wedded women?

> Oh, lass,
> You are so bewitchingly dressed up that one does not tire of looking at you,
> Why do you want "to comb your hair" instead of getting married and thus
> forego romance?

Of course, they would not sing this song, because the women who wore the light jackets made out of silk gauze and piled up their raven black hair into a chignon were already a thing of the past. But on account of a handful of writers, film directors, and actresses, these self-wedded women would be passed on to future generations as an embellished image of their beautiful selves.

(In the early part of the nineteenth century, in the southern part of Panyu and Shunde Counties, scores of young women refused to marry. They arranged their own hair in a chignon, thus indicating their self-initiated transition from girlhood to adulthood. They lived together and earned their own livelihood. In Guangdong, they were known literally as "the girls who combed themselves.")

* * *

The three of us drank tea while we talked about self-wedded women.

"This is a hot topic," the director said. He noted that a few years ago, one of the commercial TV stations in Hong Kong produced a soap opera based on this theme. When the series was aired in Guangzhou, it was very popular. The local Pearl River Film Studio was in the process of making a movie on this topic. A writer from Guangdong had written a novel about it and so forth.

Mr. Li added, "We are doing this script in order to make a prizewinning film, like, for example, *Ruan Lingyu*, the recent Hong Kong film about the 1930s actress of the same name, or *Farewell My Concubine*, the film about two Beijing opera actors. The saying has it, heaven created my human matter, so I will most certainly be of use. Good story matter such as self-wedded women is just like that. We will touch up these natural beauties with a little bit of lipstick and then they can take part in a beauty contest!"

As I folded down my upright collar, I said, "How come when you say that you want to shoot a film about self-wedded women, I think of *The Village of Widows*, the film about the remote fishing village where all the men were killed in a typhoon and the widows do not allow the young generation to have children?"

The director repeatedly shook his head. "No, it won't be anything like that. That kind of movie is much too subjective and lacking in general human interest."

Films were always a good medium for showcasing something unconventional as well as for expressing ideas, but what was this prospective film about? Was it about feminism? Or was it about a bunch of beautiful girls who, having no interest in sex with men, formed pairs and swayed through fields?

The antiquated and dust-covered lifestyle of these women would turn them into the likes of the warriors and horses excavated from tombs.

Because the material was so intrinsically beautiful, no matter what the artistic means, they would not do it justice, turning it instead into something contrived or farcical. I said shyly, "Couldn't the film's structure be modeled on *Longing for Home*, where a female journalist interviews former Japanese 'comfort women'? Without fanfare, a woman reporter would come to the countryside, where she lives together with one of the self-wedded women. The woman cooks meals for her, buys her new bedding, and as time passes, they take to each other, and slowly the old woman begins to tell her stories about the old times."

The two men listened happily, saying, "Then you should be that journalist!" Later, the more they thought about it, the more they were amused until they finally burst into laughter, saying, "How could you think of *Longing for Home*? That's too weird, really, it's too weird."

At nine o'clock we left the teahouse. The sky was completely overcast. The streets were packed with all manner of carts and cars. Gradually, the self-wedded women drifted from our thoughts.

* * *

We sat in the offices of the subcounty government, which were lodged in a warehouse. The director pulled out a letter of introduction issued by a provincial agency and passed it to an old functionary. After glancing at it, the old man said impassively, "How come you want to interview the self-wedded women again? Haven't they already been interviewed quite a few times?"

The director said, "This time around, it is possible that people from abroad will come and shoot a film."

The old man raised his eyebrows archly. "And when will people from outer space come and make a film?"

I understood these local folks. They had absolutely no use for these affectations. They had an altogether different understanding of the so-called self-wedded women and so-called female revolution. According to historical documents, they feared that their own daughters would become self-wedded women. When they saw that one of their radiant and vivacious daughters put up her own raven black hair in the fashion of a grown woman, they were bitter and resentful in the extreme. Therefore, they often engaged in open and clandestine battle with the self-wedded women's groups, planning to bring back their rebellious daughters.

In the warehouse we waited for the scheduled van, which would take us to the silk factory.

Mr. Li pulled out the completed script, once again perusing it. The director stood up and sighed with emotion as he surveyed the enormous warehouse. He said, "What a great studio! This is a natural studio! It is tall enough and it is big enough. When we come to shoot, we'll set up the studio right here."

Excited by this discovery, he went off to discuss the details of a potential rental of the facility with the old man.

A gust of air from the beginning of the century swirled through the warehouse. It was also springtime. Young women would roll up their long hair, wrap around their cloth tunics, and walk about in pairs. But in my head, they always had the faces of pretty actresses. Their countenances were beautiful and their bearing gracious. Actresses excelled at disguising misery as beauty. The only thing we would ever be able to know was a disguised life. How was it possible to not disguise life from the past? We use various means to reincarnate the past, but in the end we always just disguise it.

Mr. Li said to me, "The film opens with a scene at nightfall at a brook in a region of rivers and lakes. Two couples made up of a boy and a girl sit by the creek and are passionately in love. Lines from a folk song drift by; in the song, a boy and a girl kiss. In the shade of a tree behind the lovers, there is an old woman with her hair done up in a bun. The old woman looks at these lovers with a complicated glance. Then we will present the name of the film.

"After that the story starts."

Once there was a teacher who asked his students to write a sentence involving the character *bai*, whose meanings range from "white" to "blank" to "futile."

Among the assignments that were handed in, over eighty percent featured phrases such as "as white as snow" or "as white as paper." The teacher was extremely disappointed. He thought that not one of his students had any gifts because they lacked imagination. Thus the teacher said, "Your expressions are all very blank."

Were we in the role of the teacher or that of the students? We would never be able to know.

## 2

The van that the silk factory had dispatched to get us had arrived.

At some point in the past, this region had abounded with silk factories, but now in this affluent area, the factory we were going to visit was the only remaining one. These silk factories fostered in large measure the increase in the number of self-wedded women.

The factory overlooked the river. There was an old-fashioned dock covered with green flagstones next to an old banyan tree. The head of the women workers' union received us and said, "I don't know how many films and television series have featured this dock."

As we were standing on these flagstones, I imagined the hubbub in years past. One boat after another would bring loads of shining white silk cocoons. A group of young women who wore plain-colored silk gauze slacks and had their hair done up in chignons would wait here for the boats to dock. These women were unaware that decades after their death they would be transformed into models for stories, that they would become cultural relicts, and that they would bring a sense of joy and wonder to all living beings.

Thereafter we visited the factory hall. We saw rows of machinery, shining white cocoons soaking in scalding hot water, and rows of women workers. The whole setting did not differ from the scenes we had seen in films about self-wedded women. It was as if we had stepped into a scene that really existed. The resemblance between the real and the fictional struck me as uncanny. Such resemblance creates the feeling that time has stopped, which is an exhilarating feeling in and of itself.

The chairwoman showed us everything. She was a capable and experienced woman. One couldn't help wondering whether she, had she been born then, would have joined the ranks of the self-wedded women.

"I understand them." When she said "them," it was clear that she referred to the self-wedded women. "I will sing a song for you."

Thereupon she proceeded to sing an altogether unpleasant song in the local dialect.

> The rooster with his tail all puffed up—being someone's daughter-in-law is hard

> Even if I get up early, they all say that I rise late.
> When my tears have not yet dried, I go into the kitchen
> In the kitchen, there is a winter melon, I ask Father-in-law whether I should boil it or steam it
> Father-in-law tells me to boil it, Mother-in-law tells me to steam it.
> Regardless of whether I boil it or steam it, I can't please them, banging on the tables, they make a fuss.
> On the third morning, three cudgels are worn out from all the beatings.
> On the fourth morning, nine skirts are tattered from all the kneeling.

I knew that for the purpose of writing this script Mr. Li had already come to Shunde on a number of occasions. He had stayed countless nights in countless villages, tracking down however many self-wedded women were still alive before he finally wrote the current version.

And until now I still was not too clear on what lacunae exactly my presence during this round of interviews was supposed to address.

In the past, the silk weaving factories were called silk reeling factories. During the heyday of the silk industry in the two counties of Shunde and Nanhai, young self-wedded women for the most part reeled silk in the mills, while the older ones picked mulberry leaves and raised silkworms. Even though the working conditions in the silk factories were very oppressive, since they only had to provide for themselves, self-wedded women could eke out a modest living, and there still was something left to spare. However, in the 1920s, Japanese synthetic silk had already squeezed out the raw silk of Shunde in the international marketplace. Many local silk factories had gone out of business. However, in the lone surviving Guizhou factory, young women involved in reeling still numbered in the hundreds. Thus it was easy to imagine what a large number of self-wedded women the various silk factories had accommodated during the heyday of the silk industry.

According to the chairwoman, at its peak, her factory had employed over five hundred workers.

The women who had decided to be self-reliant would emerge from every direction early in the morning, bringing along a simple homemade box lunch. The scene made me think of all the women workers who had recently streamed into Guangdong from all over the country. However, there was a significant difference, because the self-wedded women had resolved to depend on themselves for their entire lives.

Nowadays, how many self-wedded women who had worked at this factory remained?

The chairwoman said, "There are three. The youngest among them will soon be eighty years old. Every month the factory sends someone to take their pension to them."

When they were young, were these women good looking? Had they ever been in love? Now that they were old, did they have any regrets about their erstwhile choices?

Our van sped out of the factory compound into the delightfully beautiful countryside. Amidst this quiet and open landscape, I suddenly felt that self-wedded women were not real. The unreality was that of a fairy tale. Having appeared and disappeared so suddenly on the horizon of history, these women simply seemed unreal.

The van stopped in front of a large compound that was built in the style of the Ming or the Qing dynasty.

Full of excitement, the director jumped out of the bus, inspecting the large dilapidated compound. The borders of the eaves were decorated with painted flowers and birds, which gave the building an air of classical refinement. Without being able to get the melody right, I began to sing: "My glorious youth, you are all wasted and gone like these decayed walls."

The director gave me an annoyed glance.

Without being able to stop myself, I repeated the line. Indeed, comparing the beauty of the self-wedded women to the dark age in which they had lived, all that was left now were a few ruins.

From outside the gate, the chairwoman began to call "Fifth Sister, Fifth Sister!"

An old woman in a black outfit appeared at the gate. She was so old her back was all hunched over, which made it difficult for her to lift her head. She tried her best to smile at the union secretary.

The chairwoman said, "There are guests here to see you."

Fifth Sister appeared to be pleased and said, "Please come in and have a seat."

We followed her in. We first passed a very small courtyard. Two lines of poetry were pasted on the sides of the entryway. The couplet read,

> Once you wash off your make-up,
> your attendance upon the gods has its proper measure.
> Once you get rid of the vanity mirror,
> you will realize the emptiness of all forms.

After we passed through the portal lined with the couplet, we entered a large, dimly lit hall. The hall was absolutely empty except for some blackened stoves on the far side. We entered Fifth Sister's room, which was adjacent to the gate that led into the hall. Fifth Sister lived in such reduced circumstances that they could not have possibly been reduced any further. A wooden platform that served as a bed was surrounded by a tattered mosquito net riddled with holes. Next to the bed stood a single unlacquered chest. I was struck by the fact that there was not a single picture depicting a bright future, nor was there any furniture to speak of. Something resembling a kerosene stove with a soot-covered iron pot sat on the ground.

I thought again of *Longing for Home* and the old women who had worked as prostitutes during the war. Didn't the prospects of all old people resemble each other?

The director started to question Fifth Sister, inquiring about the circumstances of her leaving home. Her dialect made it very difficult for us to understand her, so the chairwoman stood on one side and acted as an interpreter.

Fifth Sister told us that she was fifteen when she put up her hair. In order to evade the scrutiny of her suspicious family, the preparations for the ceremony had all been conducted in the spinsters' house, the communal residence hall where self-wedded women lived.

The director asked, "Does that spinsters' house still exist?"

Fifth Sister shook her head. In her wrinkled face, one could not detect a trace of melancholy.

In an article among Mr. Li's materials entitled "Self-Wedded Women and Absentee Wives," the ceremony of "having one's hair combed" was described in the following manner:

> For the ceremony of "putting up one's hair," the following objects were needed: new clothes (including undergarments and underwear), new shoes, new socks, a comb, a red hair string, a little vanity chest known as "trousseau" (above was an inlaid glass mirror, below were several little drawers which contained different kinds of combs, hair needles, powder, tassels, and so forth), and sacrificial items: roasted pork, chicken, a red envelope with money, fresh fruit, incense sticks, decorated candles, tea, wine, etcetera. These items were secretly prepared over a period of time with the assistance of the sisters in the spinsters' house.
>
> The evening before the ceremony, it was customary for the girls to stay overnight at the spinsters' house. After taking a bath in a fragrant ablution of tangerine leaves, they gathered together all the sisters of like mind, regardless of whether or not they had already undergone the ceremony, and talked with the self-wedded ones offering instruction in the "ways of the heart," like how to persevere in one's independence, how to make a living as a single woman, how to support each other. Thereafter, they provided mutual encouragement. At the first glimpse of dawn, they took advantage of the deserted roads and together went to a temple in the vicinity to perform the ceremony.
>
> Once they got to the temple, they set down the articles of clothing and the sacrificial items in front of the Guanyin Bodhisattva. They lit fragrant candles, performed the three kneelings and nine *koutous* in front of the statue of the goddess, offered an oath of their resolve to be self-wedded, vowing never to marry a man. Then a self-wedded woman who had been assigned to this task untied the girls' braids and combed them into a chignon (there were also cases where they made the braids into chignons the night before the ceremony). Subsequently, they changed into the new clothes. After their hair had been arranged, the girls once again paid obeisance to Guanyin and then exchanged bows and congratulations with the sisters who had come along. Thereupon the ceremony was concluded.

* * *

We had every reason to believe that Fifth Sister had gone through the process of this ceremony before embarking on her journey, but the focus of our excitement had shifted. Clad in dark clothes and speaking barely intelligibly, this self-wedded woman seemed a moribund relic from another age. However, that mysterious spinsters' house, that fragrant tangerine leaf ablution which would drench the body of a virgin resolved to remain independent, those shiny silk clothes, those colorful offerings, all aroused our curiosity.

Hadn't some great philosopher said that all human behavior was motivated by curiosity?

The terseness of the descriptions of the article notwithstanding, at least three scenes could inspire our director's enthusiasm.

First, the bathing scene. "After the initiates had taken a bath in a fragrant ablution, they assembled all the sisters of like mind regardless of whether or not they had already undergone the ceremony and talked together, with the self-wedded ones offering instruction in the 'ways of the heart'."

One could picture this scene in the following manner: Those freshly bathed and pleasantly perfumed girls and those women who had taken the fragrant bath in the past would huddle around the dim light of an oil lamp and excoriate the various shortcomings of men. Thereafter, the freshly perfumed girls would egg each other on, and for a while, the whole scene would be highly emotional.

Then, the walk at dawn. "Then at the first glimpse of dawn, taking advantage of the deserted roads, they went together . . ."

Here one could bring out the aesthetic potential of the medium of film even more successfully: at daybreak, in a beautiful village, some beautiful young women, dressed in new clothes, would wander along a path through the fields. Their freshly washed faces would shine like the rosy morning dew. They would walk arm in arm, their faces full of anticipation about their bright future. For this kind of morning scene, the soundtrack should not feature any music.

Then the scene of the hair binding ritual: "Then a self-wedded woman who had been assigned to this task untied the girls' braids and combed them into a chignon."

This scene could be even more heroic. As the lamp dimmed, the flowing hair would be combed into a chignon. Depending on the artistic techniques used, this sequence could be suggestive in various ways. Then once the hair was tied up, all the girls could sing together.

> The silver chest is heavy, the friendship between us is deep.
> We don't strive for wealth and fame, we just desire divine protection.
> Guandi, God of War, bestows upon us the courage and righteousness of warriors.
> Guanyin, Goddess of Mercy, assists us in preserving the chaste purity of our hearts and bodies.

On the one hand, if we used these scenes in a novel, they would all be ingenious. In fact, we might well ask how with these kinds of scenes any novel, regardless of its particular style, could fail.

On the other hand, Kundera said, "If a novel can be adapted as a film or as TV drama, then what is the purpose of the novel?"

So perhaps from that point of view, one might wonder whether a novel should exclude these sorts of scenes.

However, the two people standing in front of me were very interested in stories. They spared no effort to find out all sorts of details about the lives of self-wedded women.

Mr. Li was kneeling in front of Fifth Sister. Like a kindergarten teacher, he patiently continued to nudge her.

"Did you cry at the time?"

"Why didn't you cry?"

Seventy years ago, Fifth Sister must have been a cheerful person because she believed that she would not need a man to support herself. The spirit of that kind of woman lives on until today. For instance, a certain female film star from Taiwan has said, "Why would I work so hard to make movies? Because in the future I don't want to be financially dependent on any man." But these stars do not need to tie up their hair, and they can sleep around with men or they can despise men. That's progress and this kind of progress is quite important for women. However, at that time, a commitment to independence was complicated by the question of sex. Foregoing economic dependence on men also ruled out the possibility of heterosexual intimacy. It would seem that men issued the following directive: If you want the benefit of my company, you got to stick it out with me. Self-wedded women decided that they did not want men, not even their bodies.

Fifth Sister's building contained many rooms, both upstairs and downstairs. Each of those rooms had once been inhabited by a single or by a couple of self-wedded women. As one imagined the hustle and bustle back then, many different sights filed past: young women as lovely as flowers, old women ravaged by time, all strolling up and down, venturing in and out. This decaying building harbored countless stories from that time, none of which we would ever be able to know. Amidst decrepitude, the compound shrouded itself in silence.

We mounted the wooden stairs to the second floor. This floor was already rented out to young female migrant workers from other provinces. The rents here were quite cheap. In the small courtyard, these women had put up a clothesline to dry their laundry. Above the courtyard, some translucent pieces of tiles had caught a few rays of light. The color was a pale, sepia-like gray. The director said in an animated voice, "This light seems rather suitable for filming." He cheerfully began to examine the beams of light, revealing his professional knack for this sort of thing. This light could give rise to various associations: a certain ambivalence, old songs, Charlie Chaplin's black-and-white films, the distant era a century ago, the inequity and venality of those times, the beautiful women nearing the end of their lives.

I thought of the rows of stoves in the large hall and how Fifth Sister had told us how each woman prepared her own meals on her own stove. On the roof, there was a terrace, where someone had planted some out-of-season chrysanthemums.

After we left the decrepit compound, we all silently heaved a sigh of relief. After the van had driven quite far away, Mr. Li finally said, "When I interviewed the self-wedded women in Yuecong, the women there sang a song of their hair-binding ritual." He pulled out a piece of paper and recited the following song:

> With the first stroke of the comb, I escape misfortune,
> with the second, I avoid hardship,
> with the third, I obtain good luck,
> with the fourth, great benefit,
> with the fifth, divine blessings,
> with the sixth, long life,
> with the seventh, ease,
> with the eight, purity,
> with the ninth, resolve,
> with the tenth, a sisterhood until old age.

I asked, "Did they use wooden combs?"

The director said, "Some used wooden ones, others used combs made from bones."

## 3

The second self-wedded woman whom we were going to interview lived in a relatively bustling small town.

The town bordered on a river. Pointing to the small dock on the open terrain that we had just traversed, the union secretary noted that many shots in the Hong Kong TV series *Self-Wedded Women* had been filmed here.

I remembered a male tutor from the provincial capital who was later to have a romantic liaison with the main female character had sat here in a small boat next to the shore.

The town exuded an air of classical simplicity. Traditional compounds were numerous. Guihao, the self-wedded woman we were going to visit, also lived in such a building.

As we were walking along a street where the sound of buying and selling things did not cease, we saw some peasants putting fresh grass carp on tiny lotus leaves.

After meeting with Guihao, we realized that she was very different from Fifth Sister. Although she too was old, she seemed much younger than Fifth Sister. Her back was quite straight and her dyed hair was pulled back without a single stray hair. She looked at us with a smile.

Her living quarters were entirely different. Upon entering, one found oneself in a courtyard with many kinds of flowers and shrubs. All this greenery was refreshing to behold. Looking out toward the courtyard, the living room was full of traditional rosewood furniture, all of which was kept immaculately clean.

Thus we were sitting in a kind of traditional atmosphere.

It seemed that Guihao concealed certain aspects of her life story. She merely said that she was a different kind of self-wedded woman, namely the kind called absentee wife, who would perform a regular marriage ceremony and only later become a self-wedded woman.

When the moment of marriage approached, these determined absentee wives were instructed by their sworn sisters on how to counter the advances of the prospective husband. In addition, the sworn sisters made a special protective garment for her out of a thick white cloth, which covered her upper and lower body. After she put it on, the sworn sisters tightly sewed together all the holes with linen thread so that the groom could not possibly tear it open. She also carried sharp objects on her and would not allow the groom to get close. If the groom violently forced himself upon her, she would loudly scream for help.

I said to the director, "Wouldn't it be great to have an opening scene where a group of self-wedded women wrap the body of an absentee wife with white cloth? Such a frame would certainly be pretty and provocative."

According to the standard marriage customs of this region at that time, the bride had to stay at the husband's house for three nights after the marriage ceremony was performed. Then she was allowed to return to her natal family for one day. In the evening of that day, the bride had to return to her husband's family, and only after living there for a month was she free to venture in and out. However, the absentee wives did not follow this practice; instead, having returned to the natal family after the first three days, they were determined never to go back to the husband's house. Thus, those three days tested their resolve to withstand their husbands' sexual demands. When they returned to the fold of the self-wedded women after those three days, the sworn sisters might perform an inspection of their protective garment.

Guihao said that she was from a rich family who did not approve of her choosing the life of a self-wedded woman; therefore, she adopted this other strategy.

In this latter form of marriage, in the vast majority of cases, the woman would compensate the husband with money for her absence in exchange for being included in the ancestral sacrifices after her death.

Why didn't she believe in marriage when she was young?

Guihao did not say.

She said that her husband with whom she had not consummated relations later married another woman. She smiled as she said this, her expression remaining entirely calm.

Wasn't it possible that a husband who desired the bride passionately would throw caution to the wind and rip the protective garment to shreds? The chairwoman said, "That would have been impossible, since in this region, self-wedded women enjoyed considerable respect."

So feminism achieved a victory.

In this region, there was another custom. Rich families felt that the fact that their daughters did not get married constituted a loss of face. They would catch a rooster who played the role of a substitute groom. As was customary in weddings, the family would require the girl and the rooster to pay obeisance to heaven and earth. Then the family would put on a big banquet. Thereafter, the girl was, for all intents and purposes, considered married.

So at that time, contrary to what one might expect, roosters and grooms had the same status.

We asked Guihao whether she cooked her own food.

Guihao said, "Yes, that's what I have done all along."

From a contemporary vantage point, one could detect some revolutionary elements in the life of a woman like Guihao. She might have become a youngster who sought refuge in the liberated area around Yan'an in the 1940s or she might have become a self-paying student abroad in the 1980s. But because she was born in the 1920s in Shunde, she could only become a self-wedded woman. Wasn't this evidence of the arbitrariness of one's destiny?

Guihao pulled out a photo for us to look at. It was a picture of her and two of her sworn sisters as they went to Guangzhou to have a good time. The photo was already very old. One could just dimly see that as a young woman, Guihao had been svelte and dignified.

For a while the five of us sat in Guihao's quaint living room without saying anything. As it peeked over the wall of the courtyard, the sun shone on the red brick floor in front of us. The faces of us three women—Guihao, the chairwoman, and myself—were arranged according to age, but each of us had a blank expression when it came to the matter of our respective destinies.

When we discussed self-wedded women, we always came to an impasse, namely their sex lives.

How did they solve the problem of sex? As self-wedded women have completely disappeared, so has this mystery and thus it is bound to remain a mystery forever.

According to some legends, they passed around an elastic artifact amongst themselves. Soaked in hot water in the evening, it would expand and could be used for pleasuring oneself.

According to some people, lesbianism was widely practiced in the spinsters' houses, and given the decadent atmosphere, the women were likely to invent ways to turn ordinary tools into masturbatory devices.

Having sex is normal, but because of their unique lifestyle, it is mysterious.

That Mr. Li invited me along this time turned out to be related to this question of sex. Seeing that I was a woman, he thought that perhaps I could seize upon an opportunity during the interviews to achieve a breakthrough in this regard. But as far as this question was concerned, both the self-wedded women and the local residents were all very closemouthed.

I did not ask Fifth Sister, Guihao, or the chairwoman any questions of this sort. I figured that sex was sex and one's secret intimacies were one's secret intimacies, and that the two were separate matters.

It is said that among self-wedded women, there was a practice known as "a couple of intimates" that was lesbian in nature. In this instance, two women lived together in a single room, venturing in and out together, as though married. The young couples of intimates sang the kind of local folk songs known as "wooden fish lyrics" to express their feelings for each other. According to local custom, if a self-wedded woman had a male paramour, the punishment was severe, but nobody interfered with what a couple of intimates did. In that respect, people were quite humane.

Only then did I learn that the song "The Autumnal Sorrow of the Traveler en Route," which I had often sung in the karaoke rooms of nightclubs, was a folk song that self-wedded women had frequently sung to express their sentiments. The director asked me how to sing it. I told him that I just remembered the first few lines, starting with "The moon is bright, the moon is bright." It was a heartrending song. Showing interest, the director goaded me on, listening to me as I sang.

> The moon is bright, the moon is bright,
> The moon is bright, the moon is bright,
> The night is quiet, the hour is late, as I face the brilliant moon,
> The brilliant moon is bright and clear.
> How can I bear to be at heaven's end, far away from home,
> I am deeply grieved, my memories cannot be forgotten.

I wondered whether there could be a woman like that in my own life. Would we recognize and appreciate each other's talents, live in the same flat, sit cross-legged at sunset, and would each sing "The moon is bright" as we accompanied ourselves with the staccato sound of the wooden fish clapper? That truly was a beautiful picture.

In that picture, sex was also beautiful.

In the courtyard, we took our leave from Guihao. Behind her grew seven kinds of plants, including a pomegranate tree. She had planted them to use in offerings to the gods. Guihao said, "The roasted pork used in the offerings is getting more and more expensive."

It was one o'clock in the afternoon. The chairwoman said that she wanted to go home for lunch. She asked us whether we wanted to continue our interviews in the afternoon. Mr. Li and I both looked at the director. I had no desire to keep going. It had begun to rain and felt increasingly chilly. The director said, "Where does the third one live?" She said, "In a nearby village. Just like Fifth Sister, she can't even speak clearly."

"Is there anything special about her?" the director asked. The secretary denied it resolutely.

The director glanced at us and then said, "In that case, we won't go."

Next to an old teahouse we shook hands with the chairwoman, thanking her for her assistance. Then we went up to the second floor of the teahouse to eat.

After we sat down, I fished the cigarettes out of my black suede bag. To be frank, I was worn out. I smoked my cigarette. The river outside the teahouse was completely shrouded in rainy mist. Smalls boats moved slowly in the drizzle. This particular sight had not changed in all those years. It made me think of these old self-wedded women who would sit in this very teahouse, at this very window, reminiscing about their youth, their once plump and smooth arms adorned with green jade bracelets now all withered and shriveled up like sticks of firewood. In the past, the vendor who would sell pork on this street would stare at their gently trembling breasts and sing:

> Oh, lass,
> You are so bewitchingly dressed up that one does not tire of looking at you,
> Why do you want "to comb your hair" instead of getting married and thus forego romance?
> Indeed, as I look at you I see your lewd eyes matched by a cherry-like mouth, lass,
> Your tunic with the embroidered flowers cannot hide that pair of tender milk pearls.
> Even though you are chaste, you do not have a memorial archway erected in your honor!
> With you being as pretty as you are, what's going to happen?

The women's faces would flush and their ears would turn red. They would beat the vendor with whatever was in their hands. When the Japanese came, that vendor died of a sudden illness. When young Guihao was tightly wrapped in the white cloth her sworn sisters had given her to protect herself, her husband must have knelt down and implored her to undo that piece of cloth. The heartfelt aspirations and concrete experiences of that time had, over the years, become like the drizzly rain outside. Who knows whose lives would become unmoored over time? The faithful prostitute Du Shiniang drowned her treasure chest and herself to take revenge against a faithless lover. The self-wedded women sealed their own bodies. Who could say whether her own life would become unmoored, drifting across history?

The dishes were served. If one looked around, the happy people who filled the teahouse all seemed to belong to another world.

Mr. Li said: "Please enjoy true Shunde cuisine."

Shunde County boasted of the best food in all of Guangdong, particularly as far as fish was concerned. Thus, after the silk factories shut down, many self-wedded women went to Guangzhou or Hong Kong to work as domestics for rich families. They continued the traditional culinary style of Shunde. Since they were attentive in their service and looked after everything with great solicitude, they were very well liked by their employers. Wealthy merchants and prominent officials tended to hire "Shunde amahs" as nannies, chaperones, and cooks. As a result, the amahs from Shunde enjoyed so much prestige at that point that it became a sign of social status to retain them in one's service.

What Mr. Li had ordered were all authentic Cantonese dishes: Daileung milk soufflé, Shunde pheasant rolls, garlic eel, boiled lotus root slices, and turtle soup. Indeed, even in this small restaurant next to the river, everything was exquisitely prepared.

We all had some Cantonese rice wine to counter the spring chill.

After two cups, our conversation began to ramble.

The director said, "It's strange. How was it possible that there was a vanguard of women like that in Guangdong in the 1920s? If our film explored this question, we could call it *The Vanguard*."

Mr. Li said, "In the past, we also had an amah from Shunde. Later, she died in our house and my mother made the funeral arrangements."

Living in a large house in the Xiguan district, Mr. Li's family had been prominent in pre-1949 Guangzhou. After liberation in 1949, Mr. Li's father, who had been a seafood merchant, moved to Hong Kong, but Mr. Li did not relocate until after he had finished high school.

Mr. Li said, "My family's fortunes later declined. The amah and my mother fought daily over problems like how much pork to use in a lotus root pork dish or in a turnip pork dish."

The three of us laughed.

I said, "I have a question. What would happen if a self-wedded woman could not stand being so lonely and took up secret relations with a man?" Mr. Li said, "She could be encased in a pig cage filled with stones and tossed in the river! There was a case of a self-wedded woman who had fallen in love with her sister's husband. Once the liaison was discovered, she was put into a pig cage and was about to be tossed into the river when the man rescued her with a payment of one thousand silver dollars."

The director said, "I don't understand why traditionally the punishment for secret relations is always associated with pig cages and rivers. When you think about it, the three things are completely unrelated. Probably there were so many secret affairs, people ran out of ideas on how to punish people."

We again broke into laughter.

When we had eaten nearly everything, we saw the chairwoman hurrying up the stairs, which puzzled us greatly.

She said excitedly: "I made inquiries on your behalf and I found out that a couple of intimates is still living in Nanhai."

The director immediately asked, "Do they live together?"

The secretary said, "Yes."

Because the factory van was already otherwise engaged for the afternoon, the chairwoman could not accompany us. All we could do was to walk in this chilly drizzle for an hour on a low bank of earth between fields until we got to the main road where we would hail a cab. I saw that the white pants of the director, which had symbolized the martial action novel earlier in the day, were now splattered with yellow dots of mud.

When all was said and done, what did these self-wedded women have in common with us? As I was walking in this chilly drizzle, I suddenly was at a loss for answers. When they were young, they were affected by an infectious marriage phobia. They put up their hair in unison, combing it in the manner of a grown woman. They lived together, with everybody doing her own chores and eating her own meals. When two of them became fond of each other, people would call them a couple of intimates. There was lesbianism. There were sex toys. They wore silk gauze clothes that are no longer fashionable, they sang folk songs to the accompaniment of the wooden fish clapper. They earned their own living. The circumstances of their old age were melancholy.

And we?

We also dread marriage, but we get married and then divorce, and after a divorce, we get married again. We have discos like "The Baby Doll Club," where we women can move our bodies a little bit in a refined place sanctioned by society. There we can gather with men whom we rebuke for being part of a different species. We have our own fashions, we have our own tastes. We look askance at lesbianism.

They and us had nothing in common. Only the pathos exuding from their bodies could possibly catch up with us.

I suddenly did not want to disturb that old couple. In a village, they lived quietly surrounded by luxuriant and orderly flowers and shrubs, living out their lives as they had voluntarily chosen when they were young.

As they had gotten old, they would no longer entertain themselves with folk songs. But in those long nights, would they still sit in front of a burnt-out lamp? Would they still take out a red belt and play the game known as "Catching the Great Sea"?

This game would be particularly suitable for a scene in the film: two women would face each other, one of them would unfurl the red silk belt with both hands, the other one would catch that red string with her tiny pinkies, all the while singing likable short tunes.

But all games are played by young people.

This is what the article "Self-Wedded Women and Absentee Wives" records:

> It is very difficult to determine when these two phenomena began. A Mr. Li from Panyu made the following observations based on the local history put together by a Mr. Ren. "In the hundred years since the beginning of our Qing dynasty in 1644, the gazetteer cannot record all the chaste women in the region of Panyu. Among the most extreme cases, the girls vow to each other never to marry, then they drown themselves together in a river." This gazetteer was compiled in 1774. Hence, one can see that in Panyu the refusal to get married had already become a custom in the early Qing. The practice of not residing with the husband's family began even earlier. According to the *Biography of Mr. Qu Wengshan*, "because Wengshan's first wife, a Ms. Liu from Xianlingxiang did not reside with her husband's family, he took a second wife, Wang Huajiang." The marriage between Wengshan and Ms. Liu took place in 1662, thus indicating that the phenomenon of absentee wives was already widespread at that point in time. Around 1908, in Nancun in the region of Panyu, the current author's native place, the population numbered several thousand people, but there were only a handful of brides. In 1909, not a single woman got married, which indicates how dominant the lifestyle of the self-wedded woman was at the time.
>
> After the founding of the Republic in 1912, even though both of these phenomena gradually vanished in the immediate aftermath of Liberation in 1949, the custom was not entirely extinct. According to a survey conducted by the official Women's Federation of Guangdong Province, in Dalong, one of the larger subcounties in Panyu, there were still 245 self-wedded women among a total of 2,028 women, thus representing 12 percent of the female population. During that same time period, in the subcounty of Shayin in Zhongshan, there were still forty-six absentee wives.

# 5

# BROTHERS

Wang Anyi

*Translated by Jingyuan Zhang*

## 1

At the Art Institute, the three women considered each other sworn brothers, calling themselves Old One, Old Two, and Old Three. They spoke of their husbands as Mrs. One, Mrs. Two, and Mrs. Three.

The three Olds were the only women in the class but they outshone the men in every way. Their shared dorm room was even dirtier and messier than the rooms of the male students. They washed their dishes only just before using them, and their clothes only just before their weekly showers. When Old One came back with a plaster head she had filched from the art room, Old Two gave it a painted mustache, and Old Three drew a pair of glasses. The stolen head took its place on a table among other miscellaneous objects. They got up later than even the laziest of the boys; on Sundays and holidays the three could sleep from one evening to the next. The sunlight shone through the windows, creeping over and beyond their motionless quilts, on which the moonlight then took its place.

But on their diligent days, they got up earlier than the most energetic boys. They put on their walking shoes and quietly walked through the darkest part of the campus before dawn to climb Phoenix Hill. They did not take the paths well worn by the feet of generations, but chose to walk in pathless places full of thorny brambles and sharp stones. By the time they reached the top of the hill, the sun was just emerging from the river and a fierce wind let their hair flutter behind them. Speechless at the beauty of the sight, each stood alone, forgetting time and place. On such mornings, they were always the last to arrive in the classroom. When they sat down at their desks for the morning readings, other students were already getting up to leave for the dining hall, where a long line was forming quickly. The three seemed not to see or hear any of that. They sat like stones at their desks. Birds sang midday songs outside the windows of the deserted classroom. The three reached the dining hall just after it closed. They grinned at each other, as though a carefully planned prank had succeeded. Later in the afternoon, however, they waited ahead of others outside the dining hall for dinner. They bought quite a few dishes from the dining hall and some fruit wine from a store in town. They took the food and wine to their dormitory, and began singing like three sworn brothers.

On such a night they did not sleep. They opened their hearts and spoke about their innermost secret thoughts. What a rare and powerful moment in the course of a human life! Many people have journeyed from birth to death without a single chance to examine and express their inner feelings. People gradually come to believe that their inner selves are no different from their surfaces and that there is nothing for them to hide. At night, when they finally have a moment to themselves, they behave the same as they did in public during the day, and do not reflect for a second about their own soul before they fall into a sweet dream yonder. That is a real shame.

The three women belonged to the tiny minority who were able to take advantage of opportunities for self-awareness, and they were particularly lucky to have found one another in the great human crowd. If there had been just one of them, she might have fallen into silence or depression for lack of anyone else to listen to her words and to share her thoughts. Many chances to understand oneself are lost and buried because of loneliness and helplessness. But these three met, and were spending days and nights in each other's company. When they were together, an insight would suddenly strike when they were least prepared, provoking great excitement among them. They always seized upon these inspirations, which otherwise would vanish in an instant.

The three friends showed great concern for one another. When one of them ran into obstacles in trying to discover herself, the other two would encourage her and push her to overcome the mental block so that she could go on with her exploration.

When the conversation grew especially profound, they turned off the lights and talked in the dark without seeing one another's faces. When dawn came, they felt a bit ashamed, and did not dare to look each other straight in the eyes. Even so, they refused to acknowledge their timidity, and forced themselves to do so anyway. But as soon as their eyes met, they looked away, feeling acutely embarrassed. Quite often, they lost their bearings—perhaps because their talk had probed too deeply, or perhaps because they were affected by external circumstances. They felt their conversation had gone wrong somewhere, so they tried to change direction to find a way out of the maze. But they only got more confused. They all opened their mouths simultaneously. In their quest to be heard, they completely lost track of the subject. In the end, being at their wits' end, they all fell silent at once. Those were the most disappointing moments, which filled their hearts with boundless regret. And the effort cost them dearly, draining them for a long time of all thoughts and feelings, so that they were increasingly unable to recognize their true selves. They would resume a long period of normal and mundane life. During such days, they would regularly sleep, eat, go to classes, hand in homework, and write love letters to their "wives" at home.

The three sworn brothers were from Shanghai, Nanjing, and Tongshan County in Jiangsu Province respectively. As for their husbands, Mrs. One was a worker in Shanghai, Mrs. Two was a military officer stationed in the Northeast, and Mrs. Three was an administrator in Tongshan County's cultural bureau.

Mrs. Three began to visit Nanjing often on business trips. Before he embarked on the trip, he would send a telegram to Old Three announcing his arrival. After receiving the telegram, Old Three would make a room reservation at the school's guesthouse. When Mrs. Three arrived, he would go straight to their dorm room, wash his face, and eat the food they had brought back from the dining hall.

As usual, this particular meal was his treat. But of course it was bought with Old Three's meal coupons. Over the meal he tried to make small talk. The women were taciturn. Old Three blushed intermittently and did not dare to look into her sworn brothers' eyes. But their stern glances pierced her anyway, making her pick up on their silent censure. She felt that she had somehow wronged them. After hurriedly finishing dinner, Old Three rushed to do the dishes, although nobody was trying to snatch the job from her. The other two were annoyed. They shot each other a glance and secretly sneered. Old Three clearly sensed their discontent, but she did not dare to raise her head as she diligently scrubbed the plates.

Afterwards she sat down with her two sworn brothers on one bed, and they started a lively conversation. Her husband sat some distance away on another bed. Across a table littered with miscellaneous objects, he took pains to come up with topics he thought would please them. He attempted to flatter the other two women by calling them "First Big Sister" and "Second Big Sister." But the women frowned at these forms of address, considering them very vulgar. Eventually, Old One got up and announced, "It's time for bed." Visibly relieved, Old Three and her husband left the dorm hurrying off to their guest room. The two remaining women exchanged a glance, and with a contemptuous smile on their faces, sealed a tacit pact that excluded Old Three.

Old One and Old Two were in no hurry to go to bed. After they lay down and turned out the lights, they both stared into the darkness. Old Three's empty bed made them melancholy, as if one of their friends had abandoned a common cause. Those earlier nights in which they had poured out their hearts to one another became a weak and fragile thing, which was easily broken. Old Three had become a traitor.

Old Three and her man lay on a hard bed in their hotel room. She thought of her two brothers and of how their silence had oppressed her. She began to be angry at her man—if he had not come, everything would have remained intact, but now all was destroyed! But gradually, she forgot about her brothers and even about herself. She let go of all thoughts, and sank into a deep sleep. But in the middle of the night she woke up with a new thought. No matter how often she might call herself a "brother," and call her man "Mrs.," male was still male and female female, and no one could change that. She went back to sleep. When she woke up again, it was already daylight and past breakfast time.

When she entered the lecture hall, she saw that her two brothers were already sitting in the front row. The two had serious looks on their faces, as if they were the ardent and studious ones. At the sight of them, she was filled with remorse, feeling alone and despising herself. In her desperation, she became shameless. She boldly marched up to her two brothers, and with a victorious smile sat down next to them.

A rift had opened between them, a rift that prevented them for a long time afterwards from having those heart-wrenching talks. After much time had elapsed, long conversations would heal the rift—at least on the surface. Those talks were deeply moving, filling the brothers' eyes with tears. Each brother recounted her experience of meeting and getting together with a man, and described it as a struggle in which the self was obliterated and regenerated.

They were nearly dumbfounded when they realized that without their determined effort and protracted struggle, the selfhood of each brother would be extinguished. They were lucky that the three of them had met. They had caught and rescued each other just in the nick of time! By holding tightly to one another, they kept each other from going under. But the journey to the shore beyond was still a long one, and they must always be careful.

They tried to figure out why a man and a woman wanted to form a union at all. A man and a woman were two separate entities, but they wanted to merge into one entity. And once they merged into one entity, they still pursued their separate courses. To give the world unity and harmony, people seemed to search for partners who closely resemble themselves; little did they know how easy it was for such partners to swallow each other and dissolve into each other, like two fractions that share a common denominator. Merging completely was an unfortunate fate, but individuality came at the price of a terrible solitude that only a superhuman being could endure. Heaven had divided people in two different sexes, with the same number of people in each. From the outset, then, people had not been given the ability to endure solitude. A person feared solitude, and therefore wanted to have a partner; but merging obliterated the person . . .

Questions like these assailed them mercilessly, one after another, each linked to the next, the answer to one question becoming a new question demanding a new answer. The three brothers felt besieged and trapped, thinking that human beings had nothing to live for. The sense of hopelessness galvanized them; they felt that they had touched the core of human life, a black hole at the heart of the universe. The world was empty, but since they did not have the courage to die, they should at least try to do something for unfortunate humankind and for themselves, creating some small pleasure, however transient and fictitious, as they crossed this sea of bitterness. They should start with what was immediately around them, beginning with the most trivial things. Their hearts warmed at the prospect of dispensing kindness to everyone.

That was how a semester would end. Now either a summer vacation or a winter vacation began where they would each return to their families. They parted unwillingly. As they got ready to leave, they were in low spirits. They felt that human beings were fragile and weak. A human being combating the power of Nature was like an ant trying to topple a giant tree, or a mantis trying to block a chariot. They felt a nervous excitement in their despondence, talking and laughing as they walked out through the campus gate. Since Mrs. Two lived in Nanjing, Old Two usually saw off Old One and Old Three, and then closed the windows and locked the dorm room. She cast her last glance at the empty room, and the memory of all those bright days and dark nights came to her mind. She could not bear to linger any longer. She promptly locked the door and walked out of the quiet dorm.

There were two or three vacations when her husband, a military officer, had been sent to a remote area for business. Old Two then spent her vacation alone. She returned to school a week or two earlier than usual. Looking at the other two empty beds, she said to herself: "These two must be enjoying themselves now!"

Time weighed heavily on her, but she somehow endured one day after another. She nurtured a feeling of pride in herself, thinking that at least there was one person—herself—who could pursue her studies in solitude. She practiced sketching in the deserted art room, surrounded by lifeless white plaster sculptures. The desolation made her heart pound. She talked to herself. "You lonely soul, no one cares about you in this world. Everyone is busy with her own affairs." She thought of her man, the military officer, who must be building bomb shelters on mountains in some far corner of the earth. Anger suddenly swept over her: I am busy, too! There are so many things for me to do.

With this thought, she began to be especially diligent. She rose before dawn to go to Phoenix Hill to make sketches, taking the thorny path, tearing up her clothes, and scratching her skin. She returned to the campus only after she was totally exhausted.

She waited anxiously for the start of school, rehearsing many times in her mind the scene in which she would greet Old One and Old Three with a calm and gracious smile. In her imagination, she could not figure out what she would be busy with when Old One and Old Three saw her. What would she be busy with? She left this question hanging and continued her imaginary scene; as she was busy with one thing or another, Old One and Old Three came and called her, "Old Two! Old Two!"

But when the day for meeting finally arrived, Old Two returned to her hometown instead. She said to herself, I have waited for them for so long. It is their turn to wait for me now. It was only on the morning of their first class that she showed up at the classroom door. Seeing their surprise and joy, she felt consoled. Later when she saw the local specialty presents they had brought back for her, she was almost moved to tears. Happy days were to begin! She felt that she had her revenge against that military man who was building his bomb shelters, and so began to calm down.

That night as they lay on their separate beds, a pleasant early autumn breeze blew in through the window, making waves in the mosquito nets. In the courtyard, a cricket chirped. The three chatted aimlessly, off and on. They carefully avoided the topic of their vacation, letting its inspirations pass uncaught, and talked of other things.

From outside the window, a male student called for one of them, mimicking the brotherly appellation that they used among themselves. They felt that this profaned their relationship, and did not respond to the young man's call until he changed his mode of address. The addressee got up to open the door. It turned out that she had left a bar of soap at the washroom sink. She closed the door and slipped back into her mosquito net.

Now they were all wide awake, and they began to ridicule the boy for remembering such minutiae as the ownership of a piece of soap. Their conversation turned to the withering of masculinity in modern society. The strong male of the past was hard to find nowadays. They nostalgically enumerated the qualities that a man should have, as though they themselves belonged to a traditionalist age. They said that a man should have a broad chest and shoulders, so as to carry out the great tasks of the world and to bear heavy burdens of misery for the sake of the next generation. Trivial things should never enter a man's realm of concern. If a man paid attention to a piece of soap, then he was hopeless.

The women were completely disillusioned with men, thinking it was their misfortune to live in such a degenerate world. It was only then that they started talking about their vacations. They told caustic and jocular stories about the various antics of their "wives," rolling on their beds with laughter. If men had already extinguished their egos and were feminized, what was there for women to fret over or fear? A union between a man and a woman was like a battle, in which one devours the other, with the final victory belonging to whoever was stronger. Apparently women had won, because men had become the captives of trivial matters. But if men had destroyed their gender characteristics, how disappointing for women! The brothers laughed until their laughter ran aground. They felt that the situation was dire. When they tried to envision a world where there were only women, they were once again brought face to face with the black hole at the center of the universe. Gradually they fell silent and lay back down. It was already very late.

At daybreak, they woke refreshed. They remembered the discussion of the previous night and felt that they had reached a new level, as though they had turned into new beings: in this degenerate world, they would do something positive. Thinking they could save the world, they felt buoyed by a sense of mission. They picked up their chopsticks and unwashed bowls and marched to the cafeteria like martyrs.

The final semester came. The brothers were saddened by the thought that soon they would have to embark on their separate ways. There would never again be such days of intimacy. Even if they managed to get together now and then, it would not be the same, and they would not be the same. They felt that now, together, they were the best, the freest, the most aware that they could be in their whole life. Before, they had not known who they were. They had just gotten by, blindly following the crowds. Just when all seemed lost and they were going under, they met each other. Coming to know one another woke the true selves within them. They finally came to know what each of them was like. They relinquished apprehensions and impediments, and released their true selves.

They discussed all of this, day after day and night after night. Their discussions left room for only one meal a day, and sometimes for no sleep at night. They agonized over whether parting would make them fall back into their old state of simple-minded ignorance, where they would lose their newly realized selves in their relations with their husbands and marriage and with the world at large. They shuddered at the thought that their selves, unable to express themselves freely, would gradually disappear. They whiled away a whole day at Quanwu Lake, intently gazing at the water extending into the distance, in the hope that this moment might last forever.

However, during the final semester, Mrs. Three visited the school more often than he used to, coming almost every two or three weeks. He looked at Old One and Old Two with increasing hostility, and did not conceal his distaste for the term "Old Three." Every time his wife answered to "Old Three," he made a long face. He deliberately bossed his wife around in front of her brothers. After washing his face, he would demonstratively leave the dirty water in the basin, waiting for his wife to dispose of it. He no longer called the others "Big Sister One" and "Big Sister Two," but, instead, called them "Little Li" and "Little Wang."

Old Three now had to make a choice about work. On the one hand, she could go back to Tongshan County, where Mrs. Three had already arranged a job for her in the county's cultural center. On the other hand, she might stay on at the school and work as a college professor—a job coveted by all those of her classmates who did not already have permanent residence permits for Nanjing. That was why her Mrs. visited so often. He knew that many of her friends were trying to persuade her to opt for the second choice, that is, to teach in Nanjing, and he wanted to make sure that she would definitely return to Tongshan County.

The inside scoop was that the school wanted to chose among the three women for the job. Old One and Old Two had already reached an agreement that they would not compete with Old Three, because according to the job assignment policy, one of the two could stay in Nanjing, and the other could go back to Shanghai. Therefore a chance to remain at school in Nanjing was not very vital for either of them. But for Old Three, the job would be a turning point in her life.

Old Three was tormented by indecision. Whenever Mrs. Three came to visit her, she wanted to go back with him to Tongshan County. As soon as he left, she wanted to remain at the school and work as a professor. Old One and Old Two tried to convince her that this would be the only chance for her to change her fate. Hanging her head, Old Three replied that she understood how much better life would be in Nanjing. She also knew that once she gained residence in Nanjing, her husband could be transferred to join her. Yet she also knew that Mrs. Three would never agree to be transferred to Nanjing for her sake, because a man should not adapt himself to the needs of his wife. If a man followed his wife, he would never be able to hold his head up.

The other two sworn brothers smiled coldly. Oh! According to his logic, his woman should follow him so that he could hold his head high and crow, and what the woman had in return was silence?

Feeling somewhat agitated, Old Three began to defend her husband; that was not his view at all. The other two kept sneering and insisted that it was his view. Feeling cornered, Old Three blurted out without thinking, "If a man cannot take responsibility for his woman, isn't that a sad thing for us?"

The other two were taken aback by her remark, for they did not expect Old Three to be able to say such self-defeating things. After a while, Old One said slowly, "Old Three, you are being muddle-headed. He is not taking care of you. It is clear that he cannot take responsibility for you. He is asking you to sacrifice your future for the sake of his vanity." Old Two added, "At such a moment, the ideal act of masculinity would be to give you free reign to explore the world!" Old One laughed and said that would be a grand gesture.

But Old Three started to cry. She said that she did not want a grand gesture, all she wanted was peace and harmony between husband and wife.

This sudden revelation of an ordinary wifely ideal was a terrible disappointment for the other two. They fell silent.

Amidst her sobs, Old Three said that she could never forget the night many years ago when he walked seventeen miles on foot with an oil lamp in his hand on a day so snowy the bus could not run, from his town out to the collective enterprise in the countryside where she was stationed, just to tell her that he was willing to wait for her. Old Three slowly calmed down and smiled bashfully. "In fact, the important thing is whether there is love between a man and woman. If there is love between them, being devoured by the other is pleasant and good. What is the use of a true self, if it brings no happiness but only destruction?" Old Three said that she had been pondering this matter for quite some time now. She felt that the three brothers had been too extreme in their ideas, over-complicating everything. No wonder they kept finding an empty black hole at the center of the universe. If only they retreated a few steps, it was possible to have a goal in life. She heaved a long and deep sigh of relief and said that she now had found the goal of life. Having said that, she gathered the dirty dishes and pots to wash them in the sink down the hall. After that, she returned to the room and went right to bed.

That was a quiet night in the brothers' room. No one spoke. Old One and Old Two lay awake in their beds, and had the sense that in spite of her presence, Old Three had indeed already gone very far away from them now.

At last came the day of final parting. The three women held a miniature farewell party for themselves in their room. When they sat down at the table, a kind of unfamiliarity swept over them. They forced themselves to find trivial topics, reminiscences of their bygone school days. They poured the fruit wine into their teacups and gulped it down quickly. Soon the alcohol took effect, and they became merry again. They burst into laugher over very small matters. They recalled their first meeting: Old One was the first to arrive at school, Old Two second, and Old Three third. They did not even say a word to each other before they fell asleep. They began to talk only the next morning. The first sentence of their conversation was, "When does the dining hall open?" At this, they again keeled over with laughter.

As they were laughing, Old Three suddenly raised her head and asked them whether they could guess what she was thinking this afternoon when she was walking in the streets? The other two looked at her with shining eyes. She then said that what she was thinking was that it would be wonderful if a car hit her. The other two, upon hearing this, laughed and laughed, and then wept.

Old Three did not weep. Holding the teacup in her hands as though warming her hands in winter, she said, "You people may have glorious days ahead of you, but I shall no longer have them. In a small county town where everybody knows everybody else, a new person will be recognized immediately and will become old and familiar within a couple of days. People buy food and vegetables in the same street. Everybody knows what everybody else is having for dinner. There are no secrets to stimulate curiosity, no hope for wonders to occur." She said that her family had lived there for generations, but her ancestors were from Henan. Perhaps it was because her grandmother's grandmother's grandmother had been driven from Henan by the Yellow River's flooding. That sort of thing happened once every several hundred years. But now that the river was well under control and the residence permits were very strictly administered, there would be no more large migrations. Having said that, she began to laugh, but the other two sobbed even louder.

At that moment, the third became the eldest. She looked lovingly at Old One and Old Two as the pair wept together. "You don't know how very fond I am of you!" When she was with them, she felt free and happy. She had never been so free before she met them, nor would she ever be in the future. In the past, she had lived with her parents and her sisters and brothers. How could she have done whatever she felt like doing! Even meals were served at set times, at the ringing of a bell. It was only with her sworn brothers that she learned that it was all right not to eat on time—that it was human. What was inhuman is to be forced to eat when one has no appetite, or to be forced not to eat when one was hungry. After this day, as a wife and a mother, she would have many obligations and could not afford to be negligent. Even when you did not want to eat on time, others wanted to eat on time. There would have to be a single mealtime for the whole family, because people have work to do. Complete and thorough self-realization was impossible, in fact; it was only a topic for idle talk. It was not men who had devoured our true selves; we should not be throwing our spears in their direction. Men and women were both victims, comrades in the same trench, and should support each other. Day lilies at a trenchside were especially fragrant.

All three were deeply moved by what she said, and they cried until they could cry no more.

That was the last night at school before graduation. There was a similar farewell party in every room. In some, songs could be heard. The brothers' loud laughing and crying did not attract any attention. The following morning arrived with headaches and hangovers. The women felt depressed and spoke little. They slowly packed their luggage and left for the train station. Only Old Two was going to remain in Nanjing, and she did not want to be left alone. She walked together with Old One to the outside of the school, and bid a peaceful good-bye to her in that quiet street.

## 2

Old Two returned home and started her ordinary life by teaching at a nearby high school. In addition to teaching two regular art classes, she also tutored an evening art class. A drawing by one of the students in her evening class was selected by the National Exhibition of Artwork by Young People. Afterwards, some parents asked her to allow their children to join the evening art class.

A year later, her military officer husband was demobilized and came back to work as an administrator in one of the city agencies. He got a two-bedroom apartment from his work unit. The couple lived a stable and peaceful life, but occasionally the husband had to travel on official business.

Old Two had a few close women colleagues. Sometimes they would go to a salon to have their hair done, or they would go shopping together for clothes. One Sunday, they agreed to have an outing together at the Sun Yat-sen Memorial Arch, with their husbands and their children. Old Two, having no children of her own, simply brought her husband.

She and he were from the same middle school; he had been in the first year of senior high when she was in the first year of junior high. During the Cultural Revolution, when the factional fighting was at its worst, she suddenly received a love letter from him, in which he asked her to be his lifelong companion. It was the first love letter she had ever received. When she recovered her composure, she put his letter in an envelope and mailed it back to him. From that point on they were no longer on speaking terms, and tried to avoid each other.

But links between them grew. They gradually became indispensable to one another. If they did not see each other for one day, they would feel empty, as though something were missing. When it was time for them to move to the countryside to receive reeducation from the peasants, they could no longer contain their feelings. They met by chance in the street. They stopped. Concealing a pounding heart, they, somewhat pale-faced, exchanged mild-mannered greetings. "Where are you going?" One said that he was going to Danyang County; the other said she was going to Huaiyin County. "Who will be going with you?" "How do you think it will be?" Neither of them wanted to cut off the conversation. They asked one unimportant question after another. When one of them paused, the other immediately found another question. They stood in the street for a full two hours. Finally, they exchanged their mailing addresses and said good-bye to each other.

Later, he joined the army. Before he left, they met at Mochou Lake. This time, they embraced and kissed each other. Not quite knowing how to conduct a kiss, they merely put their closed lips together. But that kiss was more exciting and memorable than any of the numerous kisses they would have later. By the time he was promoted to be an officer, she had already returned from the countryside and worked for three years as an ironworker in a factory. She then passed the entrance exams for college and became a college student. She also got married.

On the Sunday of the outing, she took her husband to the Sun Yat-sen Memorial Arch. She emphasized the word "take," as if in this way her husband became her domestic dependent. Her two colleagues also brought their children, a girl and a boy.

The children became the focus of conversation. At first the mothers listed their children's shortcomings with barely concealed pride. They dwelt on this endless topic until noontime. Then the two children took turns performing, either singing or dancing. The six adults were the audience. They had to heap up smiles on their faces and clap and cheer after each performance. Old Two's facial muscles hurt from overuse. While smiling and applauding, she secretly made up her mind that she would never bear children in her life. She swore that she would never participate in such activities, yet she had to tell her colleagues with warmth and enthusiasm that she had a wonderful time indeed and that they must do this often. She and her colleagues finally parted at the gate of the Memorial Arches to take their separate buses home. In the bus, Old Two felt tremendously relieved, and her face became more animated.

She thought of her sworn brothers Old One and Old Three. The memories of their happiness and of their friendship almost brought tears to her eyes. She remembered that the three once swore in front of the Yangzi River, at Phoenix Hill, that they would never in their lives have children. They said that being already married they had only semi-free bodies. If they had children, they could not even keep the semi-free bodies.

How precious freedom was! A person in this world already has more obligations and social roles than she could bear. She knew that Old Three could not be relied upon, because she was one of those extremely responsible and self-sacrificing women. Her meeting with Old One and Old Two was just a temporary indulgence for her. She would go back to carry out her duties and sacrifices. Old Two thought of what Old Three said on the last night before parting, and knew it was from the bottom of Old Three's heart. As Old Two recalled, Old Three most accurately expressed her real self. But the "true selves" of Old One and Old Two had never been voiced. Those nightlong conversations about who they were became foggy and unclear when Old Two tried to recall them. She could not remember what they had discussed.

That night, she wrote a letter to Old One. She knew Old One was assigned to work as an art teacher at a normal school in Shanghai, but she did not know if Old One was still there, or if she had changed jobs, or even left Shanghai to go to Shenzhen or abroad. These days many people left Shanghai for Shenzhen or went abroad. Anyway, Old Two gave it a try: she sent the letter to the address of the normal school in Shanghai. In the letter, she told Old One about how she had been and asked how Old One had been doing for the past two years. The letter was a single page long.

After the letter was sent off, at first she kept thinking about it, but after two weeks, she put the matter aside. The time spent as a student was only an episode in her life, and that is just what it should be.

Time passed, one day after another. Her husband was promoted to Section Head and then was transferred to a higher office as a Deputy Director. He was in charge of the people at his workplace, but back home he was the submissive one. He adapted well to each of these disparate positions, and seemed to enjoy switching roles. When she was ordering him around, he was not at all annoyed. If one day she spoke with a softened voice, he would sincerely wonder whether she was ill. Sometimes he would call her "Old Two" in an attempt to cheer her up, but she did not show any pleasure. Instead she asked him not to talk nonsense, didn't he see that she was busy? Embarrassed he stopped using that name, and thought to himself, What's wrong with her? In fact, she was fine; she simply did not like him to call her that name. The term "Old Two" represented a period of her life whose meaning she had not yet quite figured out.

She did not try to think about it further. After graduation, she had become quite lazy and did not much exercise her brain; perhaps she had exhausted it when she was a student, leaving no reserves.

They bought a color TV. Every evening she went to bed at eight o'clock and, leaning on a stack of pillows, watched TV until the phrase "Good-bye and Good Night" appeared on the screen. She then fell into a sound and dreamless sleep.

She began to gain weight. Many clothes that used to fit her became too small, and other clothes that once were baggy now fit her. In order to lose weight, she made it her rule to get up at six o'clock every morning. After getting up, she would practice calligraphy, writing with her hand high above the paper. Afterwards she ate breakfast. Her husband always bought their breakfast of long crullers and soybean milk at the corner store. After breakfast, the couple would ride their bikes to work. Because of the regular life she led, she gained weight instead of losing any. They did not want to have children, so they calculated and practiced a strict rhythm method. As a result, their lovemaking became very regulated and controlled.

A student in her evening art class passed the entrance examination for college and was accepted by her alma mater, the Art Institute in Nanjing. This gave her comfort and pride, because her everyday labors had finally come to fruition. In addition, she was touched by the feeling that she now had an heir.

She invited the boy to her home for dinner. Of course, her husband cooked the meal. The child was at first rather nervous, but by virtue of a series of jokes and every other conceivable means, her husband finally succeeded in putting the boy at ease. The three people sat at the round dinner table and drank beer. The boy's young face became flushed and his eyes became watery. He stammered, saying that he had loved drawing since he was very young. He used to make chalk drawings in his family's courtyard: big horses and people in ancient costumes. His parents supported his artistic hobby, scrimping and saving to buy pens and drawing paper. Both parents, being factory workers and nearly illiterate, thought that if only their child kept drawing, he would become a good artist. It was not until he attended the evening art class that he learned what drawing and painting really were, and that what he had done by himself was just doodling. He announced that he would work very hard at the Art Institute and would never let his teacher down.

Hearing what her student said, Old Two was almost moved to tears. She got up and opened her bookcase to fetch out a big art album. She put the album into the boy's hands. The boy knew this book was rather precious and did not dare to accept such a lavish gift. But at her insistence, he finally took it and left.

When classes began at the Art Institute, she accompanied him to the school and took him to see a couple of her former professors. Her former professors received them very warmly and asked about her life. They then nodded their heads and smiled. "How time passes—you are now a teacher yourself!" They remembered her as a student who often missed classes, called two female fellow students "brothers," and slept late during the day, but at night was nowhere to be seen. In their recollection, she was a naughty one.

After she heard her teachers say these things, all sorts of feelings welled up in her. Once she had really been alive! She suddenly felt lost. She said good-bye to the boy and returned home alone.

Life went on in the same way for another year, a year in which one of her students was accepted by the Department of Stage Design, Shanghai Institute of Drama and Theater. She did not feel quite so excited this time. She felt it was no big deal; it was just something a teacher should expect. It would be the teacher's fault if her students did not pass the national examinations and could not attend college. It was a teacher's duty to make sure that her students do well in the examinations; that was all. But the place her student was going—Shanghai—made her think of Old One. She wondered if Old One had in fact left Shanghai. Old One had not written back.

During those days, she suddenly became interested in knitting. She bought new wool yarn, or got used yarn by unraveling old sweaters. She knitted day and night. When her hands picked up the knitting needles and began to knit, she would suddenly feel calmer. She thought about things with equanimity, as her hands kept knitting: forward stitch, round stitch, and back stitch. The mechanical yet relaxing movement of her hands brought her some peace of mind, which in turn made her feel happy. Even when she was in the middle of other things, as soon as her thoughts turned to the possibility of knitting afterward, a sense of joy would bubble up in her heart.

So within a few short months, she became an expert in knitting sweaters. Because of her creative spirit, she often invented different knitting patterns. Her husband wore brightly patterned sweaters to work, filling his office with color.

Someone liked the sweaters and begged Old Two to knit one for him. Old Two agreed happily. So the person rushed out to buy the yarn and brought it to Old Two's home. Old Two asked her husband to hold the yarn so that she could roll it into a ball. As she began to knit, she suddenly felt bored. She thought that making a sweater would be an interminable thing. A stitch in and a stitch out, how wearisome! She thought, at first, knitting was quite a happy and random thing; it was like a person taking a pleasant stroll. But now knitting had become a task. Every stitch was just a small step to the finish line, and there was no joy in it. She thought about her entire life and became even more depressed. Life had no ultimate aim; it was just a procession of days after days, nights after nights. It held no fresh and strange stories to excite her.

From then on, knitting no longer gave her comfort or pleasure. She longed for the end of this knitting project so that she did not have to do any knitting again. But she kept putting it off, and let the days slip by. The person did not want to press her too hard to finish. He visited her a couple of times, and saw that the sweater did not grow. Old Two was busy with other things, or simply doing nothing: not knitting. Half a year passed, and the season for sweaters was long gone. He gave up all hope (though eventually Old Two did come by with the finished sweater). So in Old Two's life the business of knitting started with joy and ended in boredom.

However, this experience caused the bitterness and anxiety she had so long suppressed to surface. Day and night now she asked herself, for what purpose do human beings live? Her mind, which had long been idle, now became active and interfered with her daily routine. She could no longer fall asleep at night. As she lay there listening to her husband snore, she became increasingly agitated. The snoring seemed to symbolize the monotonous and unaware life of the entire human race. She often fell asleep at dawn only to have the alarm clock wake her from her weary slumber shortly thereafter. She had no choice but to get out of bed.

She neither wanted to have breakfast nor fold her quilt and tidy the bed. She would just sit there stewing in her irritation until she would ride her bicycle to work. In the streets, the morning sunlight pained her tired and swollen eyes. She arrived at the school gate and saw students swarm onto the campus. Her angst expanded and became an encompassing sympathy: how unfortunate for these kids to be living in this world!

Her husband witnessed her mood swings and thought to himself, "Her old malaise has come back." He seemed to know her better than she knew herself. He knew that inside this woman's body there was an unusual force, a force that had no outlet. Moreover, this woman also lacked the common sense to reign in the force, and so it raged, like a flood barreling through a reservoir, surging first to one side and then to another, falling and rising unpredictably. Still, he was confident that the flood would stay within the dam. It was not that he had any illusion about her rationality—rather, he knew that this dam was formed not by her rationality alone, but also by many other people's rationality, including his own. Of course, that did not mean that he would relax his vigilance. Instead, he must watch her movements very closely.

Whenever there seemed to be a change, he would take preventive actions accordingly. One of the reasons why he loved her was that she was like an unguarded city: all her emotions showed on her face, making it easy for him to fathom her. He knew what she wanted and tried to meet her needs. And yet he intentionally withheld certain things, so that she would not form the habit of expecting all of her wishes to be satisfied—so that she would learn to control certain desires. She must know that she was not the only person living in this world; there were many others. She must learn to control herself, for otherwise it would be hard for her to survive.

Having plenty of common sense, he understood very well the reasons for the survival of the fittest. He believed that the virtue of a man was not his masculinity, but his adaptability to a constantly changing world. He also knew that on this matter Old Two's views were different from his own. He tolerated her and appeared to be making concessions to her demands because he knew very well that her image of an ideal man existed only as an aesthetic concept. In real life, what she needed was the kind of man he represented. Without this kind of man, it would be hard for her to take even a tiny step; she would most likely be lost in a morass of despair.

So he did not bother to argue with her about it. Whenever they did argue about it, she would take on an inspired look, as if the whole world were asleep while she alone remained alert. How very grand! When she did not want to tidy the bed and refused to eat breakfast, he did not force her to do so, but neither did he give in to her mood. He would take care of the small things such as tidying the bed, and he would buy breakfast for her as usual. It was fine if she wanted to skip breakfast and ruin her daily routine, but he would see to it that the world around her remained as impeccably regulated as before. Eventually she would begin to give up her erratic behavior. At that moment he doubled his efforts to maintain order. He kept to his regular work schedule and never came home late. He washed the quilts and cleaned the windows and the rest of the apartment in an attempt to make her feel ashamed of her absurd behavior. Gradually she would revert to the routines of everyday life.

This man believed that family and career were two equal parts in a person's life, and these two parts were means and end for each other. His aims in life were simple and clear unlike hers, which were confused and chaotic. Nevertheless, her chaos and confusion created a sense of fluidity in his life and helped avoid boredom. Of course, he could only accept this fluidity as an element of an aesthetic realm. He was a man who was very particular about aesthetic pursuits. For this he would give up other things, such as becoming a father. He even was grateful to her for making him appreciate the human spirit. She could unearth some of the humane emotions that were suppressed by the restless intensity of his workplace. Yet, such things should never disturb what he viewed as normal life; thus the value of her fluidity was only to heighten his sense of vitality. In the end, he thought that he and Old Two were a very compatible couple.

In actual fact, however, Old Two's depression had its own limits; when her spirits sank to the lowest point she would slowly recover by herself, and find that there was still some hope to reach her goal in life. So she tolerated the drudgery of an endless succession of identical days.

She discovered a talent in her drawing class, a senior who was a head taller than she and had broad shoulders, but spoke with the mumble of a small child. Thinking that the boy had a rare artistic ability, she devoted a great deal of attention to his studies. She told him that he could be better than everyone else, and that if he worked hard he had a good chance to attend the Central Institute of Art in Beijing. The boy listened to her and practiced drawing all day long, neglecting his other subjects. And she, too, neglected other students and directed all of her attention to this one. In the end, the entire art class consisted only of the two of them. They started in the afternoon and continued until early evening.

But she later discovered that this boy's talent was equally distributed among all of his subjects. If he were to concentrate on dance and music, he could do better than the average students as well. He did not have a special talent for any particular field. This kind of student could be good at any subject, and should go to a general university. So she lost interest in the boy, and did not spend too much time with him. He, being mild tempered, did not much mind his teacher's change of heart. He gave up drawing, reviewed his other subjects thoroughly, and passed the college entrance examinations with high scores.

From then on, her evening drawing class was permanently discontinued. Without this evening class, her workload was much lighter than before. At the high school, art was a peripheral subject, not even as important as physical training. In physical training classes, students had to do well enough to pass certain standardized tests, but drawing classes had nothing of that sort, in fact, there were no criteria at all. So in her class she did what she liked. Sometimes she would just place a vase with plastic flowers on her platform desk and ask students to draw the vase. She would sit there and read a novel or doodle a couple of sketches that she later threw away.

This kind of life lasted another semester. One morning as she was combing her hair in front of a mirror, she discovered some wrinkles at the corners of her eyes and a certain flabbiness in the skin of her face. She was reminded of her age and suddenly felt melancholy. She thought that her youth had almost ended without her being aware of it. She had a sense of urgency and wanted to grasp the last chance to enjoy her waning youth.

She began to learn how to make up her face. She borrowed fashion magazines and bought new clothes. Thanks to her profession, her cosmetic skills were very good. She knew exactly what colors of eyeliner, eye shadow, and lipstick to use for each kind of light, and how to coordinate her facial make-up with the colors of her clothes. Moreover, she often varied colors and proportions so that when other people looked at her, they had the sense of something new without being able to pinpoint what it was. Her face appeared to be glowing with health. Other people thought she must have something to be happy about, but actually nothing joyous had occurred. As she changed her appearance and alluringly strolled through the streets, her heart was filled with self-confidence and hope, even a sense of starting anew.

She began to enjoy going out. Before she set out, she would put on her make-up and change her clothes. She went to the movies, she went shopping, she went to visit her friends.

She even took part in another holiday outing organized by her colleagues. Her colleagues' children had all grown quite a bit; they were now attending primary school. They were all learning one instrument or another such as electronic keyboard or violin. Their parents brought the instruments to the picnic in order to have a concert on the grass. As before, she was so irked that she almost went home in the middle of the performance. After the day was over, she deeply regretted her indifference; she should not have been so jaded. That was when she lost interest in retaining her youth—but she kept the habit of cosmetics. Women did like to be beautiful. Even though she was once called "Old Two," a name for a man, she was in essence a woman. But where were those who used to call her "Old Two"? At this thought, she felt rather lost.

That night she woke up from her sleep and poked her husband. "Let's have a child—how about it?" Her husband assumed that she must have been talking in her sleep, but then his hand felt her body on his side of the bed—she had already slipped under his quilt from her own. He sat up and asked her whether this was just a sudden thought.

"There's nothing wrong with a hasty decision."

"And if you regret it later?"

"Ha! This isn't something one can regret. A child is born, and you cannot drive it back in with a stick."

Her voice was loud and clear in the quiet of the night, but it also sounded vague, as if it were not her own. He was secretly taken aback. What is the matter with her now? But his body began its movement, and soon he was overcome by passion. For suddenly she could not even wait until the next day to give birth so that her empty life could somehow be filled.

She had heard that motherly love could sacrifice all things gladly. She thought, if this "self" of mine cannot reach its full satisfaction, I may just as well let it be sacrificed in a big way. Better to be a shattered vessel of jade than an unbroken clay pot. She went peacefully to sleep.

Towards dawn, she awoke in good spirits. She got up, cleaned the room, and ate the breakfast her husband had bought. They bicycled together to work. She felt that a solemn sacrifice was accumulating within her belly, and as a result even her pedaling was cautiously slow. Slowly she arrived at school; slowly she got off the bike. She left the bike in the bike shelter and walked into the teachers' office. There, she saw someone getting up slowly from behind her desk, looking at her with a shy smile. Old Two's heart began to beat very fast. She felt that she had seen this person before, but who—? Suddenly a thought flashed across her mind, and she knew things would change.

She took a step forward. "Old One, is that you?"

She had not used this name for a long time, but as soon as it was out of her mouth, she felt as if Old One had been with her every day, and that she had called this name every day. Old One was standing behind the desk with an apologetic smile, like a child who has just done something wrong. After a while, Old One softly called: "Old Two." And then, "Look at me, Old Two! I look so awful; I am pregnant."

Old Two looked at the protruding belly of Old One, and suddenly an image of the previous night appeared before her eyes, clearer now than the reality, as if what really happened last night were just a dream. She walked towards Old One, touched her curving belly, and said with tears in her eyes: "It doesn't matter at all. How many years have we not seen each other?"

"Many, many years," said Old One. "Look at me: I am going to give birth to a child."

"It doesn't matter, it doesn't matter. We've met again at last. It doesn't matter."

They stood face to face, wishing to embrace, but they were also rather shy. Shaking hands would seem too formal. So they did not even shake hands; they just stood there. They remembered their school days when they did not get up in the morning, when they did not wash their bowls after meals but simply stacked them up, when they walked through the campus before dawn to climb Phoenix Hill, and when they watched the sun rising from the Yangzi River. Tears welled up in their eyes; those days were long ago. They wondered if there were still people who would watch the sunrise from the top of Phoenix Hill. The sun emerging from the surface of the river and then leaping out into midair—was it an eternal scene, as they used to think? At that time, they were only in their twenties, having just survived the years of misery. It seemed that the happy times had returned and would never leave them again.

"Old One, Old One, why didn't you write to me? I wrote to you! Didn't you get my letter?" Old Two cried out.

Old Two's colleagues had gone to their classrooms. Old Two's classes were scheduled for the third and the fourth period. The two of them were alone in the teachers' office. Outside the window, the sun was shining and birds were singing in the bushes.

"Old Two, I wanted to write to you, but every time I picked up a pen and spread the paper to write to you, I was at a loss about what to write. I didn't have anything new or interesting to tell you. If you read my letter, you would say 'what a boring letter!' "

"When you didn't answer my letter, I thought that you must have left for Shenzhen or gone abroad. Nowadays so many people go to Shenzhen or abroad, right?" Old Two began to weep.

"I didn't go anywhere, I just stayed in Shanghai and worked as a teacher. Shenzhen and foreign countries are very strange to me. I didn't go anywhere," Old One explained.

"If you had gone abroad, I would be left alone. Old Three doesn't think of us anymore."

At this, they thought of Old Three and the days when all the brothers were together. Those bygone days were happy days!

Old One and Old Two stood there and talked, forgetting to sit down, as if time flowed like a river around them. The bell began to ring, and their hearts trembled at the illusion that the old school days had returned.

## 3

Old One spent the night at Old Two's home. They changed the way they addressed each other: Old Two called Old One "Old Li" and Old One called Old Two "Old Wang" because they did not want to be reminded of the absence of Old Three, an absence which would remain forever. They slept on the big bed in the inner room, and Old Wang's husband slept on a makeshift bed in the living room. That night they did not sleep because they had so much to tell each other. Only Old Wang's husband slept, in the living room, but only fitfully. He did not understand how these two women could have so much to say to each other. He woke up at four or five o'clock in the morning. He did not hear any voices coming from the bedroom. He thought the two women must have tired of talking and fallen asleep. But then he heard someone say, "The sunlight is coming in." True enough, the sunlight shone through the floral patterns of the window curtains. The people in the bedroom seemed to be getting up. He heard them laughing and talking and leaving the bedroom. When they walked past, he asked them where they were going. The women were startled and began to giggle.

His wife said, "You almost scared us to death!"

He said, "I just asked you where you were going so early in the morning." The man thought that his woman was going a little crazy again.

The woman replied, "We are going to buy some breakfast. Go back to sleep."

He thought, well, the sun has risen from the west! And he went back to bed. He heard the two women open the front door, close the door, and walk down the stairs. Before his eyes he seemed to see a picture of two women walking in the morning sunlight. Strangely, he was moved. He lay on his bed for a while, and then slowly got up and put on his clothes.

The two women were walking in the street. The sun had not yet risen, but its rays had already lit the sky and the morning glow kept changing its colors. Even though they had been awake all night, they were in particularly good spirits. They agreed to keep in touch with each other from now on, writing to each other, and never again falling into the habit of not communicating.

They said that in this boring world, they should encourage each other so as to avoid going under. They could not think of anything more exciting than this in their lives, and they felt fortunate to have met again. They had never expected to meet again in true emotional union. A couple of years had passed, but they were not strangers to each other—even though daily life had eaten away at them in certain ways. For example, each had become a little conventional, even well behaved. But in their hearts there still remained some passion which rekindled their friendship.

In order to preserve that passion, they each had borne the pain of many lonely days. They had lost Old Three, and they had worried that they had also lost each other. It was this fear that had kept them from communicating with each other.

They thought, if they had lost each other, how meaningful would the remaining passion be? If they delayed and let time pass, the remaining passion would be eventually be spent.

A life full of responsibilities was so dreadful—you got up in the morning and there was already a series of things waiting for you to do. You could not miss even one step, because if you did, the whole series would fall apart. Your life no longer only concerned yourself; it had to do with other people, too. What would become of the others? What right did you have to destroy other people's order? Other people had not destroyed your order, but instead tried to help you maintain that order. One person and the next formed links in a chain, and no part of the chain allowed the others to have any thought of breaking away. When one was yoked and chained, passion and warmth were merely burdens and distractions. The two brothers each carried the burden and waited a long time for the moment of their meeting. From now on, they could carry this burden together. From now on, the two links could join forces to destroy the chain! They were very excited, thinking that their meeting was a great event marking a new era.

They said that they were going out to buy groceries, but they forgot all about that. They took a long walk, and had some dumpling soup and steamed bread in a small restaurant at New Street Corner. They walked in the direction of home, without bringing the husband any breakfast.

The sun was high in the sky. The bicycles on the way to work formed a stream, resounding with the ringing of bells. Old Wang gave her school a call and asked to change her teaching time because she was going to see her former classmate off at the train station. On their way home, they saw that some shops were already open. They bought snacks from more than one, and ate as they walked.

By the time they got home, the husband had already gone and left a note for them on the table, saying in effect that he hoped that they were late not because of some unexpected accident, but because they had forgotten about the time. He also mentioned, very thoughtfully, that he would call her school and ask leave on her behalf, so that the two women could have a pleasant time together. He also reminded her not to forget that Old Li would have to catch her train at two o'clock in the afternoon.

The two women were deeply moved by this man's open-heartedness, and praised him. After that, they started discussing the issue of masculinity, and forgot all about preparing lunch.

They tried to figure out what a man was. They said that a man was the natural companion of a woman. Between two women, there were many problems that could not be solved: sex, for example, and making a new life, and carrying on the family name. Because of this, a woman had to be with a man so that they could complete the life journey, as each individual in human history has had to do. But then, because a man and a woman should be together to accomplish all of this, a man and a woman became very close, almost indispensable to each other. A man, therefore, became a woman's greatest controlling force. Each became a prison to the other: he imprisoned her and she imprisoned him. So a man was a prison. The two women felt they had deepened their understanding of man in real life. But this realization brought them nearly to an impasse.

They were overcome by emotion, and sat quietly on the small stools, facing each other. They were supposed to be washing vegetables, but they did none of that. All the vegetables remained in the shopping basket.

The sun in the sky was moving slowly. They thought they might have to spend their entire lives in prison, and now a further young prison had just been conceived. Old Wang felt nausea but tried to suppress the urge to throw up. She thought, we are really making trouble for ourselves. They did not have any appetite. Having three meals a day suddenly seemed a tedious chore. It was time for them to go to the train station.

They slowly got up from their stools, picked up Old Li's luggage, and left the apartment. The sun at noon was so bright that it hurt one's eyes. Disheartened by their imminent separation, they walked to the bus station one slow step at the time. The bus was almost empty, and both of them got seats.

The sun made the iron shell of the bus very hot. They felt the coming of a sultry summer. Neither said a word. The bus moved very slowly, stopping at every block before finally reaching the last stop.

They got off the bus and walked across a wide square, heading for the train station. The train had already begun boarding. They decided to part with each other at the ticket gate. On the one hand, they tried to avoid an emotional scene, and on the other hand, they really were afraid of parting with each other. They calmly said good-bye, and one walked toward the train while the other walked toward the station's main gate.

Old Wang walked among the station benches very slowly, and did not dare to examine her own feelings too closely. The sun made the whole square shine, like a big mirror. She stopped in front of the entrance hall, and thought, summer is coming. Summer in Nanjing was so hot! She stepped down the stairs, feeling dizzy. She wondered if she were pregnant. She had only a vague memory of that passionate night. The event seemed very distant and unreal. She told herself that the pregnancy was not real, and then walked through the square. As she reached the middle of the square, she felt altogether lost and without hope, as though she were a lonely ship on a vast ocean. She could not see the other side of the ocean. She continued to walk aimlessly. In this state, she walked to the bus station. Somehow she got back home. As soon as she entered the apartment, she fell onto the bed and soon dropped into a deep sleep.

The train that Old Li boarded began to leave the station. Old Li was sitting next to the window, watching the people wave good-bye to the passengers on the train, and wondering what Old Wang was doing. Soon she felt sleepy and dozed off. When the train was crossing rails, it made a loud noise and woke her. She saw the last signboard of "Nanjing Station" pass by, and realized that she must have fallen asleep. It was just a matter of a few minutes, but it seemed like a very long time.

She rested her gaze on the trees that were quickly receding from the window, and let her mind wander from one thing to another. In a few months she would give birth to a baby. In fact, she had been thinking about this child for a long time. She knew that she shouldn't yearn for a child so much. When they were at school, they often said that they would not accept any further confinement in life. She was a person with a rich inner life, beyond what was easy to bear. She knew a child would mean another tremendous emotional burden—in her case, an extraordinary one. Her wish to maintain her personal freedom would be completely thwarted. But still she wanted to have a child; without a child, she would feel empty. She tried in vain to have a child for a long time. When she was finally convinced that she would never have one, she gradually calmed down. But then she got pregnant. Her heart was filled with joy; every minute she could feel the growth of another life inside her.

When she felt that life growing, what they had discussed during their school years—the complete self—returned to her again. Before this time, Old Li's self had been deeply buried. She got up every day at dawn to rush to catch the bus. Public buses in Shanghai were always jam-packed and the streets chaotic. She squeezed off the crowded bus, pushed through the noisy streets, arrived at her school, and began to teach. After work, the homebound journey was just as difficult. On top of that, she was also in a hurry to buy groceries on her way home. She would run with small steps to catch the bus, and getting off the bus, she would run home instead of walking. Before she got there, she would stop at a farmer's market and haggle with the merchants over the price of the vegetables. She then would run back home to cook the dinner. Her husband was a manager of a small factory. Every day he got home after dark. He was so tired that he spoke little to her. Sometimes she thought that the reason they could not have a child was simply that they were both very tired, even though they were both in good health.

Preoccupied with trivia, Old Li did not have the leisure time as Old Wang did to muse endlessly in the abstract about the "self." Her self had to be attached to something concrete, so that she could see her self in this crowded and noisy world. In a mind packed full of mundane events, what seemed most important was how to get from one day to the next.

When she finally lay in bed, watching the TV program winding to an end, she felt boundlessly happy. At that time and that place, any thought about the self became an extravagance, something that Old Li could not afford. If Old Li had not been an extremely sensitive person, her self would have been eliminated. Old Li had hidden her self in her heart, a heart that had room for a great many things. Among all these things, her self was well hidden, unlike that of her brother Old Wang which occasionally came out to make trouble. On the surface,

Old Li seemed calm and peaceful, but deep within the still waters, there was turbulence.

From the time when she discovered that she was pregnant, her self-consciousness emerged from the depths of her heart, and made her radiant. She felt that another "I" was lying cozily in her womb and was gradually growing. From the vantage point of having a distinct life inside her, she could seriously examine herself. She wondered what she really was. What part of her would be found imprinted on the little life inside her belly? She could not figure it out, but she kept thinking about it with great interest.

At this time, thinking about the "self" made her very happy. Her thoughts were not as empty and unspecific as the discussions that she and her friends had had in the dorm night after night, nor were they as bitter and stifled as Old Wang's. It was with the sudden happy recollection of life in school that she decided to go see Old Wang.

She volunteered to do an errand for her school and took this opportunity to go to Nanjing. Little did she expect that this meeting would have rekindled such passion between herself and Old Wang. She used to think that when they would meet they would just reminisce about the past, but this time something new seemed to have started. What was that new thing?

She wondered. She felt that she was not as happy now as she had been on her way to Nanjing. Many scenes from her life passed through her mind. She marveled at the fact that she could go on living day after day. How numb she was! She wondered if it was a good thing for her to give birth to the child. Did she want her child to continue the kind of life that she was leading? What was the point of adding another such life to the world? Could such days be changed? Would they become worse? She could not stop imagining her child living the kind of life that she had. In this way, she began to see the hardship and blindness of her life. Her heart filled with grief.

Old Li was very kind and sympathetic. When something bad happened to other people, she could empathize with them and feel their pain deeply. But if it happened to her, she would endure it with utter patience and stoicism. Her tears were shed for other people's misfortune. When misfortune happened to her, she would have a thousand ways to make herself forget it.

Such people are usually mistaken by their contemporaries for pathetic people who have lost their selfhood and live without awareness in a dark world. It may appear that they have extinguished the self entirely, and their kindheartedness is often taken as an old-fashioned and even hypocritical moralism. But in fact, these are the ones who have the self and will not lose it. Because of this, they can turn to observe others, without being like some people who are always talking about the "self." As a matter of fact, the behavior of these others is an expression of fear, a fear that their self is in danger of being lost, as if it would be lost if it were not mentioned every minute. There are still others who talk about "self" to be fashionable, wearing the word as one might wear new clothes. Perhaps, the fate of being eliminated or abandoned is awaiting these people in the near future.

But women such as Old Li did not find modern terms like "the self" very easy to use. She was not even like Old Wang, who was able to accept new things and constantly talked about "the self." Old Li's view was that the self was a natural and ordinary thing; there was no particular need to mention it. That was why she had so much kindness and sympathy. However, if a woman like Old Li turned her attention to the self and raised the question of "Who am I?" then the question had more than ordinary depth and significance.

Plots and fields swept past the train windows, and the sun was already setting on the horizon. The train's speed seemed to change the movement of time; she felt that the sun stayed on the horizon and did not sink. Gazing at this profoundly beautiful scene, she felt melancholy. She started wondering what Old Wang was doing. She must be asleep, the light in her room becoming dimmer and dimmer.

The sun sank below the horizon. Old Li recalled that at dusk the streets in Shanghai were very crowded. Her husband went to work on a bike. There were many streets in which he could not ride his bike. He had to make many detours in order to get home. By the time he got home, he was fatigued and querulous. Seeing him like that would always make her worry on his behalf. She acknowledged that her domestic chores were increased because of her husband. If she did not have to take care of him, her life would be much simpler. For instance, in the evening, she would not have to cook three dishes and a soup, and then warm a cup of rice wine. She then remembered her conversation with Old Wang that morning about how men and women were prisons for each other. She had forgotten to tell Old Wang that this prison was a prison of love. Just as Old Wang was burdened by responsibilities, Old Li was burdened by love.

How heavy love was! Love needed self-awareness more than it required responsibility. Responsibility did not have to include love, but love always included responsibility. Thus love was a double prison. Sometimes she just wished that she had been an orphan. If that had been the case, she could at least avoid the double love for her father and her mother.

She imagined an orphan's life as carefree: waving a little whip, he herds a flock of sheep. Owing to the legends and fairytales that she had been reading since childhood, an orphan in her mind's eye was always a shepherd boy. Oh, to be a shepherd boy!

She did not understand why there should be so many people in this world. Moreover, these people did not exist in isolation, they each had connections with others. In such a connection, Old Wang saw responsibility, whereas Old Li saw love. And she was so unfortunate as to live in the city that was the most densely populated and the hardest to move about in. Shoulder to shoulder, people crowded the narrow streets. The finest sentiments became increasingly coarse because of this constant contact and rubbing against each other. People tended to be less patient, less self-controlled. Self-respect was trampled amidst quarrels and insults. Those pitiable people! She closed her eyes.

The train rocked and shook as it went. She had hoped to sleep for a while, but she couldn't. When she again opened her eyes, the lights in the carriage had been turned on. Dim yellow light gave the impression of nighttime. It was still daytime outside, and the shepherds were herding their sheep toward home.

She silently said to the child inside her belly, is it a good thing or a bad thing that I will give birth to you? She thought that she and the child and the child's father would be tied down by one another. It used to be just the two of them, and now there would be another one added. The relationship suddenly became complicated. She mused, from now on, she would not only wait for a man to come home to dinner, but also wait for a child to come home for dinner. If she returned home late, not only would there be a man waiting for her to make dinner, but also the child. Waiting consumed so much of one's patience and feelings. If she had been a homeless person, roaming the world with a patched bag, then no one would wait for her to come home and she would not wait for anyone to come home either.

She could not figure out why, in such a world with so many people, a husband and a wife would form extremely intimate relationships. One person must penetrate the other's body, and such penetration determined the fate of their eternal union. To affirm their permanent solidarity, the two produced a child. From then on, there were three people closely connected in this world. Anything done by one of them would surely affect the other two. Hence, they could not act on their own. Old Li felt this blood connection and experienced the piercing pain of a knife wound. She silently said to herself, my dear folks, I cannot forsake you!

Still, she longed for freedom, and dreamed of being a wanderer in the world. Because the pressure of love was especially heavy on her, her longing for freedom was also particularly strong. She could not take love lightly, just as Old Wang could not take responsibility lightly. She thought that love was a very grand and yet miserable thing, and believed that a great deal of pain and anxiety in the world was caused by love.

It was night when the train came to its final destination. As she wondered what Old Wang would be doing, she trailed behind the forward flow of passengers. After a while the train car became empty and quiet. She got off the train and walked down the long railway platform. A half moon hung in the sky, illuminating the black rails and the dark green train. The crowds swirled toward the gate; she heard the din of swiftly tramping footsteps; she heard the roar of human voices. Suddenly she became oblivious, drifting with the torrents like an abandoned boat. Without knowing how she had gotten there, she found herself outside the train station.

She was familiar with the road. Without a second thought, she made it to the bus station. A bus was there, and she got on. The ticket collector boarded the bus and asked the passengers to buy tickets. Then the driver came. The bus started moving. She dozed off, standing in the bus. Half asleep, she overheard various arguments. People were quarreling and quarreling, and then started laughing. Immediately their combined voices filled her mind, drowning all of her thoughts. Her last thought was, has he returned home?

She got off the bus at a secluded alley. No one was in sight. There was only the dim streetlight and the city's distant roar. She walked toward home. Her apartment was on the second floor of a building facing the street. She saw the light in her apartment from a distance. She craned her neck and quickened her steps, wanting to get home at once. Now she saw the warm light through a flowery curtain from the windows of her apartment. She felt a lump in her throat, and her eyes were wet. She realized that for this tiny light she would give up the freedom of her life.

She walked through a back alley and arrived at the back door of the building. As she was about to put her key in the lock, the door opened. It was her neighbor seeing off some guests. She had no time to greet her neighbor, but went in the door and walked upstairs. Her steps on the staircase produced a creaking tune. She pushed open the door to her apartment. It was a heartwarming evening.

Her husband told her that he had come home early in anticipation of her return, though he was supposed to have dinner with his colleagues. He had bought some groceries on his way home, and had made dinner. But now the dishes were cold. She ate the cold dishes and reheated the rice, and listened to her husband's recounting of the trivial events that had taken place during the two days of her absence. She felt a loving pity for his tedious childish talk. Suddenly, she felt her spirits sink. She did not finish the bowl of rice; she washed herself and went straight to bed. Her husband asked if she was ill, but she answered that she was just tired. She closed her eyes and soon fell asleep.

At this time, Old Wang in Nanjing, having overslept in the afternoon, could not sleep at all. Propped up in bed, she was watching the last program on TV.

Old Li's husband, listening to the soft snore from his wife, sighed with compassion. It was really hard to be a woman. He thought of the many difficulties of being a woman. Many of them were greater than those of a man, and yet a man could do nothing to take the difficulties from her. He thought that this woman was not very fortunate to be married to him, but instead suffered a great deal without complaint.

His parents did not have much space in their apartment, and he had quite a few siblings. When they married, they lived in a small corner of a friend's garage. It was agreed that they could use that place for only a month. After a month, they each returned to their respective parental families. Like two unmarried lovers, they could meet only after dark in the woods at the riverbank. She always consoled him.

She was kind, and also perceptive in her judgments of other people—unlike most kind women, who are rather dull. She had the ability to make other people happy. Her descriptions of events were always very lively and interesting. Even if they were just hearsay, she seemed to have experienced them herself. That was a sign of her imagination and creativity. When she was teaching children, other teachers liked to come and sit in. He often wondered if such a woman's talent was not wasted. She could have become another kind of woman. But what kind of woman?

Sometimes, when his work was going well enough to leave him some spare time to think things over, he would observe that his woman was in fact not what she appeared to be. He knew that under her tranquil surface, there was a hidden and potentially very destructive current. Whenever he thought of this, he felt somewhat terrified and inadequate. So he tried not to think of these things.

The lucky thing was that she was always calm and composed, and her serenity filled the house. Because of this, he was grateful to her. He thought to himself that no matter what happened, he would always love her and treasure her presence.

He knew that she was a person who appreciated another heart full of love. She always gave his loving heart a tenfold return of understanding. But it was a dangerous thing for a woman to have such profound understanding. He felt uneasy, and often he was gripped by a dark premonition that one day when he came back home, she would no longer be there waiting for him; or that when he was waiting for her at home, she would never return. Where could she have gone?

Whenever such fear got the better of him, he hurried home, heedless of the vehicles in the street and the curses of his fellow passengers. He pushed open the back door and dashed upstairs. When he opened the door to the apartment, he saw her sitting there, facing the roofs bathed in the evening sun, as she was working on a watercolor painting. Seeing him come in, she asked why he was home so early and if everything was all right? With his throat constricted, he lowered his head and mumbled that he had forgotten to bring something to work and therefore came home to get it. She tried to help him look for the thing, but he pushed her aside. He grabbed something at random from the closet and said that he had found it. He walked downstairs. When he once again boarded the bus for his factory, he saw that he had grabbed a ball of red yarn left over from her knitting. He wept.

Other times when he was more clearheaded and objective, he thought that he should give his woman's dangerous undercurrent some opportunities for release. He understood that suppression only amplified the dangers. So he would mischievously bring home the worst troublemakers from his factory to drink with him. Those men could tell wild and dissolute stories, use very vulgar words, and make trouble in a hundred different ways. During such nights, his home was full of noise and laughter until the neighbors knocked at the door. But his wife always maintained her composure and serenity throughout, thus causing even the worst of them to behave a little in front of her. Her husband then felt ashamed of himself for being so absurd and malicious.

He gingerly got into bed, carefully lay down next to her, and turned off the light. Alone for the past two nights, he had often woken up at night. Now that she was back from Nanjing, he felt relieved. Like a little boy, he curled up next to her and went to sleep.

## 4

Old Li's memories of her school days had been revived. Unlike Old Wang, who could recall the past events and let them go at any time, Old Li was the kind of person who would not let go of the past once she was reminded of it.

Because of the recent encounter and their newly reestablished contact, Old Li began frequent communication with Old Wang. They exchanged letters almost once a week. Each letter was three or four pages long, covered with small print. Writing letters and reading them became a happy event in their lives. They mailed their letters to each other's schools. They spent all their time reading and writing letters—whenever nobody else was around. Each week they spent three days reading letters and three days writing them, with one day of rest.

In their letters they marveled at themselves. Why did they have so much to talk about? For they each had a husband, and a husband was supposed to be closer than a friend. But what they talked about with their husbands was very limited.

In their next round of letters, they both realized that there was a profound reason for this. Because a woman lived together with her husband day and night, they became very familiar with each other. Whenever one had a thought, the other knew about it without any words being spoken. But gradually, people became lazy and passive, thinking that it took no effort to know what the other had on their mind. Whenever one person realized that something was wrong, and wanted to raise the issue for discussion, she or he felt that it would look silly to the other, and therefore held back. All fresh topics and thoughts were dispersed by daily life. Everyday trivial events filled the space between husband and wife; any abstract discussion would be awkward and alien. The bond of understanding between husband and wife was based on corporeality; it was a physical thing. The material infrastructure made them give up the superstructure—the spiritual world. Dialogue on the spiritual and ideological level could only take place between two parties who maintained a certain distance. And the two parties had to be people of the same sex, because exchanges between people of different sexes inevitably went astray, with ideas overwhelmed by sexual desire, and spiritual communication eventually blocked and replaced by physical communion. The only possibility for spiritual dialogue was between people of the same sex.

The two women each spent over a dozen long pages in solving this puzzle of theirs. When it was solved, they felt extremely pleased. They happily wrote;

communicating with a girlfriend gave them the illusion that they had returned to the time of their youth.

Every young girl has a close girlfriend. The two girls talk about anything and understand each other. They share everything and are inseparable. But later, such intimacy is disrupted by the fact that they each fall in love with a person of the opposite sex. They start betraying each other, learn to lie to each other, and spend more time with their boyfriends. They keep their secrets inside their own hearts. Thus begins a period of divided loyalties.

Old Wang and Old Li seemed to draw upon the emotional intensity and the sexual innocence of a friendship between girls, but at the same time these two mature women enriched it with their contemplative powers. In their letters, they imagined themselves to be free girls who could do whatever they wanted without any hindrance. When they buried themselves in their letter writing, they forgot about their surroundings. In the letters, their ideals were set free; their ideals could be realized.

Old Li's child was about to be born. But as for Old Wang, that night when she had sex with her husband produced nothing—the new life inside her was only in her imagination.

One night at three o'clock, Old Li gave birth to a baby boy, whose loud cries excited her greatly. On the same night, Old Wang could not fall asleep for some reason; she felt very irritated. When Old Li's letter arrived a few days later, she remembered that night, knowing that her discomfort must have been induced by her sixth sense. Human emotion was a mysterious thing, she thought.

She wrote back to Old Li, saying that she wished to be the child's godmother. She had not read the Bible and was not religious, but she had learned from reading foreign novels that a godmother was something like an adoptive mother.

She went all over town looking for presents, and finally bought a small long-life charm made of jade. As she was looking at the long-life charm, tears streamed from her eyes. She thought, now we have a baby.

In her mind, she had already excluded the baby's father. She thought of the baby as having two family members: his birth mother and his godmother. She thought that they should educate the child well because he was the product of their spiritual union. She held the long-life charm tightly in her palm—and decided to go to Shanghai. She believed that Old Li, having just given birth, needed her around to take care of her.

Summer in Nanjing was unbearably hot, and it was vacation time, so Old Wang's husband agreed to let her take a few days off and go to Shanghai. He bought the train ticket, packed her clothes, and saw her off at the train station.

She did not notify Old Li of her coming. Her sudden arrival at Old Li's home delighted Old Li in the extreme. She held out her hand from the bed. Old Wang helped Old Li to lie back in bed and would not allow her to get up. Immediately she began the work of attending to Old Li in her month of confinement.

The first thing she did was to fire the nanny hired by Old Li's husband with the excuse that this old woman was a plotter and a schemer, more interested in scamming the mother and child than in taking care of them. She assured Old Li's husband that she would take care of everything in the household.

In fact, she had no idea how to attend to a woman in her postpartum confinement. She had heard that a woman during confinement should not be exposed to air currents. So she closed all the windows, though the temperature was ninety-three degrees. She put a hot wet towel on Old Li's forehead, and boiled very hot eggs for her to eat. She washed Old Li's body three times a day, and forbade her to move her arms or legs, saying that if she used her strength she would have pain in her limbs later on. She held Old Li's arms and legs to wash her. Old Wang herself hated the heat, and had a short temper anyway. She sweated from morning to night. She insisted on staying up all night to look after Old Li, but in fact it was not necessary. Soon, snores could be heard from Old Wang in her bamboo chair. Suddenly she would wake up and ask if everything was okay.

"Everything is fine," said Old Li.

"Then why aren't you asleep?"

"Old Wang, I was sleeping all day."

"You go to sleep now. I'll stay awake," replied Old Wang. But then her eyes closed and the snores could be heard again.

Every day Old Wang got up early to get fresh milk in the neighborhood, and then she went to a market to buy groceries. Not knowing how to clean a fish, she cut her finger trying. She learned how to bargain with Shanghai merchants, even picking up coarse language in order to be more successful in her dealings with them. People wondered whose family had hired such a fierce nanny. But she was very gentle when she changed the baby's diapers. She often warned Old Li's husband to be gentle with the child. She said that once there was a careless father who took off his baby's penis when changing the diapers. She seemed to have made up the story on the spur of the moment. Because she lacked experience for such work, she was extremely nervous. As soon as a diaper was changed, she washed it and hung it outside. She would prepare for heating the milk half an hour before the job should be done. She was unusually diligent and patient, but she was always in a flurry, finishing one thing while destroying another. During these days at Old Li's home, many plates and bowls were broken. Boiling water seeped through the wood floor to the apartment below. But all the neighbors were moved by this woman from Nanjing. They did not complain about her clumsiness, but instead gave her useful advice and helpful hints. By the end of the month of confinement, she had become a skilled domestic worker.

Old Li's husband was grateful to Old Wang. He had not thought that women could have such devoted friends. It was one thing to do things capably; it was another thing for a person to be sincere. He did not know what he could do to repay her. She did not let him do anything; she said that he was very clumsy. He went to some trouble to get her a ticket for some foreign films, but she was unwilling to go. She wanted to stay with Old Li all the time.

It was a very hot summer, and the Li family only had one room. The husband set up a canvas cot by the roadside, leaving the room to the two women and the baby. He slept alone under a tree. Looking at the dim light from the windows above his head, he had conflicting feelings. On the one hand, he was grateful to this woman who came to help. On the other hand, he was a bit annoyed at her because it seemed that she had divided his family. He felt rather pathetic, as if he had been exiled, spending the night under a tree.

Another thing that surprised him was that the woman called his wife "Old Li." When at first he heard this, he thought she was calling him, and replied: "I am sorry, my surname is not Li." Unexpectedly, she said, "I am not talking to you." Calling his wife "Old Li" sounded weird and ugly to him, as though his wife was no longer his wife when she answered to this name, but rather some man or some other person. He was not accustomed to this. He pretended not to hear when Old Wang called out "Old Li." But he also felt that he should not feel so repelled, because of what she had done for his family. So he calmed down.

That night, Old Wang fell asleep and then woke up to see Old Li looking at her with her eyes wide open. Old Wang asked, "Is everything all right?"

Old Li smiled. "Everything is fine."

Old Wang then asked, "Why then can't you sleep? You go to sleep, I'll stay awake."

Old Li begged her: "I cannot sleep. Let me stay awake for a while."

Old Wang's heart softened, and she said, "Okay, I'll let you stay awake for a while. It's so late—what shall we do to stay awake?"

Old Li said, "Let's talk. You've always been busy since you came, and we've never had a chance to talk with each other."

"Okay, let's talk. But what shall we talk about?"

They were silent at first, hearing only the ticking of the clock. The night was very quiet. After a while, Old Li said, "Life is really a strange thing."

Old Wang knew what she meant but asked her anyway. "What's so strange about it?"

"You see, it can reproduce a person," Old Li said.

Old Wang ridiculed her. "You mean, like reprinting a book?" Old Li chuckled, but Old Wang suddenly became melancholy. "In fact, it should be a reprint of two people; it's not accurate to say that it is a reprint of one person only."

Old Li said, "According to what you say, it should be a reprint of six people. You see, the mother is always a reprint of two people; and the father is also the reprint of two people—"

"Then it is a reprint of innumerable people. In our veins flows the blood of so many unknown relatives!" She shuddered at the thought, and hunched up her shoulders as if in fear of the cold. They looked at the sleeping baby, and felt that he had somehow become a creature so strange as to be beyond recognition. What was really ours? They looked at each other.

Old Li shuddered and said, "Maybe we've gone too far. You see, there are places where one should not dig deeply."

Old Wang expanded on that topic. "Yes—we may come to a bottomless abyss; and once we fall, that will be the end of us." But they always had embarked on the dangerous road, full of curiosity and the spirit of adventure, and therefore were unwilling to stop the exploration. They went on to ask themselves, was the first human being a very pure person? Where did human beings come from? This was a more dangerous exploration; they found that humans were not just the reproductions of other humans but also the reproductions of animals such as monkeys and fish. In their bodies flowed the animal blood from the primeval forests. They discovered that the "self" of a human being was not pure at all, but was contaminated from infancy. In fact, a human being could not be held responsible for the word "I." At this thought, they were frightened, and felt a sense of despair. They pushed their discussion to the point of seeing human life as a process of purification, of departure from animals, and suddenly noticed dawn outside. They breathed a long sigh of relief—after the long and dark night, they finally saw the morning light! They felt new joy and hope.

They took turns kissing the baby, who had just opened his eyes in the early morning. They thought this baby was the most beautiful life in the world, and the highest form that humanity had yet achieved. They believed that a good life should be assembled from the good aspects of many lives. The compilation depended partly on nature and partly on reason. This way, there would be a possibility of obtaining a better life than the old one. They recalled last night's scene; hand in hand, they had traveled a dangerous path and reached the peak of the mountain. Side by side, they had braved the waters and reached the shore beyond. Each had thoughts of gratitude for the other: without your support and company, I would never have the courage to embark on the dangerous path, let alone complete the journey to the end. I would either die in a dark pit along the way or withdraw at the beginning and be haunted by nightmares of failure. We have had an adventure of the soul, and it will always be ingrained in our memories. Whenever we need help, this memory will give us aid and comfort.

On the day when the baby was one month old, Old Li's husband prepared a big dinner to celebrate the occasion. It doubled as a farewell dinner for Old Wang, because her school in Nanjing would begin very soon. Old Li did not invite any other guests; there were only the three of them and the baby. They drank fruit wine and beer. Gradually, they became a little tipsy.

For Old Li and Old Wang, it was as though they had returned to the last night at school upon graduation. There were three of them then too, and they were also drinking fruit wine, laughing and crying. In a blink of an eye, several years had passed. They felt melancholy, and spoke of the experiences they had shared, completely forgetting the presence of Old Li's husband. They talked about cutting classes and sleeping late. They roared with laugher; they wept. They had lived a carefree life then, without burdens or responsibilities. As they were talking, they began to notice Old Li's husband and started to treat him as an audience. They rushed to speak, interrupting each other, and occasionally pulled his arms to make him pay attention. The water was boiling on the stove, and he was about to fetch it, but they prevented him from leaving. Sometimes they would have the same thought at the same time and begin to laugh without speaking at all. Old Li's husband had no idea what was going on. Finally they let him go get the hot water. When he came back, he saw the two women face to face, their eyes filled with tears.

They said, even a single day of such carefree living was a fortunate thing, but they had lived that kind of life for over three years. So now they had to pay twofold for it with the heavy tedium of their ordinary days. They wept.

He thought the two of them must be crazy. It was the first time he had seen his woman lose herself so. He felt sad, feeling that she had suddenly become comical and ugly beyond recognition. He moved from the table to the armchair behind them, lit a cigarette, and silently watched them perform. He felt that they were staging a comedy, but they were not trained to do a professional job. He could not laugh; he felt rather disgusted.

The women finished the last of the fruit wine, the special dishes, and the soup. They became quiet as though they were tired. The moment of quietness was very still. No one spoke. The baby was asleep.

Old Wang said, with tears in her eyes, "This summer is indeed memorable!"

"Yes," replied Old Li, also with tears in her eyes.

Old Wang proposed, "Let's spend our next summer together."

Old Li said, "OK, we'll go to Qingdao, Beidaihe, and Dalian."

Old Wang chimed in, "We won't invite anyone else, just you and me." They were quite taken by the vision of spending their summer at the seashore. But Old Li's husband felt these seaside prospects represented a horrible craziness. He decided to sabotage their plan at all costs.

But then their plan for the summer was already abandoned, because they felt that the summer seemed too far away. They advanced their travel plan to the winter vacation. Now they started having different ideas about where to go. One said that they should go to Guangzhou for the Flower Exhibition, and the other said that they should go to Harbin to see the lanterns sculpted from ice. They started arguing and neither would budge an inch.

They saw the husband sitting there and wanted him to be the judge. Grabbing his arms from both sides, one said "Go to Guangzhou," and the other said "Go to Harbin!" He looked at the two women, with their flushed faces and their glassy eyes. He thought fearfully, these two crazy women! Fortified by wine himself, he pushed them away and said rudely, "Go back to where you came from!" The two women reeled and almost fell, but they began to laugh together. He laughed with them, masking his momentary anger.

Next morning when he got ready to go to work, the two women were still asleep, one lying in bed and the other curled up on the bamboo couch. On the table he saw the leftovers from the previous night. He could not help feeling irritated. In addition, he had a splitting headache. Skipping breakfast, he rode his bicycle to work.

When he returned in the evening, he saw that the apartment was clean and the floor had been mopped. On the table were some delicious cold hors d'oeuvres. The baby was bathed and powdered, lying on the cool mat. His wife too had had a shower, and now wearing her clean clothes, she was sitting at the lamp reading a book. The woman from Nanjing was gone. Suddenly he felt that the space in the apartment was much larger than before, and he was very glad. He thought, our life of the past month was chaotic; everything was upside-down. After washing his face, he sat down at the table. His wife placed the food on the table. The early autumn's wind blew gently from the window. As he was watching her, he felt moved. He thought, my wife is back; she had been captured by ghosts last night.

That evening, neither Old Li nor her husband mentioned the name of Old Wang. He did not ask if Old Wang had left, nor did she tell him that Old Wang had gone.

After Old Wang left, Old Li resumed her normal life. She found a baby-sitter; in the morning, she took her child to the baby-sitter's home, and in the evening she brought him back. During the day, she was back at her old job.

The two women seemed to have exhausted their conversation during the summer. For a long time, they did not write often. The occasional letters were nothing but ordinary greetings. The baby took much of Old Li's attention. She watched him grow, little by little. The child seemed to learn something each day. One day he could say "Mama" and "Papa"; the next day, he could wave good-bye, and the day after he would lose his temper and make his parents suffer. Old Li felt that her labors and hardships were rewarded and was happy.

And then the baby would get sick: either diarrhea or fever, sometimes both. Whenever it happened, he had to be sent to the hospital. Holding the baby on the way there, she was terribly worried, and thought, my treasure, if anything should happen to you, I would die too. She felt that her life was linked with this fragile young life. As a result, she felt her life was weak and she could die at any time.

When her child was sick, she could not sleep a wink. Her mind would turn to thoughts of death. She worried that her child might die while she was asleep. The thought pained and terrified her. In fact, the child just had a cold.

Old Li's husband thought that her anxiety was excessive, even bordering on the neurotic. Her usual coolheaded calm seemed to have disappeared. She became hot-tempered. Sometimes she would blow up at him, blaming him for coming home fifteen minutes late. She was on tenterhooks all day long as though she expected a disaster to happen any minute.

Thinking that her worry was a result of physical exhaustion, the husband tried to do more housework to lighten her burden. He changed the child's diapers like an experienced nanny.

Sometimes when the child was not sick for two weeks at a stretch, Old Li would relax, and then she would feel happy. When she did relax, the child would often get sick, as though on purpose. The child would run a high fever at night so that the couple had to rush him to the emergency room. She then began to think that she should not relax, because whenever she did, her child would get sick. Hence, during the days when the child was not sick, she felt especially nervous and tense. When the child got sick, she would feel relieved. The whole business was getting pretty ridiculous, but there was nothing that she could do.

To comfort her, the man said, "Our baby looks so healthy these days!"

Instantly her face changed color, and overcome with fear, she asked him to stop talking like that. She said, "Don't say that! If you do, our baby will become sick."

Sometimes he took the opposite tack and said, "Our baby does not look well." She would become even more worried, and take out the thermometer to check her child's body temperature. As a result, he did not dare to say anything and began to be nervous himself.

One night he said to her, "We have been married for so many years. At first we wanted to have kids, then we gave up and decided we didn't, and then the child came. It's all the will of heaven. So no matter whether our child is alive or dead, or turns out to be good or bad, he has his own fate. There is nothing that human effort can change."

When she heard this, she started to weep and asked, "What do you mean by that? Do you mean that when a child is sick, his parents should not take care of him but should let him suffer or even die?"

He tried to defend himself and said that was not what he meant, but to no avail. She was growing more miserable and despondent. She felt everything was unreliable and unstable. He found her very irritating, but he forced himself to console her. She did calm down a bit. When she was calm, she seriously thought that she was wearing herself out this way, like an overly taut string that was about to snap. She tried to let go and relax a bit, but her child was spoiled; he had become weak and overly sensitive. Whenever he went out without a hat, he would come home coughing badly. She tried getting cough drops instead of going to the hospital, but the coughing developed into whooping cough. Her regret was so great that she would never dare to be careless again.

Old Li was extremely exhausted. She thought, since I had the child, I have had to do everything very carefully. It has been like walking on thin ice or at the edge of an abyss. Every day has been full of dangers. I should have been a homeless wanderer! This idea flashed before her eyes and was gone like a shooting star. She looked at the child with sorrow and said to herself, if I went and roamed the world, what would become of you?

Whenever she was exhausted, the thought of a wanderer's life came up to distract her. She thought, one day when I cannot take it anymore, I'll just leave. It was as though she had a way to retreat, and she could then become calm. But her ability to endure hardship was limitless. The day when she could not take it anymore would never come.

When the child grew a bit older, she sent him to a nursery school near her own school. In the morning, she would hold up the child as a plea to board crowded buses. But no one would get up to give his seat to a woman with a child in her arms. People on the bus were packed together like sardines. Sometimes, when she was tightly holding to her child, someone would take advantage of her by rubbing against her lower body. She really wanted to swear aloud, but she couldn't; when a bus was so crowded, it was only too common for people to touch one another. The school was very far from her home, so she had to leave home very early in the morning to catch the bus. In the cold winter days when she had to drag the child from his warm bed, she almost wept. She thought of giving up her work, but she could not. It was impossible for her husband alone to support the three-member family. On the bus, when the child began to cry because he felt crushed by the crowd, she would weep too. People around them would just watch them and sometimes ridicule them. But finally someone would offer them a little help, for instance, by giving her a push from behind to help her get to the door at her stop. Even though such help was trivial, she still felt consoled, thinking that there was some warmth in this world. Old Li was very good at appreciating any warmth around her, and at enlarging it with her own compassion, thus helping her endure.

During this time, she seldom wrote to Old Wang, nor did she have time to answer Old Wang's letters. Sometimes she would send postcards with her child's footprints. Gradually, Old Wang accumulated a series of prints of growing feet. This satisfied her imagination.

Between the two women, there was no end of wonderful ways to communicate. Endowed with imagination and sensibility, they could easily pick up on inner feelings. If these two women had not met, their abilities to communicate would have been lost for lack of exercise. They lived in a rough world indeed, and if they were too sensitive they would not be able to survive. They had to be tough and shrewd as they developed their finer qualities. They then used their practiced abilities in dealing with their husbands, inducing their husbands to yield to their demands and thus feminizing the men a little. If the two women had not had each other's support, they would have remained crude to the end. But they did meet, and together they cultivated fine and tender flowers on a small private plot in their hearts.

This private plot was gradually expanded. They remembered each other's birthdays, and exchanged homemade birthday cards with beautiful and meaningful words. Sometimes they did not write letters, but one would just send the other a note asking her to look at a certain line on a certain page of a certain book.

What Old Wang found was, "Finally, what I had feared came to pass." She knew that Old Li's child was sick again.

What Old Li found was a poetic line: "A lady's sorrow, having allowed her husband to seek office." Then Old Li would know that Old Wang's husband was away on official business.

Their husbands had no idea about all these goings-on between their women. If they had learned of it, they would not have understood; they would have laughed at the women. Realizing this from the beginning, the women decided not to inform their husbands of their ongoing friendship. They sent the letters to their workplaces, and when they returned home, they made no mention of receiving letters.

For no matter how old a woman grows, she never loses a certain childlike simplicity. If this simplicity is not recognized, it either dies or is transformed. Men do not bother to participate in these games with women because they do not have the childlike quality, nor do they have the patience. In today's world, because of jealousy, pettiness, reserve, and other hindrances, it is very hard for a woman to find a woman companion. If she does find a woman friend, that friendship will never be replaced by any man.

## 5

During the winter vacation, Old Wang came to Shanghai again. She felt she bore a responsibility for her godson.

Before she took the trip she resumed her old hobby of knitting; she knitted many pairs of pants and socks for the child and stuffed them all into her suitcase. As soon as she arrived at Old Li's home, she began to try her knits on the child. The child was rather vexed by her shaking.

This time, she put on the air of a "godmother," did no housework, and sat crossed-legged with one foot poised in the air. This time, she lived a life of being served. She did not go to sleep at night and did not get up in the morning. When Old Li's husband got up in the morning to have breakfast before work, she would remain sound asleep with a sheet over her head. Slumber seemed to be contagious. Gradually, Old Li also gave up getting up early in the morning. At night she would chat nonstop with Old Wang.

Old Li, Old Wang, and the child occupied the big bed; Old Li's husband slept on the couch. When he listened to their chatting at night and watched them sleep during the day, he thought they were bizarre. During weekdays, he would leave home right after breakfast. This way he avoided being bothered by the two women. But on Sunday morning, when the sun was high and shining brightly into the windows, the two women were still asleep, the room was a mess, and he could do nothing—he really felt rather annoyed. Nevertheless, Old Wang was their guest, after all, so he could not throw a fit; he could only hide his fury. Sometimes when it became too much for him, he would say, "Ladies, it's time to get up. The sun is shining on your buttocks!" The two women made a clear chuckling sound. He realized that they were not fast asleep at all, and that they were just lying there for the sake of mental tranquility. His unhappiness increased.

During the time when Old Wang was there, Old Li's attention to the child was clearly relaxed. On windy days, she would take the child to see the exhibitions in the Art Museum. It seemed that because the adults paid no notice to him, the child did not even fall sick.

Old Li's husband saw all of this and was seriously angry. He felt that this woman Old Wang seemed to wield magic powers over his woman. Whenever his wife was with Old Wang, she would go a little crazy and could not do anything right. For example, his wife would overcook the food if Old Wang was in the kitchen with her. He really wished that Old Wang would go back to Nanjing at once, but it was just the beginning of the winter vacation and it looked as though she would not leave till the very the end.

Finally Old Li's husband hit upon an idea: why not invite Old Wang's husband over for the Chinese New Year's Festival? If he could come, there would be someone to control Old Wang. As Old Wang had lived peacefully with her husband for so many years, her husband must have ways of containing her. Old Li's husband resented the fact that their peaceful life was disturbed by Old Wang. He also realized that this woman's presence tapped into the dynamic force hidden deep inside Old Li's heart. If not for this force, Old Wang would never be able to disturb his family life. Of course, then Old Wang and Old Li would not have been friends. He wondered why on earth these two women had met, since the world was so big and human paths so many. They really had good luck in finding each other.

His suggestion about the upcoming holiday surprised the women, but they were immediately enthusiastic. They said that they had never done it before, but two families celebrating the New Year's Festival together would surely be very interesting. The only difficulty would be that there was not enough space for both families in the one room.

Old Li's husband said that it did not matter, because he could sleep on the bamboo couch and Old Wang's husband could sleep on another couch. Though it might be crowded, it was the New Year's Festival after all! The Festival should be a time bustling with noise and excitement.

Having agreed to Old Li's husband's proposal, Old Wang wanted to go send a telegram to her husband that very night, and Old Li wanted to go with her. Old Li's husband told them that he would stay at home to look after the child while they went out. So the two women excitedly left the apartment, and rushed to the telecommunications center. They sent an urgent telegram to Old Wang's husband in Nanjing.

Old Wang's husband received the telegram at three o'clock in the morning. At first he was worried that something must be wrong. When he saw the telegram was an invitation for him to go to Shanghai for the New Year's Festival, he was relieved. On the morning of the eve of the Chinese New Year, Old Wang's husband, holding the presents of roast duck and chicken and other things purchased for the occasion, squeezed up the creaking stairway leading to Old Li's apartment.

Old Li's husband liked Old Wang's husband instantly. They were about the same age and had many things in common. Old Li's husband observed that Old Wang did indeed begin to restrain herself after her husband's arrival. In the afternoon when she was going to the grocery store, she did not ask Old Li to accompany her, but asked her husband to go with her instead. She also joined in the cooking that night and made some egg dumplings. Whenever she started being unruly, her husband would gently remind her that she was a guest in someone else's home.

Old Wang's husband's words struck a cord in Old Li's husband's heart; he liked what he heard. Old Li's husband discovered the reason why Old Wang was annoying: she had regarded someone else's home as her own. For this reason, she had been self-indulgent and unrestrained. Old Li's husband forgave Old Wang a little because her husband was very polite and reasonable.

During the New Year's Eve dinner, Old Wang proposed a drinking game and Old Li's husband agreed. Old Wang's husband wondered at his wife's jubilation in playing the game: Why was she so happy now? All the irritation she felt in Nanjing was gone, as if she had returned to her own home. She was so pleased, so content!

He carefully observed Old Li and her husband. At first, he suspected that Old Wang's happiness derived from the presence of Old Li's husband, but then he found that that was not the case. Old Li's husband was polite to Old Wang, but his politeness carried a kind of indifference.

He then observed Old Li and noticed that Old Li really pampered Old Wang. Whenever Old Wang acted wildly, Old Li would look at her fondly and encouragingly. This reminded him of the night when Old Li was at his home; the two women had talked until dawn. He said to himself, these two women were really attracted to each other. But what attracted them to each other?

As he was thinking, Old Wang had already lost the drinking game and drunk two or three glasses of wine as punishment. With a reddened face, she bent down with laughter, "I can't do it anymore!" But Old Li forced her to drink another glass of wine. Old Wang said, "You, husband and wife, are trying to make fun of me!" And then the two women started laughing boisterously.

After this tomfoolery, the two women took a deep breath and began to talk to each other in a more quiet manner. The two men also started talking to each other. Old Li's husband thought, Old Wang's husband is here; at least I can talk to someone and I don't have to watch the two women's performance anymore. The two women were saying how time passes; the year has gone by in a flash. The two men then said, soon another year will be over. The two women said, we have done so much in the past year; what shall we do in the coming year? The two men said that they had been pretty busy in the past year and soon they would be busy again in the new year. The two women said that the TV program for the Festival was getting worse each year. The two men said that the TV program for the Festival was getting no better over the years. The two women turned to the men and laughed at them, how come you guys mimic what we are saying? The two men replied, smiling, it is you who mimic what we say. The four of them began to laugh. Afterward they conversed separately, man with man and woman with woman.

Old Wang and Old Li talked about having an exhibition of their paintings. The theme of the exhibition would be "Brothers." They could hold the exhibition either in Nanjing or in Shanghai. They discussed the practical details: the cost of renting an exhibition hall, the cost of printing the handouts, and how much they would charge for admission. They became rather discouraged by all the details.

They drank some wine, ate some delicacies, and listened to the men talking about international and domestic politics. Then they took heart again, believing that the financial problem could be solved. They could open art classes and ask each student to pay tuition of fifty yuan per semester.

But then they worried that they would be very busy with the art classes for the semester after they collected the money. In the end even though they had financial means, they would have no time to paint enough paintings for the exhibition! In addition, if one student paid 50 yuan, ten students would pay 500 yuan, and a hundred students' tuition would only be 5,000 yuan. It was too little. Moreover, how could they teach a hundred students? Did they want to give up their jobs?

Their eyes lit up at this idea—they could quit their jobs! Having to work was such a bore! Day after day, month after month, year after year, they were doing the same kind of work. As they spoke of quitting their jobs, they suddenly felt a thrill; many years' suffering would thus end. Why had they not thought of this before? After they quit their jobs, they would be free to do whatever they wanted—for instance, they could organize art exhibitions. But then the problem of money popped up again; if they quit their jobs, they could never make ends meet. At this, they became rather depressed.

After a while, another new idea took shape: they could travel, and make drawings and photographs of peasants. They could go to Guangxi, Sichuan, Yunnan, or to the western part of China: Shaanxi, Qinghai, and Tibet. They argued for a while about the travel route: whether to go up north or to go down south. They could not come to an agreement, and so put the issue aside. They continued to fantasize: if they were to travel, they would have art work and also money. Maybe they could also hold an exhibition of their travel photographs. They were intoxicated by their beautiful dream, and merrily they drank one glass of beer after another. On the eve of the New Year, they had found hope and a purpose in life.

At midnight, firecrackers could be heard all over town. They, too, had braided together firecrackers for the occasion. They tied the braid to a bamboo stick and dangled it out the window, joining in the symphony of popping sounds. Immediately the room was filled with sulfurous smoke that made them cough and laugh at the same time. They could not help thinking that this would be a good year.

On the fourth day after the Festival, Old Wang's husband had to leave. His holidays were over and he had to work the next day. He asked Old Wang to go back with him, but Old Wang replied that her school would not begin until the tenth and she would like to stay for a few more days. Old Li's husband was hoping that Old Wang's husband would be able to persuade her to go back; however, Old Wang's husband did not insist, and left by himself. Old Li's husband was disappointed and a bit miffed.

That day was spent quietly, as if people were tired after all the holiday excitement. No one wanted to talk or to cook. They heated up some leftovers from the previous days and had a casual dinner. They all went to bed very early. The two women, as usual, chatted for a while but soon fell asleep. The sound of televisions from their neighbors was heard until midnight, but all was quiet in their apartment.

Somehow, both Old Li and Old Wang felt a little guilty—as if they had done something wrong, though they did not know what. They also felt that they had missed an opportunity, but they had no idea what kind of opportunity they had missed. They felt a little regret, but they did not know what they were regretting. Feeling uneasy, they were on their best behavior. They got up early the next morning, made breakfast, and cleaned the apartment, thus putting Old Li's husband in a better mood. He left for work with a pleased look on his face.

It was a bright day. Old Wang proposed to Old Li to go for a walk in the park with the child. Old Li thought it was a good idea.

They went to the nearest park and brought the baby along in the baby carriage. It was quiet in the park. Some old people were doing shadowboxing. Some young couples were playing with their children. Old Li and Old Wang sat on a bench facing the sun; the baby carriage was next to them. The sky was a brilliant blue, dotted with a few white clouds. Yellow winter jasmine was already in bloom, and the frozen earth at its roots had softened. Birds were singing somewhere in the park. Old Wang and Old Li were moved by the scene. They felt relaxed and became talkative. They wished that this beautiful scene could last forever; why could time not stop? They said that the Festival was joyous and great fun, except that there were simply too many people and too much noise. Now that everything had quieted down and they could finally sit face to face, this time together was very precious.

Old Wang said, "I am glad I did not go back to Nanjing with my husband."

Old Li said, "I am happy about that, too."

They felt that their discomfort had been completely groundless, and that in fact everything was peaceful and beautiful. Their hearts brimmed with thankfulness, and they said again and again what a great piece of good fortune it was that they had resumed communication. If it were not for their mutual encouragement, it would be terribly hard to go on. They also discovered that their friendship enabled them to hold on to something of the romantic and poetic, which would otherwise have been ground away by the monotony of daily life. Their relations with their husbands were physical relationships, and weakened their grasp of things creative. Men were strange creatures.

They discussed that with emotion. Every man was a product of pragmatism. Men had only goals, no process. They brought women along with them to their destinations, without paying much attention to the scenery along the road that they had traveled. They of course acknowledged that men were more practical than they were. Such was life; if one relaxed a little and did not work hard, he would lag behind. Without a solid material base, beautiful dreams could no longer exist. They then thought that the reason for men's practical struggle was to protect women's poetic dreams, and that this was in fact a great sacrifice. Women should be firm and keep their own camp. It was up to the women to keep this camp, not up to the men. Men had done what they could.

After a while, the women realized that they were wrong; men did not shoulder all of the tasks of the practical struggle. They had shouldered only half, and women shouldered the other half. Their spiritual exploration began to peter out. They complained about the men, but actually men were not entirely to blame, since it was all part of a broader social problem.

Nevertheless, no matter what might happen, the two of them should help each other and keep reminding themselves to avoid the death of their spiritual side. They treasured their friendship highly, for it was vital, pure, and lofty. Their friendship was not like that between a man and a woman whose relationship is driven by sexual desire. It was an intellectual and rational relationship, the highest form of human relations.

Suddenly, Old Wang had an absurd idea, and asked Old Li, what if they both fell deeply in love with the same man? Old Li thought for a while and said that she would withdraw and leave the man to Old Wang.

Old Wang pushed further. "What if this love was so deep that neither of us would give up the man?"

Old Li said, "Kill the man."

Her reply moved Old Wang to tears. Little did they know that their conversation had actually reached the edge of a dangerous precipice. Their friendship had already reached a turning point.

While they were talking to their hearts' content, they failed to notice that the child was bouncing up and down in the baby carriage. The clear sky and bright sunlight made the baby very merry. He tried to stand up, and his action rocked the carriage. A few times the carriage nearly tipped over, but then it caught itself and landed safely. The child was startled the first time, but after a few times he came to enjoy the adventure. He liked the moment when the carriage was going to topple, and tried to recreate the dangerous situation and relive the experience of coming to safety. Gradually he got the hang of it and was pretty successful in his maneuver. His thirst for adventure increasing, he doubled his efforts to rock the carriage. His luck was pretty good and the carriage did not fall. This self-created game bored him eventually; he did not really want to play it anymore. However, in the grip of a kind of inertia, he could not bring himself to stop. Mechanically he rocked the carriage, one time after another. It was already noon, with the bright sun right in the middle of the sky. The baby felt a bit sleepy and wanted to sleep, but his body was still rocking automatically. Finally, the carriage toppled over, and bounced on the concrete floor. The baby did not sense any danger, and for a moment he felt an extreme and powerful happiness. But he hit the side of his head on an exposed tree root. Blood shot out immediately and blurred his vision. He did not feel any pain, but the blood scared him and made him realize that something important must have happened. He burst into tears and screamed.

Old Li and Old Wang turned their heads and saw the child bleeding on the ground. Old Li yelled: "My child!"

Her scream made Old Wang shudder. When Old Wang looked at Old Li, she saw a stranger: her face was ghastly pale, her teeth clenched, her brows raised. She looked absolutely hideous.

She rushed to the child's side, attempting to pick him up. But the child's body was half inside the carriage and he was wearing a thick cotton-padded coat. She could not pick him up at first. She lost it. Her hair was all over her face and some strands were stained with the child's blood. She looked like a ghost.

Old Wang went over to help her, but Old Li yelled at her: "Don't touch my child!" Old Wang was taken aback. She felt her heart was being smashed to pieces, but she controlled her pain and continued to help with the carriage.

Old Li pressed the child to her chest. The child was still bleeding. He lay in his mother's bosom, felt secure, and stopped crying. He stared quietly at the blue sky. Old Li's face now had blood on it too. She was not sure where on the child the blood came from. She tried to stop the bleeding with her hand. Soon her hand was bloody. She began to cry in a coarse voice.

Other people in the park came around and tried to comfort her. They helped her locate the wound. When she saw the tender white bone in the pink flesh, she stamped her feet and howled.

Someone handed her a handkerchief to press on the child's wound and told her that a clinic was located at the rear gate of the park. A person who knew the way rushed with her toward the hospital. On the way, that person grabbed the child from her, and dashed ahead toward the hospital. Old Li followed him with unsure steps, wailing like a peasant woman. Everyone was looking at her, thinking that this woman must have gone mad.

Old Wang pulled the carriage and followed Old Li. She felt great sympathy for Old Li and wanted to help her but she did not dare to do anything. She felt that Old Li deeply loathed her, as if the whole incident had been caused by her alone. Old Li would rather accept assistance from strangers, and even let a stranger take away her child, but she yelled at Old Wang: Don't touch my child!

Old Li's cry echoed in Old Wang's ears, making her feel like a criminal. How she wanted to help Old Li, to compensate for her sin! But Old Li would not give her a chance.

When they were crossing the road, Old Wang saw Old Li dashing toward the wheels of a truck. Old Wang tried to pull her away from the truck, but Old Li waved her arms at Old Wang as though she wanted to pick a fight. Old Li had sudden strength, and her push almost knocked Old Wang down. After Old Wang got back on her feet, she saw Old Li miraculously reaching the other side of the road. The traffic on the road did not let up. Old Wang waited for the cars to pass and watched the back of Old Li disappear into the distance. Her heart sank. She knew that at that moment something of absolute importance in her life was irretrievably lost.

It was not until the child had stopped bleeding, had taken medicine to prevent infection, and had fallen asleep at home, that Old Li regained her self-control. Her cheeks had two vivid red spots, like a tubercular patient in the terminal stage. She paced incessantly in the room, now touching the clothes hanging outside to find out if they were dry, and now checking the big thermos bottles to see if there was still hot water. Old Wang wanted to ask her not to waste her energy in this way, but she did not dare to utter a word. And Old Li seemed to have forgotten completely about the presence of Old Wang, neither speaking with her nor looking at her.

That day the sun was especially gorgeous, and the days were getting longer. At five o'clock it was still very bright. The child was in a deep slumber. He slept on his side, with one finger in his mouth and a bandage over his head, like a hero.

When Old Li's husband's footsteps were heard from the stairs, the two women began to panic. They exchanged glances but as their glances met they realized how far apart they were. Their hearts pumping, they looked at the door in terror. They did not know what would happen, but their hearts were filled with ominous premonitions.

Old Li's husband opened the door and walked into the apartment. He saw a very clean and quiet apartment, with dinner on the table and the baby asleep. Such a peaceful scene was rare in the past few days. He very happily said, "Let's have dinner!" He sat down at the table and took a few morsels with his chopsticks. He was waiting for his wife to urge him to go and wash his hands before the meal, but since she made no move, he had to stand up again to go and wash his hands himself. This little disappointment did not disturb his good mood. He was still very happy. He returned to the table, and bellowed for them to come and have dinner. He even spoke to Old Wang: "Your husband must be eating dinner alone at home. Come on, why don't you two have dinner? I have already put the food on your plates. Are you waiting for me to spoon-feed you?" He could not help laughing at his own remark.

The two women then stood up and slowly walked toward the dinner table. On the way, they exchanged glances a second time, and this time they saw fear in each other's eyes. They resented each other, but did not know why.

Old Wang straightened her back, raised her head, and said very clearly, "We had a disaster today; the child . . ."

Old Li's husband immediately turned to look at the child and saw the bandage on his head. He tried to keep calm, put the chopsticks down slowly, and asked what had happened. Old Wang retold the event in one breath, and then stood at attention in front of Old Li's husband, as if she were going to the execution ground. Feeling a surge of anger rise within him, Old Li's husband became livid. He now saw that his good mood was a result of their deceit; he had fallen into their trap. The beautiful evening and all other such evenings were simply destroyed by them! Crash! He threw his bowl on the floor. Startled, Old Wang turned her head to look at Old Li. Old Li had already retreated to the bed. She sat there, staring into emptiness, as if she had seen nothing going on around her.

Old Wang restrained herself and said, "Why did you break the bowl? We did not let it happen intentionally. All boys bump against things, and all boys grow up."

Old Li's husband gave her a cold sneer. "According to you, my child's fall was a good thing and I should thank you for it."

Old Wang sneered back. "You don't have to thank me, nor do you have to resent me. I did not drop this child of the two of you!"

When she said "the two of you," she felt pain in her heart, realizing that Old Li would never come to her rescue. Old Li was sitting there quietly, absentmindedly watching the two squabble. Old Wang experienced another chill.

Old Li's husband heard what she said, and could no longer control his wrath. Since this woman entered their lives, there had not been a single day of peace. He pointed his finger at Old Wang and yelled, "Yes, you are the one to blame!"

Old Wang screamed, "That is not fair!" And then there was a lump in her throat and she could not say anything more. She did not want to cry. She had so many reasonable points to make, but she could not say a single word. Her lips trembled and her face twitched with the effort to hold back her tears.

Old Li's husband felt that this woman was ugly and evil: Why was she staying here and not leaving? This was not her home! Why didn't she go away? He impulsively yelled at her. "*Get out!*"

When she heard this, Old Wang's tears dried up. She forced herself to smile and said in a trembling voice, "I am not leaving here. This home does not belong to you only." After that, she went back to sit on the couch.

She cast a glance at Old Li. In fact, her remark was intended for Old Li, to seek her assistance, but Old Li did not hear anything. She just sat there, blank and numb, with one hand lightly patting the child. The child was now awake and calmly sucked his fingers. Old Wang pulled her feet up on the couch and stared at the back of Old Li. She murmured to herself, "It's over, Old Li; it is all over." Tears streamed down her cheeks and soon her entire face was wet.

That night Old Wang did not go to the bed, but huddled on the couch. Old Li's husband took the bamboo armchair. Old Li and the child took the big bed. None of the three adults could fall asleep, each having too much to think about.

Old Li's husband was feeling a little regret, thinking that maybe he had overreacted. He had lost control in a moment of desperation, but he had no intention of apologizing to Old Wang.

Old Li had turned into a commonplace housewife within a day. She had no thoughts for anything but her child. She got up countless times that night to give the child water, help him go to the bathroom, check his temperature, and make him take the medicine. Whenever she got up, she would see the two bright eyes of Old Wang shining in the dark like those of a cat.

Next morning, Old Li's husband ate his breakfast and went to work. Old Wang still sat on the couch. Old Li called her to have breakfast. She cast a strange glance at Old Li, but made no reply and kept sitting there.

Old Li looked at her, sighed, and cleared the table. She then sat down on the bed and began knitting a cashmere jacket for the child. The child had already forgotten his adventure of the previous day. He was jumping gleefully up and down on the bed, waving a wooden sword. The sunlight beamed into the room.

Old Wang's face was very pale. Old Li was worried about whether Old Wang was sick. She tried to find a topic for conversation, but Old Wang did not reply to anything except by nodding or shaking her head.

Old Li realized that Old Wang must still be angry with her. She gradually recalled what she had said to Old Wang when they discovered the child's fall in the park. She also began to recall the quarrel between Old Wang and her husband. She felt miserable. Several times she tried to express her thoughts, but she did not know where to begin.

In just one day and one night, Old Li felt she had gone through a tremendous transformation. She did not know what kind of transformation, but she knew that something had happened. She did not know if there was anything that she could do to save their precious friendship. Several times she wanted to come close to Old Wang and stroke her boyishly short hair, as she had often done in the past. But Old Wang's unfriendly glare kept her away.

At noon, Old Li made some noodles, but Old Wang did not eat anything. Nor did Old Li have any appetite. She ate a little bit and gave up.

In the afternoon the child fell asleep. Old Li said to Old Wang, "Please watch the baby for me. I'm going to do some shopping; I'll be back soon." Without waiting for a reply, Old Li fled the apartment, and ran down the stairs to the street.

In her hurry, she had not thought about what she might buy. She decided to buy some toilet paper, but she found that she had not even a penny with her. Of course she was trying to apologize for telling Old Wang not to touch her child the previous day. Old Li walked at random in the sunny streets for a while before she returned home.

When she opened the door, she saw her child asleep on the bed, and Old Wang still sitting on the couch. Gingerly, Old Li asked Old Wang: "Do you want to eat anything?"

Old Wang turned and then shook her head. There were tears in her eyes.

When evening came, Old Wang stood up, washed her face and combed her hair, and helped Old Li prepare dinner. When Old Li's husband came home, Old Wang joined them for dinner.

At night, she slept on the couch. Old Li and the child slept on the bed, and Old Li's husband slept on the bamboo armchair. Because he felt apologetic toward Old Wang, Old Li's husband willingly took the uneven bamboo armchair.

This arrangement lasted for three days. During those three days, Old Wang said nothing to Old Li, but she did sometimes speak to Old Li's husband. Whenever she did this, Old Li's husband would feel rather flattered and would respond quickly.

On the tenth day after the New Year's Festival, Old Wang went back to Nanjing as previously planned. When Old Li proposed to see her off at the train station, Old Wang kept silent, saying neither yes nor no. But when Old Li snatched the suitcase away from her, she let go of it.

They walked behind one another to the bus stop and waited for the bus to come. Neither of them said anything as they boarded the bus, or on the bus, or as they got off. They walked in silence through the square. The winter wind was chilly. They were both reminded of another parting, when Old Wang had seen Old Li off at the Nanjing train station. They turned their faces away, not daring to look into each other's eyes. Old Li accompanied Old Wang to the departure gate, and watched her hand her ticket to the guard. As Old Wang was about to go in, Old Li suddenly held her and dragged her out of the line.

"Let me go!" Old Wang struggled to get free and cried out in a hoarse voice. Other passengers began to stare at them.

Old Li grabbed Old Wang's arm with both of her hands, disregarding other people's curiosity and disapproval, and said, "I love you, really; I love you!" Between them, the word "love" was never used, because the word "love" had been desecrated by sexual intercourse between men and women. But now Old Li used it.

Tears rolled down from Old Wang's eyes, but she said, "It's late; it's already too late now."

Old Li also wept. Through her tears, she said, "No, it's not late, not late at all."

"It is late; it is too late!" Old Wang cried, her tears streaming down. "There are some things that are extremely beautiful but very fragile. Once broken, they cannot be repaired." After she said that, she tore herself away from Old Li, and rushed back toward the gate. Soon she was out of sight.

They never met again. After a couple of years, Old Wang gradually got over her pain. She traveled to the Three Gorges alone. She remembered that on that lunar New Year's Eve, she and Old Li spoke of a trip to the Three Gorges, and also about having an art exhibition entitled "Brothers." She smiled and shook her head, as if to shake away those past events. In the years since then, she kept changing jobs, moving from one to another, but she was satisfied with none of them. In the end, even she had no idea what she really wanted. Her boat moved through the Gorges, with steep cliffs towering on both sides. Far above, between the tall cliffs, appeared a thread of blue sky.

# 6

# LIPS

Liang Hanyi

*Translated by Kimberly Besio*

They stood beneath a low weathered wall. Amid the darkness, white gardenias silently let off an eerie, faint fragrance. Above, white clouds, as ominous as the gardenias, rapidly surged across the night sky. The weather report this morning had predicted a typhoon.

He lowered his head. She retreated several steps, goose bumps rippling up over her entire body. A wave of uncleanliness swept through her.

"Disgusting!" As she reviled him, she took to her heels, and as rapidly as the surging clouds, fled toward the brightly lit street.

Shuiping had more than once been disappointed in her affections. Whenever an occasion for intimacy arose between her and a man, she would quickly escape. No one quite understood why. The years of her young womanhood had slipped away amidst countless missed chances. Shuiping had no regrets. Every morning she would stand in front of the white porcelain basin which was scrubbed so abnormally clean that it was almost as if it emitted her reflection in miniature, and she would stare at her lips.

Shuiping would brush her teeth five times every day—after every meal, before going to sleep, and upon getting up in the morning. Even when she was at work, there were no exceptions. She always kept a set of toiletry items by her. While working, it was her wont to pick up a blue-flowered handkerchief that she kept in the corner of her desk and to lightly wipe her lips.

Unless it was absolutely necessary, she would refuse to wear lipstick. She abhorred that slimy feeling of having a layer of something upon her lips, as if they weren't her own. Therefore, she had come up with her own particular style of make-up: she would only apply eyeliner, eye shadow, blush, and powder. But she would leave her lips a blank. It gave people the impression of something cut off, fragmented, and unfinished—much like Shuiping's own life.

Being kissed either too early or too late can both be a sign of an inauspicious life. Shuiping had had the experience of being kissed. Afterwards, she had repeated the terror of that kiss in countless nightmares.

The dream always took place in a dark mountain hollow; monsters and goblins would be arrayed all around her. As she fled, people as directionless as if they had lost their souls would rapidly pursue her from behind. In the end, in a canyon lined with towering strange and malformed crags, she would finally be tightly clasped by one of them. The opaque and androgynous demon would deeply and greedily lick her, gnaw her, thrusting its tongue straight down her throat. Suddenly, blood would well up from her lips. The demon would suck, not stopping until she had been drained of all her blood, making her as dreadfully pale as a corpse.

To be kissed that way in a dream was somehow rather shameful, especially for an unmarried woman of twenty-eight or twenty-nine. She wasn't sure how others would view her, if they knew of this. Would they say that she was abnormal, a sex-crazed old maid?

She had actually only been kissed once in her entire life. Since she didn't like to think of that incident, it was as vague as if it too were a dream. There had been several times when Shuiping, upon recalling that moment, had even thought that it was merely one nightmare among several, and that perhaps it was entirely the product of her imagination. Possibly it was only a dream that after several repetitions she had taken to be true as if it had really occurred.

That dream was different from the other dreams. In other dreams she had walked into a deep, impenetrable darkness, but this dream gradually faded into a paleness enshrouded by mist.

There was something ghastly about that dream. Swathes of white extended in every direction—white walls, a white chair, a white picture frame, and white sheets. At the front of the table there was a single, half-withered rose, poking its head out of a translucent glass vase, spying on everything that occurred around it.

The white sheets moved, and from underneath them appeared a pale thin face. The tightly pursed lips, like the half-withered rose, were a decadent, almost black, crimson.

"Qingwu!" Shuiping called her name. A pair of bright eyes flew open. Due to her illness, her eye sockets were hollowed out and suffused in a sickly, bruised purple color. But once those eyes were opened, it was as though two brilliant pearls were shining out of a black cave. They seemed to scorch the mouth of the cave, leaving burned ashes piled up around the edges.

Qingwu had already entered the final stages of tuberculosis, but due to fever, her lips had burst into a bizarre crimson. As she stared at her, Shuiping found that she had never before seen Qingwu look so beautiful.

During Shuiping's freshman year in high school she and Qingwu had been in the same class. One the class president, one the vice president, they had sat, eaten, and lined up together. The two had lived in different districts. Qingwu would insist on seeing Shuiping onto her bus, and only then would she board her own bus home.

A peculiar sensibility undulated between the two of them. Due to their innocence they didn't dare guess, even less did they dare imagine what it meant.

Even though they saw each other all day long, Qingwu was constantly writing letters to Shuiping. In those letters, she would often lodge the shy feelings of friendship that she didn't dare articulate directly between the lines. After class was dismissed, Qingwu, who was sensitive to the point of neurosis, would always use an excessively cold tone to talk about the soul-stirring feelings found in poetry.

Shuiping would listen, half taken, half bemused. The unusual tone of voice would transform the sentiment of the words, conveying a chill beauty reminiscent of a snowflake.

Coming from Qingwu's mouth, the only thing that would remain of the line "The remnant leaves at the village on the creek—dancing red dots full of pathos" would be a single thin leaf, marked by the scars of sorrow.

In their sophomore year they had been assigned to different classes. Every day Qingwu would still come to Shuiping's class with her cloth-wrapped lunch box; sitting at her side, she would—with cold detachment—talk about the most heartrending matters. After school, with her book bag on her back, she would still stand outside of Shuiping's classroom, waiting for Shuiping.

Through the window of the classroom Shuiping would look out at Qingwu's silhouette as she stood motionless, lost in thought. In the drizzle, the silhouette would taper into an attenuated sliver. In her hand would be a twig splashed with a delicate green, the stem having turned an inky black after being soaked by the rain.

"That's a present from Qingwu!" As soon as she thought of this, Shuiping would feel vaguely unsettled.

It seemed that whenever Qingwu came, she would always have to bring a little something. Qingwu would always randomly pick up a sprig of something from her environs, and after school was out, would bring it to Shuiping. In the winter, when there wasn't anything to be found, she would bring along a dried up twig.

As exams approached, Qingwu would go to Shuiping's house to study. They would study until late at night, and Qingwu would naturally stay over. On the first such occasion, Qingwu changed into Shuiping's water-colored nightgown, but she wouldn't dare sleep next to Shuiping. Clutching a separate blanket she kept her distance, choosing a corner of the bed to lie down on. Shuiping wanted her to move over next to her. Qingwu replied, "That would be too presumptuous!" Upon hearing this, Shuiping was puzzled. She sensed that Qingwu felt awkward and confused. She didn't know what was bothering Qingwu, but at the same time didn't feel like reasoning with her anymore.

Afterwards Qingwu entered the hospital.

It must have been that Qingwu's past actions had gone too far. Within the girls' school, gossip circulated. Classmates would gather together and begin to whisper to each other. In low voices, they would use obscurely weird, even downright filthy and obscene words to describe Shuiping and Qingwu. Shuiping was called into the counselors' office for individual counseling several times. In the elections for the following year, Shuiping, who had always been the class president, lost for the first time.

"Shuiping! Come here!" Shuiping could hear Qingwu calling to her from a swath of emptiness that was as vast as a landscape painting. She leaned down, and pressed near, listening attentively to Qingwu's weak voice. Qingwu's two arms abruptly came up to tightly encircle Shuiping's neck. Her dark red lips radiated heat.

They pasted themselves to Shuiping's ear as Qingwu whispered a request. Shuiping suddenly blanched. Without waiting for Shuiping to reply, Qingwu's lips had already slid down Shuiping's temple and fastened themselves tightly on her lips. Shuiping couldn't struggle free. All she could think about were her classmates' disgusting rumors. Her long-standing nightmare had finally become a reality.

Qingwu seemed to have given into a feverish abandon. Dry, rough, and faintly tasting of medicine, her tongue searched Shuiping's mouth, wriggling, almost as if she had summoned up all her life's remaining strength, and concentrated it in a single kiss.

"Qingwu!" Shuiping screeched, and forcefully struggled free of the arms encircling her neck. In the course of her struggle, she knocked down a vase of roses. The red flower petals scattered all over, like so many withered red lips.

"You're disgusting!" Shuiping fled to the doorway, turned toward Qingwu, who was flailing around in an attempt to sit up, and contemptuously spat out this one remark.

Shuiping never went back to see Qingwu again. During the month before Qingwu died, there was only one thought that ran through Shuiping's mind: "Qingwu is filthy!" The sensation of feverish lips and the moment of the tongue stirring within her mouth admixed with the uncleanliness of the medicine remained upon her lips at all times.

She felt that Qingwu's behavior had ruined their beautiful friendship.

Before Shuiping could prove anything, Qingwu passed away. Taking with her that one and only kiss in her whole life, and in spite of its innocence, she passed away amidst guilt, self-blame, and heartbreak. The outcome was so ugly that it alarmed Qingwu. She had been filled with sincerity in wanting to complete her last reluctant good-bye to this world. But in that look of loathing she had instead discovered the ugliness of life.

Nothing had been resolved by her death. Marked with the imprint of Shuiping's lips, the dead woman's lips were little by little withering and rotting in the dark. Whenever Shuiping thought of this, she was secretly terrified.

As time passed, the curse of the one who had died continued its hold on the one who was still alive.

# 7

# FEVER

Hong Ling

*Translated by Paola Zamperini*

Right after four a.m., with a bewildered mien, a girl ducked into an inexpensive hotel in a deserted part of town. Her pale little face was trembling with cold, her hands were clutching a heavy black coat. Her movements revealed, besides agitation, an eerie quickness. Her nervous fingers firmly held onto the worn surface of the wooden counter. Although from the hotel's appearance it seemed that riffraff would not be admitted, the place still looked exceptionally desolate, quite unlike the more typical gaudy love motels. The stern-faced girl at the front desk barely opened her sticky eyelids to glance at this strange guest; in fact, it could already be considered a sign of exceptional interest that she cast more than one glance at that bone-colored face.

The young girl, whose body was shrouded in a frigid hue, would have left people with a chilly and frosty impression, if it hadn't been for her thin lips: set against her ivory-white face, their virulently red luster came as a shock. Having the beautiful luster of blood drops about to fall, these lips gave people the mistaken impression that her entire body, from head to toe, sent out an uninterrupted powerful red glow.

Combining the sharpness of the waxing moon and the softness of the waning moon, the contours of her lips, finely inlaid on her fair skin, looked like the marks of the aerial path of a red phoenix bathed in fire, speeding with irresistible momentum on an earth devoid of the color of blood, stirring up a barely controllable, barbarous, and violent blaze in its wake.

This is what the young woman who filled in as a front desk clerk, her eyes still heavy with sleep, thought as the girl rushed into her room and quickly closed the door behind her. When she sat back down in her chair and entered again the realm of sleep, she couldn't help dreaming of the fiery glow of beautifully red logs, embers still ablaze, on a ground covered by silvery snow, a glow that became unruly and turned into a wild blazing fire that scorched the surface of the earth. The burning hot white snow hissed and screeched.

The girl dejectedly leaned against the door in the ugly room, and slowly sank to the floor. She took off her impermeable coat, breathing heavily yet peacefully. Yes, she had a fever.

Fever? It was really a downright megajoke, funny enough to do away with all the clever and witty creatures that did not lack a sense of humor! How could an ageless and immortal vampire that had the body temperature of frozen water get sick all of a sudden, and come down with a fever of all things?

She laughed hoarsely and with difficulty. Panic-stricken, realizing that the current of heat coursing through her belly and her chest almost came spurting out along her bronchi—the vampire covered her mouth with the back of her hand, and forced herself to swallow the pungent and bitter magma, fearing that her mouth would really give off a poisonous blaze that would not have left a single part of her flesh intact.

No, it would not only have destroyed her flesh. The fire of her heart, hidden for a long time, had already gnawed away her viscera till her skeleton had disappeared. Each drop of sweet juice sucked from the neck of her prey was absorbed in a flash by the petrified cells, dried up like rust, leaving her unable to get the least satisfaction. Her body temperature, which had increased in the course of the night, made her restless and uncomfortable. Finely intertwining a mountain of knives and a bed of needles on every inch of her skin, the purgatory's unceasing punishment reminded her that lack of desire was the source of all original sins—especially for a vampire.

Having passed through centuries in which countless skeletons were piled high, the eternal companion that she had been at last able to find had died of a hemorrhage while having an abortion, as she stood by idly and indecisively, deprived of her powers by the daylight sun.

More than once, she had eagerly hoped that those blood drops overflowing from the stainless steel operating table could bring her back to life as they seeped through to the coffin under the earth and emptied into the crack of her mouth from which her canines protruded slightly. Alternatively, she had hoped that she could do the human women she loved a small favor—in the climax in which the desire to live forever was mixed with that of wanting to die, she could use her sharp teeth to gently probe the soft and moist vagina, her mouth like a greedy sucking disk, and while she would suck out the scarlet bodily juices, she could also swallow into her belly the lump of tissue attached to the uterus that had not yet assumed the shape of an embryo. This way, she solved their problems and she could also nourish herself!

Oh, if it were like this, if it were like that. If she were to take any action, she could bring back to life all the women she loved, bringing them back "forever"!

Those unshakable regrets and reveries had made it impossible for the girl vampire to sit or stand still. Immensely terrified, she had roamed through the bright metropolitan night scene amidst the tall and large neon ads which a few days earlier had still cheered her up. That night, when she had happened to see this dilapidated, ghostly little hotel sticking out unexpectedly from a back street in a neighborhood that she had wrongly believed in ruins, she suddenly conceived a vicious idea. Perhaps she should spend the night there, and experience first-hand how things stood when one faces the sun.

Sooner or later, her steadily increasing body temperature would become a fiery hot cattail and burst through her natural body. Thus it was better to forge ahead, disregard the consequences, and test the strength of the sun. Perhaps the flow of light outside her skin and the bright fire inside her would annihilate each other. Even if there might be nothing left of her but a pile of smelly ashes, there was nothing else in the world besides sunlight that could cure her weird disease.

The room's window was facing the direction in which a perfectly round sun would very soon gradually rise—the bright yellow sphere of fire that had always passed her so closely that they almost rubbed up against each other was about to float out from the bottom of her persistent line of vision. The blazing rays were on the verge of piercing her body, which was shaking and trembling uncontrollably. The vampire, not without joy, imagined the peculiar pleasure of the rays lacerating the skin. At last, she too could taste the wild gallop of the heart just like her prey when she sucked their blood.

She lifted up her head to look at the clock on the wall. It was already six-thirty a.m. As she looked through the big transparent windowpane just in front of her, the sky was a hazy and misty dove-gray color.

What? She couldn't figure it out. If there was no sunshine, there was no daybreak.

She stood up subconsciously, and pushed with her back the service bell on the wall. All of a sudden, the glowing screen of what seemed a small TV lit up in the middle of the room. Flickering in front of her eyes, the smiling face of a middle-aged woman, who looked like the manager of the hotel, inquired what service she required.

The vampire haltingly asked about the time of the sunrise. When she heard the question, the face of the manager twisted suddenly, assuming a strange and suspicious expression. Her casual tone changed, and she answered in a cautious manner:

"From the last year of the twentieth century, after the ozone layer in the atmosphere broke, the surface of the globe has been covered by a protective screen to eliminate the light in order to protect the health of the skin of the inhabitants of the whole earth. It's already been fifty years. Now daylight and nighttime are accurately determined by human intervention. . . . Miss, are you all right? You don't look well. You have a fever, don't you?"

# 8

# IN SEARCH OF THE LOST WINGS OF THE ANGELS

Chen Xue

*Translated by Patricia Sieber*

When I first laid eyes on A-Su, I decided that she and I were kindred spirits. We were both angels who had lost their wings. Our eyes were fixed on heights only attainable through flight. Our bare feet trod on a blistering and firm soil, but we had lost the sense of direction ordinary humans would have had.

Through the windows, the streetlight seeped into the dark room, softly illuminating A-Su's naked body. She had put her arm on my shoulder, and as she lowered her head, she looked at me. A head taller than I, she had two bright eyes, which were burning like two unsteadily flickering flames.

"Caocao, I want you very badly. I want to find out what kinds of secrets are hidden within your body. I want to know you, to savor you, to penetrate you . . ."

A-Su's husky voice slowly made its way into my ears. I was inadvertently overcome with dizziness. She started to undo my buttons one by one, then she took off my shirt, my bra, and my short skirt. My underwear seemed like a white flag, fluttering lightly between her fingertips.

Getting naked and becoming extremely intimate with her—all that was fated to happen in the instant when I first saw her.

She embraced me softly. My eyes faced her erect nipples. Indeed, she had a pair of breasts so beautiful they made me feel ashamed. Compared to her, I seemed like a prepubescent girl. So what secrets could this puny self of mine possibly harbor?

As we were lying on A-Su's soft and large bed, both of her hands felt their way around my body, venturing hither and yon. As if muttering an incantation, A-Su mumbled to herself: "These are Caocao's breasts." "This is Caocao's nose."

Gliding down all the way from my eyes to the nose to the mouth and to the neck, her fingers resembled the magic wand of a divine fairy. Shivers of pleasure would emanate from every spot her fingers had touched.

"Caocao's breasts."

Her fingers stopped at my nipple and lightly drew a circle around it. After a slight shiver, a warm and moist tide suddenly and unexpectedly engulfed it. It was A-Su's lips. She sucked the nipple softly.

At last, she stroked apart the dense pubic hair in my crotch. Layer by layer, she pried my private parts open. Step by step, she drew closer to the core of my being.

"It tastes like tears."

When A-Su was sucking on my genitals, my tears had dropped into my crotch. Amidst the salty wetness of tears, I reached an orgasm unlike any I had had before. It seemed like a nightmare during a high fever. I fainted in feverish delirium, and as I fainted, I let out piercing screams and amidst those piercing screams, I was wrenched asunder.

I felt almost as if she had presumptuously penetrated my body, that she was ruthlessly pounding against my very being. She even seemed to want to break my every bone. Indeed, it was she. Even though she was a woman who did not have a penis capable of erection and ejaculation, she was able to penetrate my innermost being, touching depths beyond what any penis could have reached.

I have always dreamt of my mother, ever since I completely escaped from her.

We were in the suite of a luxury hotel. Her long hair, dyed russet, was fluffed up and curled; her eyes, highlighted with black eyeliner, sparkled wildly. A few other women, alluring just like her, donned heavy make-up and sported nothing but a bra and underwear as they wandered back and forth in the room. They snacked, smoked, and chatted idly in high-pitched voices.

I sat on the soft round bed, hugging the pillow, desperately chewing on my fingernails. My eyes only dared to look at the short white socks on my feet. I had not seen Mother in over a year. What on earth had happened to her? She originally had a head full of pitch-black long hair and a pair of fine long single-lidded eyes. Her nose was still as pronounced as it used to be. I could also make out the mole she had, a black dot the size of a rice grain next to her right eye. Still, this woman looked so unfamiliar. The strong smell of her perfume and the russet hair brought me to the verge of tears.

"Caocao, be a good girl, Mama has things to do. Go to the restaurant downstairs and eat some steak or go watch a movie! Play for a while and then come back to find your Mama, all right?"

She twisted my hair to help me redo my braids. Then she stuffed five hundred Taiwanese dollars into my hand.

I walked out in a daze and bumped into a man at the elevator door.

"What a cutie you are! You have to watch where you are going!"

He was a very tall man who wore a Western-style suit. I saw that he opened the door to Mother's room. He slammed the door shut. The room resounded with her laughter.

I neither went to eat steak nor watch a movie. As I sat in the train going home to my grandfather's place, tears ceaselessly streamed down my face. I tightly clasped the bills. My ears rang with the sound of her laughter as I watched the scenery outside the window fly past. I realized that my childhood had already come to an end.

That year, I was twelve years old.

After I completely escaped from her, I always dreamt of her. Time after time, in the dream, the train never reached the station. My tears would fly out the window and would be scattered like sighs. The clouds in the sky were scalding red and boiling hot. That was her reddish hair.

"In between your legs, there is a mysterious hollow. It is extremely sensitive, prone to trembling, and apt at making spring water well up. That place holds a mystery for me that I am very eager to explore. Dearest Caocao, I want to make you happy. I want to know how women achieve happiness from here."

A-Su put her hand into my underpants and stroked me. With a cigarette in her other hand and with her eyes squinting at me as I was writing, she smiled.

I could barely hold the pen steady.

Previously, I had always thought that my mother was an evil and dissolute woman. I hated her. I hated the fact that after I lost my father, she unexpectedly made me lose my respect for her as a mother. I hated that she made an about-face and became a stranger at precisely the moment when I felt most alone and abandoned.

I hated that even when I hated her she was still kind to me as though everything were as before.

After I met A-Su I finally knew what was called "doing dissolute and evil things," which I found, to my surprise, I had longed for for a long time. As it turned out, my mother had neither been dissolute nor evil.

A-Su was the incarnation of my innermost desires. She was a fantasy come true. What she represented was the source of my life's happiness and pain, that is, the womb that originally conceived me. After my umbilical cord was severed, I always repudiated that womb, I cursed it, but after the womb's death, it was the grave where I was buried.

"I am writing because I want to love."

I always thought that inside my body a sealed self was hidden away. What force had sealed it up in the first place? I did not know. And what did that self look like? I did not know. What I could vaguely sense was that beneath layers and layers of obstruction, something stirred uneasily. In my strangely twisted dreamscapes, in the sleep-talk uttered in a moment of weakness, in the uncontrollable pain that assailed me in the wee hours, that self appeared, lonely and hungry for love.

I wanted to love, but I also knew that before I had found myself again, I was a person incapable of loving anyone.

Thus I was writing in hopes of uncovering that hidden self. I wrote as though I were masturbating. I wrote as though I were going mad. When I was finished writing, one by one I tore the pages to shreds as though I were ejaculating. In that act of destruction, I attained an orgasm that I could not have possibly obtained through sexual intercourse.

The first story that I did not tear to shreds was "In Search of the Lost Wings of the Angels." A-Su was a step ahead of me and snatched the pages away from me. At that time I had only written half the story and I felt that I did not have what it would take to continue it, but she read it that very night and after she finished it, she made wild love to me.

"Caocao, finish it, give it a chance to have a life."

A-Su put the pen in my hand, embraced my naked body, and placed me gently on the chair before the desk.

"You should not fear your own genius, because this is your destiny."

I saw a genius wearing a monstrous mask, precariously crawling out of a filthy pool of mud. The genius took pains to extend both of its scrawny arms, they reached forward, again and again, crookedly facing pages of text whose blank squares extended like a long ladder.

In the past, I had slept with countless men.

The year I turned seventeen I came to know about intercourse through the body of a man ten years my senior. Without the slightest hesitation I let him stick it in between my legs. Although this caused a sensation of pain that is difficult to describe, I was still instantaneously and intensely happy when I saw a pool of lush red blood on the bed. It was the joy over a revenge of sorts. Finally, I would no longer need to cry about all the absurd suffering that my mother had passed on to me.

Once I was no longer a virgin, I felt liberated. I slept with countless men because I had found a means by which I could retaliate against her.

I wore the green school uniform of a particular high school that all young girls aspire to. My hair was cropped at ears' length. I had inherited my mother's beautiful features. Even though I was not as tall and lanky as she was, it seemed that my frail and petite physique touched people even more.

In the eyes of bystanders I was completely innocent and good-natured. The men who were fond of me always said that I resembled a radiantly translucent angel, and so I readily captured their hearts.

An angel? Heaven knows how much I hated this false appearance of myself as well as all the other attributes reminiscent of her.

My classmates were so young and pure, but by the time I became an adolescent, I was already old.

"Heavens! How can you be so completely unmoved?"

That's what the man who taught me about intercourse said after he had ejaculated.

He once again penetrated me very roughly. He savagely bit my tiny nipples, thrashed against me, and shook me as though he had gone mad. He alternately cursed me loudly and then implored me, until he finally lay prostrate on my chest and began to sob as though he were a helpless child.

"You monster! That I could love you this much!"

He kissed my badly swollen crotch and swore that that he would neither torment nor hurt me again.

I knew that actually it was me who tormented and hurt him. Later on, he became impotent. He said that there was a knife in my vagina that had cut off his penis and buried his love.

A knife? Yes, there was a knife not just in my vagina but also in my heart! The knife would cut off all bonds with other people in this world. Whenever anybody got close to me, they would risk getting drenched in blood.

I cannot remember when I went to that bar for the first time. In any event, it was one of those nights when I was utterly bored. In a befuddled state I staggered into a bar. To my surprise, their Bloody Marys turned out to be exceptionally good. They always played jazz music from long ago, the guests were few and far between, and what's more, no one paid any attention to each other. Everyone simply minded their own drinking and smoking. Nobody would come over and ask, "Miss, would you like to dance?" Of course, this was also the case because there was no dance floor to begin with.

So in this way, during the day, I carried my books in and out of the Literature Building, resembling an ordinary junior, while at night, I would hang around in the bar. I would drink the Bloody Marys he mixed, smoke, and incessantly write the stories that were doomed to be torn to pieces. His name was FK; he was the bartender behind the counter. He had a long fair face that did not allow one to guess his age. His hands were extremely shapely. When he caressed someone, his hands were as smooth and nimble as though he were playing the piano.

Later I would occasionally go with him to his small apartment, which was as tidy as a cat's nest. I drank liquor for which I did not need to pay. I listened to him play the piano, which could make one's bones melt. Later as we were lying on the squeaky box-spring bed, I would listlessly make love with him. His beautiful pair of hands could not elicit any music from my body, but he nonetheless continued to mix delicious Bloody Marys for me. Like a baby-sitter, he looked after me on all those sleepless and crazed nights.

"Caocao, it's not that you lack passion, it's just that you happen not to love me."

FK was one of the few men who was neither enraged nor disappointed by this circumstance.

When I saw A-Su, I had had six Bloody Marys.

When she opened the door and entered, the air in the entire bar was shaken up, even the rhythm of FK's cocktail shaker was out of sync. I lifted my head to look at her; all I saw was her back. She was talking to FK at the bar. When she suddenly turned her head around, her gaze collided with mine. Her long russet hair swirled around, turning into a large expanse of red spray.

Russet-colored hives rippled over my body.

I drank one Bloody Mary after another. In the blood-colored liquid, I saw her hand beckoning me. I felt that her lined and wildly shining eyes gazed at me with a curious smile. I felt that her body was about to burst through the fabric of her tight, low-cut formal black dress. I felt that her husky voice was whispering dirty words into my ear. In my trance, I realized that my underwear was completely soaked. Surprisingly, the person who aroused a consuming desire within me turned out to be a woman.

She was the spitting image of what I remembered of the part that could not be touched. Under her intent stare, I seemed to have returned to the womb. I felt moist and warm and I could hear the sound of the pulsating blood vessels.

I plunged headlong into the glass, fully intending to kiss her lips.

In my dizzy stupor, I could taste the Bloody Marys that had been disgorged from my stomach into my mouth. I saw how she came closer one step at a time. Suffused in a rank body odor, a tall voluptuous body engulfed me, blotting me out . . .

When I first opened my eyes, I smelt this rank odor. This was the sexiest thing I had ever tasted.

I had a splitting headache. I made an effort to pry open my tingling eyes. I discovered that I was lying on a gargantuan round bed. Coming in through the French windows, sunlight bathed the room, making it bright and warm. I struggled to sit up, surveying my surroundings. This was a large room of roughly two hundred square feet. The simple and striking decor consisted of furniture whose red, black, and white hues blended with each other. Amid all of it, I found myself alone, as though it were a wondrous dream unfolding in color.

I was certain that this was her apartment; it simply had to be. I was still wearing the same clothes I had worn the night before, but apart from the headache I could not remember how I had gotten here.

Suddenly, the red lacquer entrance door swung open. I finally saw her coming toward me. Her face was not made up. She was wearing a t-shirt and jeans. She was even more beautiful than I had imagined her.

"I am A-Su."

"I am Caocao."
She had come!

When I tasted semen for the first time, I knew that in this life I would never be able to reach orgasm with a man.

After I had just moved in with Mother, I would often see male strangers drift in and out of Mother's room. Once, after a man had left, I opened the door to her room. I saw the messy bedding, I heard the sound of running water from the bathroom. It was she, taking a shower. The wastepaper basket next to the bed was stuffed with toilet paper. As I approached it, a rank odor wafted toward me. That was the odor of semen mixed with other bodily fluids, I just knew it!

I ran back into the other room and violently retched without stopping.

Why did I still want to open the door to her room? I don't know whether I wanted to prove something I already knew. It was as though I only wanted to painstakingly, desperately remember—to remember the dubious relationships between my mother and those men so that I could persevere in opposing them in my own life.

I was thirteen then. I had just had my first period, but I already knew about too many things which young girls should know nothing about. Other than what I had learned about sex in the health and hygiene class in junior high school, such knowledge was tainted with guilt and hatred.

As far as the past was concerned, I have never been able to recount it chronologically. My memories are fragmentary and episodic. The facts have been twisted in my imaginings and in my dreams. Suspended between shame and revulsion, things are hazy and formless. Even if I attempted to trace them to the source, I still could not piece together all the details.

I remembered that the chaos began when I was ten years old. The age of ten. It runs through my life like a categorical dividing line. To the right of that line, I was an ordinary child of an ordinary family; to the left, I allowed myself to become enslaved to fear and loathing.

That year, on his way home from work, my young father was injured in a car crash. The other driver made a getaway, leaving my father lying unconscious in a pool of blood for goodness knows how long.

Mother madly rushed about without concern for anything but my father. She swore that she was going to nurse him back to health, but after half a month, amidst the sobs of my mother and my grandfather, he let go of their hands and passed away.

A month later Mother disappeared without a trace.

I was living at my grandfather's house in the countryside. I turned into a mute child. Whenever I saw my aged grandfather and his tearstained face, I was unable to say anything. I could not cry, either.

I was terribly afraid. I feared that once I opened my mouth, this nightmare would turn into reality. I'd rather endure various forms of pain in the hopes that one morning I would open my eyes and discover that all of this was nothing but a scary dream which would fade away together with the darkness of the night.

I did not speak. Day after day, the sun rose, but everything was still real. Whenever I woke up in the morning, the sun would shine into my eyes as before, but what I found before me was an increasingly feeble grandfather, the black-and-white altar photo of my father, and a mother whose whereabouts were unknown, but about whom the villagers spun various tales.

"A-Su, why can't I simply love her or hate her? Why don't I give her a chance to live on?"

I was sucking A-Su's breast. I longed for my infant years, I longed for my mother's ageless breasts, which were as beautiful as A-Su's. I thought of the love, which had been severed as soon as I had left the womb. Before I knew it, I started to sob.

From the very beginning I knew that A-Su made a living off men's desire for her. But while she roamed amidst the covetous glances of men, she cultivated her own beauty and pride. Nobody was able to possess her.

She said that the night she had found me in a drunken stupor and had brought me back home, I had laughed and cried and thrown up all over her. After I had woken up, I had sat on the bed in a daze for quite some time before she pushed open the door and came in.

"I am A-Su and from now on, why don't you live here? I can see right away that you are a spirit without a home."

Yes, A-Su, you were right, I did not have a home. The apartment that my mother had bought for me was an empty nest. Only my books and my bodily shell inhabited the tiny, overpriced room in the basement of a building close to school. As for men like FK, their variously appointed apartments were nothing but temporary havens; with an angelic mien, I would drift through this world, indistinct like a solitary ghost. I really was looking for a tomb to house my empty and fallen soul.

Various men shuttled in and out of A-Su's large room, yet I thought of home there. A-Su's rank odor pervaded the entire space and made me feel quite safe.

This is how I entered her wondrous world. During the day I got in her Jaguar to attend classes. In the evening, I accompanied her to scores of parties for rich businesspeople and influential officials. At night, I would wake up and find a prominent architect I knew from the newspapers lying naked between us, his penis shriveled up like a wretched old man's. Compared to A-Su, what dissolute and evil things had my mother done?

Apart from her beauty and her clever and callous finesse, A-Su's most important weapons were her shamelessness and her indifference. She neither trusted men nor did she feel anything for them, which meant that she invariably had the upper hand in any games of conquest.

All my pitiable mother had was a messy bed and a broken heart.

Their pockets lined with cash, men were longing to conquer A-Su's body. A-Su was longing to bring back to life the dead love within me, and I, what was I longing for?

I longed for death. After Mother's death, I wanted nothing more than to be buried with her like a funerary object.

I sat at the counter in the bar, writing. The Bloody Mary that FK had mixed on that day was as sour as heartburn. It was practically undrinkable. It was the first time I had returned to this place since I had gotten together with A-Su.

"FK, you are perverse! Your Bloody Mary tastes like horse piss!"

When I lifted my head to look at him, I noticed that he had become feeble and aged.

"I have known A-Su for over two years. In all this time, I have never seen her look at anyone with this kind of an expression in her eyes. Caocao, she has fallen in love with you."

FK sat down beside me, gulping down half a glass of vodka. "In the beginning, I only wanted her body. Even that wasn't easy, I spent a lot of effort and money waiting for her to be in the mood to sleep with me. Of course, there were guys who were worse off than me. They would throw money at her. In a flash, she was gone, and there was no way that they could even dream of touching the tip of her fingers. After I made love to her, I lay next to her and I wanted to hug her badly. She unclasped my hands and got up. With a lowered head, she looked at me and smiled faintly before she recited a poem by Baudelaire.

"Caocao, I knew then that I was done for. I did not just want to ejaculate in her body, I had completely unexpectedly fallen in love with her.

"She said, 'Don't waste your money, it's no use.'

"She was right, it was no use. All along I thought that she was a cold-blooded creature, now I finally figured out that she loves women! So there is no hope left for me."

A sadness that I had not previously seen suffused FK's face. So A-Su had fallen in love with me? I knew that, but what did it mean? What did it mean? When I started thinking about the delicate relations between the three of us, it all seemed completely absurd.

Had FK's beautiful hands been able to elicit music from A-Su's body?

A-Su, you love women. Does that mean you love your mother? Was it possible that you had suffered endlessly because you could fathom neither your love nor your hatred for her?

Once I started attending junior high school, Mother requested that she fetch me so that we could live together. That is how I came to attend a famous middle school.

Regardless of where we stayed—be it a hotel, a guesthouse, an inexpensive apartment, or some luxurious summer villa—I always had my own room and an inexhaustible allowance. I did not have any friends, just a room full of books and records and my taciturn self.

We seldom spoke with each other. She and some old friends would often come back late at night, completely inebriated. They were a group of pretty and fashionable women who, with their high heels in hand, would cry and laugh on the streets.

When I was woken up at night, I discovered that she would sit at the foot of my bed and weep. I quickly pretended that I was asleep, but I could not go back to sleep anymore. The next day, I would doze all day long in class. Upon coming home, we would again coldly look at each other.

My feelings for her died the year when I turned twelve. No matter how hard I tried, all my efforts just made us more miserable. For one thing, I had to confront the pressure of an endless battery of examinations at school; for another, I also wanted to reject her loving concern for me. Just when I became an adolescent, my nascent sexual desires tormented me to the point where I was barely human.

Finally, I passed the entrance examination for the high school of my choice, which allowed me to move out of her sphere very naturally. When she read the acceptance letter, she gave me a rare and radiant smile. The day after, she bought me a set of novels in translation. The blue covers of each volume tumbled and tossed before me like waves of seawater.

"Don't constantly lie reading on your bed! You will ruin your eyes!"

She placed the books one after another on the bookshelf. She spoke without looking at me. I also picked up a book, but somehow I was unable to put it up on the shelf, even though the shelves weren't all that high.

I cried for the first time in a very long time, behind her back, silently. The tears dropped on the page, one by one. The book in question was Camus' *The Stranger*.

I moved into an apartment building near school that catered primarily to students. I began to play various games between me and men. I was like a diseased flower, whose pistil, at the moment of full bloom, had already withered.

"Caocao, I love you. Although I know that you don't need my love, I still love you. If I can't love you, I would have no way of making my life complete."

Dispirited, I was lying on pages of writing paper that were scattered all over the floor. I wailed over my failure to express myself adequately. A-Su stretched out her hand and lifted my chin. The expression beneath her unkempt bangs was very vacant, as though a gigantic black hole was about to swallow and eclipse me. I was apprehensive. Was this how she looked when she loved someone?

I clasped her in my arms, kissing and caressing her without stopping.

A-Su, I don't understand. I do not understand what there is to love about me. I do not understand how you love me. I understand even less why the women who love me always fling themselves in the arms of men and why they become gradually vacant and old when faced with me. If neither one of us loved the other but we just energetically made love, couldn't we live a little bit more happily?

I did not understand love, I only knew that this body of mine which had been ice-cold and numb in the embrace of men had been revived by A-Su's caresses. It had begun to be consumed by an inner fire. It had become sensitive and wild as though all of its pores had opened up and were breathing heavily. The slightest touch or motion could make me tremble or scream.

"A-Su, I want you, even though I still cannot love anyone. I want you. You are the woman for whom I have waited all my life. Only through you will I once again be reunited with myself."

I really don't remember the details about Mother very clearly.

During high school, I shuttled back and forth between school and men. During class I always assumed the attitude of a top student. I traded one boyfriend for another. The things that troubled ordinary high school students I could easily overcome, but of the things that I truly desired I could not obtain a single one. The novels that my mother sent me sustained me whenever I was on the verge of a breakdown. When plagued by insomnia, I would resort to reading Kafka while masturbating.

Each month on moonless nights, Mother and I would eat dinner together. In a restaurant awash in soft lights and light music, we would sit face-to-face, smoking silently or uttering little of consequence.

I don't know whether it was an excess of pepper on the steak or the sting of the smoke. I saw that her eyes were moist. The flesh beneath her sockets had started to turn blackish-green. Underneath her heavy make-up, a profusion of fine wrinkles lined her face so that whenever she laughed, it seemed as though she had fallen into a puddle of mud. Altogether, she cut a sorry figure.

At times the phone would ring at night. On the other end of the line, her voice was choked with sobs. The smell of alcohol would transpire from the receiver so obtrusively that my head started to seriously ache.

I knew that we had already reached the end of our lives. Even though we just needed to stretch out a hand in order to save each other from the extremities of despair, in the end, neither offered the other a helping hand, or perhaps we had already exhausted ourselves in holding out our arms, but in the end, misconstrued each other's whereabouts?

I had never been able to look back.

That is to say, until I met A-Su.

A-Su was the spitting image of my mother. As a result, every time after I made love with her, I would dream of events which I had either repressed or forgotten. One by one, they would clearly reconstitute themselves in my memory. Intoxicated by A-Su's lewd laughter, I became subconsciously aware that I had misunderstood my mother.

Step by step, I drew closer to my mother's naked spirit and finally it dawned on me how cruelly and unjustly I had treated her all along.

It was me, my selfishness and cowardice, which had forced us into this abyss of misery and pain.

I remembered. Mother, I gradually remembered your face, how it looked after you removed the make-up. With eyelids swollen from crying, your eyes had turned into fine slits. You were exactly like the person from my childhood years whom I had missed so badly!

It was the summer vacation of the year I passed the university entrance examination. I had a job at a restaurant that served Western-style food. I had started to let my hair grow and I had learned how to drive a car.

In mid-September, as I was leaving work one evening, I saw Mother sitting in front of the restaurant in an Austin Mini. Somehow her tall physique and the diminutive car seemed incongruous. I got in. I saw that she was not wearing any make-up. She was entirely dressed in white. She drove very attentively in the darkness, while I had no idea where we were headed.

We came to Father's cemetery. Since he had been buried, it was the very first time that she and I had come there together.

That night, the cemetery was so tranquil and peaceful. Amid the tall stalks of wild grass, fireflies flitted back and forth. Underneath the silvery light of the moon, clad in a white shirt and a white skirt, she leisurely traversed the wild grass. She resembled a beautiful female ghost, lightly floating above the ground.

"This is Caocao, our child. Isn't she beautiful? And she is as smart as you were.

"She has not forsaken you. She has gotten into university. We can finally consider her a grown-up.

"And I miss you terribly . . ."

Amidst a gentle evening breeze, her clear and bright voice sounded lighthearted, like the songs little schoolchildren hum on their way home after class.

I saw that Father's name was engraved on the tombstone. The various wild grasses on the grave mound resembled his unkempt hair. The father that I had already forgotten suddenly appeared in front of my eyes: he was riding the same old bicycle, wearing his black-rimmed glasses, and shouting at the top of his lungs long before he had reached the gate of our home:

"Caocao, Papa has come back!"

He was as young as he was then.

I turned around to look at my mother. I discovered that she had cut her hair short. With her beaming face, she looked like a good-natured child. As she squatted on the ground, she gently stroked the tombstone with both hands as though she were caressing the chest of the man she loved deeply. Her face glowed with happiness.

In that instant, I suddenly wanted to hug her tightly, telling her in a loud voice that I loved her. Actually, I had loved her all along. No matter what she had done, she could not alter the love I had for her.

However, I did not do any of that. Even though my heart was about to burst, my whole body was immobile like a rock, unable to budge. Everything, everything was already too late.

I don't know whether I could have changed her mind if at the time I had dared to embrace her and let her know my true feelings. I think it is unlikely. Things could not have changed at that point. At that point, I was only temporarily moved. I had not yet truly forgiven her nor myself.

Three days later she committed suicide. Her naked body floated in the bathtub. A blood-red stream had gurglingly surged forth from the wrist of her right hand.

After I lost her, I received substantial savings, a flat of over six hundred square feet, and that Austin Mini.

Once I started attending college, I became a person without a past. I would spend the whole day drifting in and out of an alcohol-induced daze. At the same time, I began to write as though I had gone mad.

All along, A-Su had been an enigma. Our living together seemed like a dream. If I wasn't following her as she drifted through various grotesque and gaudy settings, I was in her flat with her where we were incessantly drinking, smoking, making love as we tumbled and rolled from place to place, joking, or whispering half-formed sentences into each other's ears. When A-Su went out, I either wrote as though my life depended on it or I was completely absorbed by the daydreams in which I pieced together my past. No normal or concrete particulars gave even a semblance of structure to our lives. We never interfered with or even inquired about each other's secrets, with the result that neither one of us knew the other's full name nor anything about the other's background or past history.

"There is nothing more stupid than wanting complete and thorough understanding from another person."

That was A-Su's motto.

All along she was an enigma, but what was at the root of this enigma was unimportant. I never concerned myself with getting to the bottom of other people's secrets; all I cared about was the implicit meaning their mystery held.

I vaguely sensed that there was something waiting for me somewhere, waiting for me to draw near and once I did, I would be able to understand. For so many years, I had painstakingly sought after it, but in the end, my efforts had all been futile until A-Su appeared. Her appearance was a signpost to guide me. But what was I looking for after all? What would I be able to understand? I did not know.

"What we need is a pair of wings. Once we find them, we can once again soar freely."

That's what A-Su had said in the beginning. So I applied myself and wrote a story entitled "In Search of the Lost Wings of the Angels." Now the story was drawing to a close, but A-Su, what about our wings?

"Caocao, you only have to write continually, then on paper, you will see me, and you will see yourself. I did everything because I wanted to reveal this one thing to you, namely the importance of writing. You must never cease to write. You don't have a choice, it's your destiny. The very first moment I met you, I saw the frenzied expression of a writer on your face.

"It was that frenzy which brought me into your life."

"A-Su, I know that I must write. But what about the wings that we have already lost?"

That night was the last time we spoke to each other.

"They must be somewhere."

She clutched my hand tightly. Her palms sweated faintly and trembled slightly.

I had a dream about A-Su.

In the dream, we were floating in the air, we were enveloped by a layer of something cold and translucent like ice. As we ventured hither and yon, our bodies caught on fire and we rolled around, utterly consumed by this scorching heat, making love with complete abandon. To us, life was so supple and spirited, but in the eyes of bystanders, we were nothing but smoke and ashes, which no one would pay any heed.

Suddenly, A-Su let go of my hand and flew away. With my eyes wide open I watched her flutter away, soaring as she flew, but I did not have any means to break free from the fetters. On the contrary, I felt that the pressure on all sides grew even more intense.

"A-Su! Save me!"

My own scream woke me up. All I remembered was how A-Su had tossed me a single phrase from the air:

"Caocao, in everything, you need to depend on yourself."

After I woke up, I found myself in the basement room where I had previously lived.

Piles of writing paper covered with words were strewn all over the desk. The title read "In Search of the Lost Wings of the Angels." On the last piece of paper two words had been written in English in capital letters: THE END.

The story was already finished! "A-Su, look, the story is finished," I shouted loudly. A-Su? Why had I returned to this place while A-Su had disappeared without a trace? In the story, it was all elaborated in detail, but where had A-Su gone in the end?

I neatly arranged the pages of the manuscript and decided that I was going to look for her.

As I stepped out the door, the dazzling sunlight pained my eyes. I stood transfixed in the intersection. One car after another flew past me. When the red light went off, the green light came on, when the green light went off, an orange light came one. As I gazed at the crowds of people rushing past, tears suddenly rolled down my face.

I could not remember. I could simply not remember where A-Su lived. I did not have the slightest clue. The street? The number? The floor? I did not have the faintest idea. I made every effort to track down all the details in the story, but that yielded absolutely nothing. I did not even know her name!

How could that be?

I thought of FK. He would surely know where to find her.

"A-Su? Who on earth is A-Su? A pretty woman I would certainly not forget, but I don't know of anyone called A-Su."

FK vigorously shook his head.

"No, and no again. There is no A-Su. Caocao, aren't you drunk?"

I had lost her! I clasped my arms tightly around the manuscript. I staggered around on the streets, disoriented. A-Su's rank odor still clung to my body. How could I possibly mistake that seductive smell?

After nightfall I returned to my apartment. I sat on my bed as if paralyzed, while thinking through every aspect of A-Su.

"My name is A-Su."

I could still remember very clearly the sound of her voice when she spoke. A low, husky sound, which, when she laughed, would become brash and sonorous. When we walked together on the street, all the men would look at her but she only had eyes for me. She repeatedly sized me up from head to toe, as though she used her eyes to strip me of every piece of clothing. Her way of looking at me made my face blush and my heart jump, but I was unable to do anything about it.

"Caocao, how is it possible that you are this beautiful? When I look at you, my underwear gets soaked."

Having brought her head close to my ear, she was whispering into it. Then she playfully bit my earlobe.

I still remember that A-Su loved lying on my small tummy while her fingers stroked my genitals. As she lay there caressing me, she sang.

> "Good little goat, open the door
> Open it a little more quickly, I want to come in."

With effort, I suppressed my moans. Trembling, I continued with the next stanza.

> "I won't open it because I can't open it
> You are the big wolf and I won't let you in."

We rolled around in the bed, laughing so hard we fell on the floor where we madly made love, only stopping when our energy was completely sapped.

I remembered that after A-Su read my story for the first time, she lifted up my face with both hands, contemplating it for a very long time, before she heaved a long and deep sigh.

"Ay! Caocao, you really drive a person mad!"

I was remembering everything, wasn't I? A-Su, I wrote the story for you, but where have you gone?

I don't know how many days had gone by. During the day I always roamed the streets, searching for a glimpse of A-Su in everyone. At night, when I was in bed, I recalled A-Su's smell again and again.

However, gradually my recollection began to blur. I had no real means to determine whether she had truly existed or had simply been a dream.

"Somewhere."

I thought of what A-Su had said, "Somewhere." That's where the solution would inevitably be found.

So where?

I had to find it. I jumped on the bus, rode on the train, I might even have gotten on a plane. I didn't know how to go about it, but I did know that there was a sound beckoning me and that I was gradually drawing closer to it.

To my consternation, I discovered that I had come to a graveyard.

A grave? So what I had been looking for was a grave.

Next to my father's grave there was another grave. I got closer to it. Some characters were engraved in the marble tombstone that towered above the ground:

Su . . .

Su as in A-Su.

Qingyu . . .

Su Qingyu was my mother's name.

Mother, I have come back. After I had been escaping from you for many years, I have finally come back.

I lay face down on my mother's grave, all curled up as though I were in her womb. I mumbled, telling her about all my feelings for her which I had not previously revealed. It was as involved and consuming as though I were just learning to babble. After I had drifted and wandered around for a long time, I felt for the first time that the ground underneath me was stable and dependable. I could finally clearly discern my feelings for my mother.

I love you. Unconditionally.

I faintly heard the sound of A-Su's laughter resound from the horizon. When I lifted my head, I saw that the clouds had gradually clustered together into a familiar form, flapping to the left and to the right.

It was a pair of wings.

# 9

# ANDANTE

He An

*Translated by Patricia Sieber*

It was the second day of the week, the twenty-second day of the eleventh month. Yinping glanced at her watch. It was eight o'clock. If one were to break the number eight into smaller units, then this moment would translate into 1122233, which seemed like a quote from a nearly forgotten but suddenly apropos advertising slogan. The year in the Western calendar—that is, 1994—did not fit well with this set of numbers. By contrast, the year in the calendar based on the founding of the Republic of China in 1911—that is, 83—was quite suitable. Eight equaled four plus four. If one reversed the order of the two fours and the three and then added that line from the commercial, then one arrived at 1122233344. That was a perfectly symmetrical arrangement. Adding up the numbers from left to right coincidentally enough equaled five times five. These kinds of mathematical games had never baffled her. It was too bad that she and Chunliang had not foreseen this. Otherwise, they could have prepared five kinds of fruit, five kinds of sweets, five kinds of salty snacks, five kinds of drinks, plus five kinds of eating utensils. Wouldn't that have been perfectly beautiful?

What if it wasn't beautiful? In her heart, another voice asked, "Then should this party not take place?" Yinping turned around and ignored the question, looking over the reception hall that could accommodate sixty or seventy guests. The room did not have any windows. It made one feel as though one had been placed in an exquisitely beautiful paper box.

She smiled as she approached the guard. She reminded him that the party would start at half past nine and asked him to open the door somewhat earlier. The brown-haired, green-eyed guard complimented her, saying that she was dressed up like a pretty sweet-faced woman out of a film. She nodded her head, laughing, "Right, it is all make-believe!" Without waiting for a reply, she left the room to go to the concert hall.

She hurried through the corridor, her feet barely touching the ground, climbed the stairs and rushed toward the back stage. Chunliang had already begun to play Bach. She never waited for people. "If you waited for everyone to settle down in their seats, your hands and feet would turn ice-cold, so you just assume that they are not coming." Nobody could insist on anything in front of Chunliang, but as soon as she stepped onto the stage, her features would soften instantly. At that point, she would become, in the words of one of her favorite expressions, "happy and pretty."

Standing behind a half-covered side entrance, Yinping stared at Chunliang's profile highlighted by the black color of the piano. Set against shades of black satin, her nape was suffused in an opal luster.

Since they had known each other, Yinping had never seen Chunliang's short hair cover her nape. She had no particular feelings for Chunliang's hair, but she was crazy about Chunliang's neck. When she was little, she would often gnaw on a chicken neck. After she had torn away the wrinkled skin, she would carefully rip apart the silky tendons underneath one by one. Often when she kissed Chunliang, the memory of this habit would return and arouse a burning sensation in her groin.

The night before, Yinping had climbed across the queen-sized bed, stealthily moving toward the piano chair. After quietly listening to Chunliang play for a few minutes, Yinping's index finger followed Chunliang's hairline past the side of her neck. Chunliang did not pay any attention to her. When she brought her head closer to nibble on her neck, Chunliang neither overtly responded nor did she push Yinping aside. When she began to feel amused because she discovered that the regular rhythms of Bach truly could not keep up with the pace of her breathing, Chunliang automatically switched to Chopin's languid melodies. Subsequently, even the notes from Chopin's airs became increasingly muddled. The music then changed to the flowing and lighthearted rhythms of Ravel. This went on until Chunliang suddenly covered her neck with her hands and screamed in a shrill voice, "That's too much! Stop giving me hickeys! How can I face people tomorrow night?"

Yinping had followed her to the door of the bathroom where she caught a glimpse of an utterly discomfited Chunliang wiping off the imprint of Yinping's lipstick with a wet towel.

"Don't you know that I am already nervous enough?"

Chunliang's voice was so tense that it seemed to give off sparks.

Of course I know how nervous you are. Yinping silently heaved a sigh. In the past two weeks, I have been at fault ten times more often than usual. Even if I don't do anything at all, I can still make you angry. Yinping returned to the room to grab the pajamas with purple and gray stripes.

Ever since they moved in together, they had saved quite a bit on clothes. The closet was full of outfits in dark colors. "If I wear pastels, I look like a translucent ghost," Chunliang grumbled. Yinping could not have agreed more. She remembered how on many mornings, the slanting sunlight would filter through the blinds and shine on Chunliang's body. In those moments, Chunliang would seem like a well-rested spirit on a spring morning on the steppe. Without anyone noticing, she might turn into a wisp of smoke, which would gradually disappear in the rising heat of the early morning sun.

Once Chunliang had changed into her pajamas, she was a lot calmer. Yinping squatted in front of her. "Don't worry, you won't mess up!"

"What if I hit the wrong key just then?"

"Even if you make a mistake, you don't let on. People won't be able to hear it."

"You can't fool me. How could the professor not hear it?"

"She knows your level of accomplishment."

"My classmates will also be able to tell. They might poke endless fun at me."

"Hmm." Yinping scrutinized the expression on Chunliang's face. "Haven't you told me that they have always admired you? This time, they are likely to say, 'This Wang Chunliang is truly formidable. Even at her graduation concert, she dares to improvise.' "

At this Chunliang smiled. She returned to the bedroom to engage in a methodical conversation with Bach.

Yinping's gaze found Chunliang's advisor below the stage. From the pleased expression on her face, Yinping gathered that Chunliang had been off to a good start. Chunliang brought out the serene smoothness of Bach's music; besides, the make-up hid the hickey.

After Chunliang and Yinping had become lovers, there was one occasion when Chunliang had squeezed Yinping's hand and laughed heartily. "Guess what happened to me today! I was chatting with a student from Mainland China when she said tactfully, "You really are interested in beauty." It took me the longest time to figure out that she was criticizing me for being too enamored of good looks. People from the Mainland really have an idiosyncratic way of talking." Chunliang laughed so hard that her forehead almost hit the surface of the table.

To accept Chunliang's "interest in beauty" had in fact been a great deal more difficult than Yinping had anticipated. Last year Yinping had moved into Chunliang's dorm. They had often strolled to a traditional market, where they ordered dinner. On the way there Chunliang was busy sizing up all the female passers-by. She would mutter, "The phrase that you pointed out to me in the paper last time is very apt: 'It's too bad that women are so heartless. For no reason they put on a show for everyone, leading on men.' I rather like women. Both their inner and outer selves are more appealing than men."

"What do you like about me?"

"I like that you are so pretty."

"I mean really." Yinping could not help but resist.

"I mean it." Chunliang responded in an offhand manner. Yinping's chest felt as though she was choking on an egg yolk.

"What's the matter?" Chunliang's line of vision shifted back to her left cheek.

"I thought that beside good looks I had other likable qualities."

"Well, in that case, what would you want me to like about you?"

"For instance," Yinping hesitated. "If there were a woman who looked like me but was mean, selfish, and vulgar . . ." She swallowed with difficulty. "Could you fall in love with her?"

"I could probably love her for two months—you know, such women can sometimes be interesting, too." Chunliang began to chuckle.

Yinping was not the slightest bit reassured. "What about the reverse scenario? What if you got along very well with a woman who wasn't all that good-looking?"

Chunliang thought for a moment: "I would probably treasure her as a friend, but . . ." She pulled Yinping through the crowds thronging the entrance of the market. "But it is unlikely that I would fall in love with her."

After they finished the dinner they had been eating in silence, they went back to the parking lot the same way they had come.

"Is it that important to know which exact part of you I've fallen in love with?" Chunliang held the steering wheel as she passed car after car.

"Well," Yinping let some time pass before she spoke quietly, "how do you know that what I like about you is your beauty and your talent? How do you know my falling in love with you wasn't just a coincidence?"

Chunliang's naked upper arm seemed to suddenly stiffen. "You have a point there, I acknowledge that." Yinping was almost prepared to put aside all pretensions and to reveal her deep-seated misgivings: well then, at what point will you coldheartedly disappear and take the beauty of our time together with you? In the end, she did not say anything. She knew that Chunliang was not given to reflecting on long-standing problems. If she had asked, it would have led to an embarrassing situation from which no one stood to gain anything.

Once in the middle of the night, Chunliang had woken up for some unknown reason. She saw Yinping sitting on the bedside with her arms wrapped around her knees.

"Have you had a bad dream?" she asked groggily.

It had in fact been an extraordinarily vivid dream. Yinping had dreamt that many colorful tents had been strewn across a radiantly green grassland. Chunliang had shuttled between the different stands until she had stopped in front of

Yinping. In the dream, Yinping solicitously sold her wares, in fact, she was so solicitous she hardly seemed herself. Even though Chunliang did not buy anything, she did not leave. Instead, she just stood there warmly smiling at Yinping. The lingering glow of the evening sun cast a golden border around her short hair. The long gown let the white light shine through as though it were filtered through the translucent wings of a cicada. It seemed as though Yinping's heart was set on fire, but at the same time she couldn't do anything about it. She was not sure how long she would have to idle away her time together with that spirit before her.

The dream was not real, but her past was. Yet how different was her recollection of the dream compared to her recollection of the past? In her memory of the distant past, Yinping could in fact not be entirely certain about what had actually taken place and what she had only dreamt of. Even if she were able to clearly distinguish between dreams and facts, she could not ascertain which feelings felt more real, the ones in her past or those in her dreams. When she attended Wenzhen's wedding, she felt completely calm. All she could think about was Wenzhen's joy and happiness. In her dreams, she had attended the wedding several times. In some of those dreams, she had cried until her heart broke, in others, she had silently sat on the side with an impassive face. So did she want to give her blessing to Wenzhen or did she want to curse both her and her husband? In the end, would she willingly continue to lead a happy life together with Chunliang in accordance with Chunliang's ideas of love or would she forcibly repress her grievances, only venting them in her dreams? Perhaps her emotions were likely to always be too complex and confused so that it was necessary to rehearse the same scene over and over in order to bring out all the different aspects and angles.

Yinping's vision slowly shifted from Chunliang's neck to her fingers, which were whirling back and forth between the ivory and ebony keys. Yinping liked Chunliang's pinkies best. If one held them up together, they were slightly bent. On the outside of the fingertips, each of them had a little black mole. On Chunliang's left hand, she was wearing a ring made of braided platinum and gold. Whenever they caressed each other, the ring would brush against Yinping' shoulders. Then it would feel as though an ice-cold stream poured into the hot flush of Yinping's excitement. Yinping tried to imagine their togetherness as Bach's right and left hand—the repetition of a similar theme, like a query taken up time and again, which was answered and exchanged, then once again further explored, thereby satisfying an innately similar desire through different approaches. However would they be able to reach a symmetrical and harmonious resolution? Or, as another voice asked in Yinping's head, were symmetry and harmony the only desirable outcome?

* * *

As Chunliang got up to bow toward the applauding audience, she looked over her shoulder, blinking mischievously at Yinping who was standing in the wings. In the front row, some members of the audience began to laugh.

After the applause subsided, Chunliang returned to the piano and began to play her second piece, Gershwin's "An American in Paris."

Toward the end of 1990, when Yinping met Chunliang for the first time in a choir, Yinping had just moved to Boston. Her roommate had insisted that she attend a Chinese-style hot pot dinner and Yinping failed to convince her otherwise. At the party, someone began to sing "Story," a composition by Huang Zi, which had been popular when Yinping had been in grade school.

> "I remember I was little then, I loved to chat, you loved to laugh.
> Once we sat shoulder to shoulder beneath a peach tree, the wind rustled in the branches, the birds were in the leaves.
> Without noticing we fell asleep, in our dream countless flower petals fell."

Yinping remembered that Wenzhen also had used to love singing "Story." She had inadvertently begun to hum along.

"You have got a good voice! Next month we'll have a performance and presently our choir lacks a mezzo-soprano." A young woman set out to pick up a mouthful of cabbage with her chopsticks. "How about it? On Friday evenings at seven-thirty. I can come get you. Oh, I forgot to tell you, my name is Lin Kerong. I study counseling at Boston University. You are Yinping, right?"

Yinping looked at her, panic-stricken. As she had listened to her, she had felt dazed. How was it possible that the manner of speaking of this Lin Kerong resembled Wenzhen to the point where every cell in Kerong's body appeared to imitate Wenzhen's mannerisms?

Their conductor was called Wang Chunliang. Yinping discovered that most members of the choir both loved and feared Chunliang. Naturally, there were also people who were put off by her arrogance.

At eight o'clock when they took a break, as Yinping lifted her head, she saw Chunliang's silhouette disappear at one end of the hallway.

"She is a lesbian." A choir member deliberately affected a secretive manner and said, "Someone saw her stroll hand in hand with a brown-haired green-eyed foreign woman in front of the Music Academy."

"Holding hands? What about it?" Another female student who had just arrived from Taiwan asked, "Doesn't the shopping area near Taiwan National University abound with girls who hold hands with each other?"

"That's different. You don't know that Americans want to avoid being misidentified as homosexual at all costs. So unless you are one, who would dare to walk on the street in such an intimate fashion?"

"Even if it's true, what's the big deal?" Lin Kerong impatiently butted in as she approached them. "She is here to conduct the choir. Why would you want to make those other matters your business?"

The woman who had first brought up the topic disapprovingly curled her lip. "You never know when something might happen."

In the spring of 1992, the members of the choir clashed over personnel issues. When everyone heatedly debated the issues up for a vote, Yinping and Chunliang's line of vision often crossed on the row of bright red cornel trees in front of the window. The cornel trees reminded Yinping of the phoenix flower tree in front of Wenzhen's old flat. When the leaves were all gone, Yinping withdrew from the choir, returning to the small world of her lab and her dorm.

Before she had left Taiwan for the U.S., Yinping had decided to switch her major to biochemistry. Toward the end of October of her first year abroad, Yinping began to wake up at four or five o'clock in the morning. Once classes ended, she was in a daze. She figured that the pressure from her language and literature classes was too great. Predictably, in December, once her grammatical mistakes became fewer, her appetite came back naturally. In her second and third year abroad, these symptoms returned promptly with the advent of autumn. In the fall of her fourth year, she did not hesitate in the slightest to hand over the responsibility for her emotional health to a psychiatrist and to an antidepressant.

One afternoon when she had arranged an appointment in spite of her general bewilderment, she came out of the doctor's office and sauntered along the street. A woman who was playing a banjo sang an old English air called "Greensleeves," which described a courtier's grief over having been abandoned by a beautiful woman.

The song reminded Yinping of her last year in Taiwan. During the late fall of that year, "Greensleeves" had accompanied Yinping as she filled out one application form for study abroad after another. It had accompanied her as she pulled out the pictures of Wenzhen smiling mischievously from her photo album and threw them into a paper bag. "Greensleeves" had accompanied her as she bore the damp winter rain, the sticky spring rain, and the fierce typhoon rains. Just before she left the country, she threw the record with that song into the trash can in order to prove to herself that she had the ability to forsake the past.

Then all of a sudden the third stanza of "Greensleeves" was followed by animated and cheerful conversation. A delicate figure appeared between Yinping and the woman with the banjo. Chunliang directed with both of her arms, making her short dress move about. The dress had long sleeves, which were as green as grass and were dotted with yellow flowers. Like a long shot in a film that simultaneously suggested closeness and distance, Yinping envisioned a field of dandelions extending on a riverbank all the way to the horizon.

"That's right! I am destined to be the spring of your life!" When Yinping recalled her impression of that encounter, it seemed as though Chunliang had been as confident as though she was singing a song.

"This is Judy, my classmate and ex-lover." Chunliang said in English, introducing the woman who had been singing "Greensleeves." She continued, "This is Ping, my current dream lady." Judy smiled graciously at Yinping. Without waiting for Yinping to nod and utter a greeting, Chunliang pulled her away, waving good-bye toward Judy.

"Where do you want to go?" Chunliang started the car. Yinping shrugged her shoulders, letting the other party decide where they were headed. Amazed by the woman next to her who had so brashly and exuberantly come into her life Yinping wondered where she was supposed to find a place for Wenzhen in her mind.

During all these years, Yinping had in fact indirectly heard news about Wenzhen. She knew that Wenzhen had had two children and that she had, together with her husband, been accepted into a doctoral program in Germany. Yinping figured that Wenzhen, a Libra, was probably extremely content: a boy child and a girl child—what a perfectly symmetrical arrangement! Yinping also liked children. However, the thought of Wenzhen's children was intolerable, making her feel humiliated, ridiculed, and embarrassed all at once. Their existence reminded her that a man could touch Wenzhen's body more profoundly than she could. These children mocked the whole idea of eternal love, in which she had so sincerely believed, but which was in fact a cliché so hackneyed not even TV soaps bothered to incorporate it into their scripts anymore.

In Yinping's junior year in college in Taiwan, the old Japanese-style courtyard houses in the alley where Yinping had grown up were leveled to make room for a multistoried building. The Liu family, which had previously been living next door, now lived downstairs from Yinping's family. When she was faced with the tall four-storied building for the first time, Yinping felt at a loss. The fences and fruit trees on the right side of the alley were all gone, and the magnolia tree in the front yard must have either been tilled under or perhaps it had been moved elsewhere only to be burnt there. That magnolia tree had watched over her and Wenzhen as they had grown up together.

The two of them had attended the same school all throughout high school. In their sophomore year, Wenzhen had suddenly grown tall. On the bus, Wenzhen would hold the ceiling bar with her right hand. She would lay her left hand around Yinping's shoulders. Regardless of how badly the bus shook or how crowded it was, all Yinping had to do was to hang onto her book bag and stand there firmly until they got off.

When the weather was nice, they would walk home. They would chat and assign points to the women who walked past them.

Wenzhen was particular about proportions, while Yinping's eyes usually went directly for the woman's skin. She looked and looked and finally her eyes would settle on Wenzhen's body. Wenzhen's arms had a healthy and bright luster. Her earlobes were soft and thick, just like the dough patties Wenzhen's mother, Mother Liu, made when she prepared dumplings. Under the sunlight the pink color of the capillaries shone through Wenzhen's honey-colored eyelids, which held her long and thin eyes firmly in place.

Most people at some point experience a time in their lives when they feel as adventurous and unfettered as Gershwin's *American in Paris*. The sense of being completely free had left Yinping when she had burned Wenzhen's photographs. By contrast, Chunliang seemed to have resolved to be a pretty and cheerful "American" her entire life. When Chunliang occasionally brought up earlier, painlessly resolved episodes of her romantic history, she would throw up her hands and wear an indifferent "That's the way I am" expression on her face. Yinping could not help but wonder whether Chunliang was secretly hinting at a future outcome or perhaps even revealing the forecast for the next day. Would their future also be derailed in this fashion? When the Charles River began to freeze over, Yinping became more and more attached to the warmth emanating from Chunliang's fireplace. At the same time, she paid less and less attention to the various ways in which Chunliang evaded the question of their future together.

She had learnt how to masturbate in Chunliang's arms. "You have to listen to the rhythm of your body," Chunliang whispered into her ear: "No one knows better than yourself where exactly you need to be further stimulated. . . . You don't need to rely on anyone else to achieve an orgasm, you know, we are all self-sufficient." As the twitching lodged itself successively more deeply in her body, Yinping knew that she had already reached the climax of physical pleasure. Behind her she heard Chunliang softly moaning. In a flash, she recalled another poignant moment—as Chunliang's wet and soft tongue had circled around the most sensitive spot of her body, an ice-cold finger had suddenly entered between her gums and her palate. When she made love to Chunliang, her orgasms were not as intense as when she masturbated, but she was deeply enthralled by the way Chunliang's touch elicited light and recurrent tremors from her body. Only then did Yinping not worry about the future nor did she reflect on how to come up with the perfect farewell gesture nor did she imagine how Chunliang would in the future tell their story to another woman.

Not long after Wenzhen began attending college in southern Taiwan, she told Yinping that she had found a boyfriend. His name was Zhang Zewei and he was a native of Tainan. In her letters, Wenzhen reported regularly about all aspects of her life although Yinping rarely wrote back. In her sophomore year, Yinping sent a Christmas card to Tainan, "I too have found a boyfriend." She did not even bother to sign it. He was a physics student and they had for some time practiced singing duets together. Without caring one way or another, Yinping did some things together with him like eating or going to the library.

In their senior year, Zhang Zewei had been sent back from the military outpost on Jinmen and reassigned to serve in Zuoying, a more comfortable posting in a small town in the south. Around New Year's, when Yinping had returned to her dorm room after watching the sandstorm from the top floor of the library, she unexpectedly received a certified express letter:

"His vacation started yesterday. He kept me company as I tried to meet the deadline for my papers. Even as midnight approached, I still wasn't done. He had fallen asleep on the bed. When it dawned, I was woken up by the sound of him slipping into my sleeping bag.

"He said that we had been together long enough and that he could not hurt me—he had even brought a condom. I figured that this was nothing too serious and in any event, it was bound to happen sooner or later.

"After he went back home, I crawled into bed and fell asleep again, returning to that feeling of being engulfed. However, unexpectedly, in my dream the person I was with was you. Just like he had kissed me, I kissed and caressed you. After I woke up, without knowing why, I started to cry and could not stop. I don't know how I can explain this to you or how I can face you. Yet I don't feel the same about him anymore. The whole day I think of no one but you."

In the following month or so, Yinping quietly broke up with her boyfriend, Huang Zhaohong, and left the choir. However, she did not hear anything from Wenzhen. In fact, Wenzhen did not even call her to arrange for them to return to Taipei for the Chinese New Year's holidays on the same train as they had done in previous years. One day, after she finished her experiments in the lab, she walked around the pond on campus several times. She figured that Wenzhen perhaps had regrets and that she should after all not mistake a scene from a dream for the real thing.

The last weekend before New Year's, Yinping bought two train tickets to go from Hsin-chu, her college town, to Taipei and put them in her wallet. She frowned. If Wenzhen did not show up the following day, should she go back to Taipei by herself or should she buy a ticket from an unlicensed bus company and travel down to Tainan to look for Wenzhen? Suddenly steps began to resound from the end of the hallway. Yinping dashed over to open the door, and as she had hoped, Wenzhen was coming toward her. However, the person in front of her was considerably thinner and paler than all the faces and postures of hers that she remembered.

The next day, Yinping was awakened by a tingling sensation.

Wenzhen's finger painted a picture on Yinping's chest. "When we get rich, we will buy a piece of land and build a small single-storied house on it. We will plant a magnolia tree in the garden . . ."

Yinping laughed as she leaned back toward her pillow.

However, Wenzhen did not leave Zhang Zewei. Still, Yinping did not grumble too much. She knew that Wenzhen had to reject her entire upbringing in order to enjoy their brief moments of happiness and passion together.

When Mother Liu called Yinping and her mother to come downstairs to help her daughter Wenzhen with her choice of a gown for the engagement party, Yinping finally began to blame Wenzhen. Unexpectedly, Wenzhen was allowing other people to carelessly violate the bond between the two of them. A month later, Wenzhen brought Zhang Zewei home. Wenzhen asked Yinping to make arrangements for the music at the wedding ceremony.

"You have nerve to torture me like this." After Zhang Zewei had left, Yinping could no longer suppress her indignation.

"It was my mother's idea." Wenzhen looked helpless. "You know my mother . . ."

"If it's that awkward for you, maybe I will go and tell them," Yinping retorted coldly.

"Ping—" Finally, Wenzhen's eyes overflowed. "I know you hate me, but I am truly afraid. I fear that other people may find out about us, but I also hate myself for being so mean."

"All right." Yinping felt unable to brush her off. "I will help you with the tapes."

Wenzhen had been silent for quite some time before she lifted her head and said, "Won't you soon be leaving the country?" She laughed mournfully. "Please leave a memento for me. At least I will be able to tell myself that you don't hate me that much after all."

Yinping remained noncommittal. Her eyes followed Wenzhen as she opened the door and left.

The wedding had taken place in Tainan. The redbud and phoenix flowers had been in full bloom on every tree in every street throughout the entire town.

As Yinping stood there in a trance, Chunliang laughed boisterously: "Why are you standing here so absentmindedly? Did I play too well?" As she spoke, she gave Yinping a big and tight hug.

After the second half of the performance started, Yinping ran into Judy backstage. They spoke softly in the hallway. Judy asked, "In a little while, why don't you come dance with us?"

"No, as soon as the party is over, I will go home."

"She must have treated you very badly these last few weeks." Judy blinked at her. "In the past, if one of us had a performance scheduled, the other would live elsewhere for three weeks." They smiled at each other. When they heard the applause and voices clamoring for an encore, they walked over to the reception hall.

* * *

Sitting in the bus on her way home from the concert, Yinping discovered that the fog outside was whirled about as fiercely as the rain and fog in a typhoon. If only Chunliang were here. She always buried Yinping's hand in her pleasantly warm palms.

Chunliang liked holding Yinping's hands. Yinping in turn liked the feeling of being liked in that way.

"Can you guess what advantage there is to being left-handed?" Chunliang had once asked her when they were in the car.

"What, you can hit someone with both hands at once?"

"How could I be that silly!" Chunliang's right hand landed smack on Yinping's thigh. She did not even have time to scream before her left hand was once again tightly held.

"All right, what wonderful advantage could that be?" Yinping spoke softly in order to appease Chunliang.

"The advantage is," Chunliang shot her a quick glance, "that I can drive and hold your hand at the same time. Even if you learn to drive, you don't have that ability.

"Or else we can always walk. When we are old and incapable of driving. Just imagine, two old ladies walking hand in hand and singing a marching tune." They both laughed so hard they almost ran a red light.

Yinping had suddenly asked, "Do you think we will still be together then?" Chunliang did not respond, but neither did she let go of her hand.

Yinping pulled the bell before the second traffic light and got off the bus. Leisurely she stepped on the snow that was as powdery as cornstarch. She unlocked the door and stepped into her and Chunliang's place. When she entered the kitchen, she picked up the refrigerator magnets that Chunliang had brushed down in her hurry. They had collected these magnets on their various trips together: oil wells from Texas, the Old Faithful from Yellowstone. The one they liked best had been sent to them by Chunliang's sister from Washington, D.C. In between two cherry trees in full bloom hung the picture of her sister's twins: two four-month-old baby girls, one with a dimple on her right cheek, the other with one on her left, both smiling exactly like Chunliang. As she looked at this picture, Yinping was lost in thought. It was too bad that they could not give birth to a child that resembled both Chunliang and her so that when they both grew old, they could enjoy the pleasure of seeing themselves growing up in the child. She picked Brahms' violin sonata and turned on the CD player.

The sound of a car engine could be heard. Yinping couldn't help herself and opened the curtains. To her surprise, her eyes fell on the figure whom she had hoped for. She went into the kitchen to boil some water, keeping her ears attuned to the tinkling of Chunliang's keys.

"It's already over?" Yinping served two cups of fruit tea on the coffee table.

The cuckoo clock indicated that it was only a quarter after midnight. When she put down the teacups, Chunliang kissed her passionately. Yinping could feel the taste of wine in Chunliang's mouth.

"I missed you. So I pretended that I was tired."

"I should have stayed longer and kept you company." Yinping watched Chunliang as she blew the bits of fruit away and took a sip of the hot tea.

"It doesn't matter. I know you did not feel comfortable there."

"I should have stayed." Yinping did not know why she suddenly became contrary.

"Why? We can both do as we please."

"Yes, but that's an important aspect of your life, and I am quite unable to be a part of it."

"I don't know how to conduct experiments, do I?" Chunliang frowned.

Yinping let quite some time pass before she spoke again. "Don't you want to take your usual shower?"

It was unclear when the music had stopped. Yinping went over to the CD player and pushed the play button followed by the repeat button. This way she could have the idiotically infatuated Brahms blare all night!

"Is Brahms that appealing?" With the rocking chair, Chunliang tapped out a rhythm that deliberately did not accord with the music. Yinping felt dizzy.

The seventy-year old Clara Schumann, Robert Schuman's wife, with whom Brahms had been in love all his life, had written a letter to the fifty-six-year-old Brahms: "We played your Regenlied Sonata again and I was deeply moved by it. I wish that the last movement could accompany me in my journey from this world to the next." Yinping wondered whether Chunliang was able to understand such enduring love.

"Well, he insists on a kind of feeling in which I no longer dare believe." What was it that Yinping was trying to insist on in front of Chunliang?

After a long chilly silence she looked helplessly at Chunliang. "I am really tired. Can we go to bed now?"

Chunliang's voice was suddenly choking with emotion. "This is your home, you can do whatever you like. I just want you to know that even if there is no such thing as forever, I could not possibly not love you." She got up and moved toward Yinping. Yinping kept her eyes closed as tears streamed down her face onto her chest. "I always do my utmost to grapple with the incessant trivia and conflicts so that they won't destroy everything we cherish and enjoy." In English, Chunliang added: "You know I am fighter, don't you?"

"I know, but I have never been a fighter."

Chunliang laughed. Her long and slender forefinger gently rubbed Yinping's temple. "You don't have to be. If you'd stop being such a drag and preparing for a break-up, things will be just fine."

* * *

When Yinping woke up, she realized that it was already light outside. Chunliang lowered the blinds and yawned. "I want to sleep. And you? Don't you want to call into the lab and ask for a day off?"

Yinping looked at the watch beside the bed and shook her head. "I'll make some coffee. I'll come back earlier than usual and catch up on my sleep in the afternoon."

Before she left the bedroom, she turned her head to look at Chunliang, her fair-skinned body was all curled up in the middle of the flowery sheets. This time, once asleep, she would sleep for quite some time. Yinping told herself that when she would come home in the afternoon, Chunliang might very well still be lying in the same spot. As before, the sun filtered in through the shutters and fell on Chunliang's body, but this time, Yinping felt very relaxed. Chunliang would not vanish into thin air—Chunliang was gently and firmly materializing in her world, she would be there until Yinping came back, or most likely even a bit longer, until that day which would inevitably come some day.

# Critical Biographies

## CHEN RAN

Chen Ran was born in Beijing in 1962 into a family of intellectuals. At her mother's behest, she began to study music intensively in 1969 with a view toward becoming a musician. After her parents' divorce in 1979, she became caught up in the literary renaissance sweeping through China in the wake of the Cultural Revolution (1966–1976). During her preparations for the university entrance examinations, she began to read widely in traditional Chinese and nineteenth-century foreign works of fiction. At the age of twenty, she began publishing poems. After beginning her formal university studies in Chinese Literature in 1982, she immersed herself in reading modern poetry, literature, and philosophy, developing affinities for modernist writers such as Franz Kafka and Virginia Woolf.

In 1985, she wrote and published her first short story in a leading literary journal. After receiving a B.A. in Chinese literature in 1986, she worked as a university lecturer, as a newspaper reporter, and as an editor for the China Writers' Association Press. Her stories were gathered in collections published by major literary publishers from 1989 onward. In the early 1990s, she traveled to Australia, England, and Germany, lecturing on gender specificity, gender transcendence, and writing. In 1996, she published her first novel, *A Private Life* (*Siren shenghuo*). In 1997, her stories, the novel, and her essays were collected in *Select Works of Chen Ran* (*Chen Ran wenji*) accompanied by an admiring foreword by Wang Meng, a major modern writer and erstwhile Minister of Culture, and by a psychoanalytically oriented afterword by Dai Jinhua, the prominent feminist intellectual. Living a relatively reclusive life in Beijing, in addition to writing full time, she cultivates friendships, reads classical Chinese philosophy, religion, and medicine, pursues Western psychoanalysis and modernist philosophy, and maintains an interest in magic, myth, and the paranormal.

Although Chen's work had been favorably regarded from the outset, the story "A Toast to the Past" (*Yu wangshi ganbei*) established her reputation. Published in 1991, the story not only touched upon a number of controversial topics—divorce, extramarital sex, a young woman's serial sexual relations with father and son—but anticipated many of the hallmarks of Chen's style. Characterized by formal experimentation, "A Toast to the Past" and later stories combine both philosophical introspection with an intensely sensual lyricism of everyday detail. Occasionally admixing different narrational points of view, Chen's stories privilege first person female narrators. However, as some critics and Chen Ran herself have noted, biographical similarities between protagonists and the author notwithstanding, such a narrative strategy should not be interpreted in confessional (*si xiaoshuo*) or autobiographical (*zixu zhuan*) terms. Instead, Chen Ran's relentlessly exploratory fiction simply insists on the specificity of female experience as a site from which to explore the complexities of the modern individual psyche. Insofar as Chen's fiction moves effortlessly between locations in China and in other countries and insofar as her outlook is informed by Western psychology and Chinese philosophy, her protagonists embody the predicaments shared by educated denizens of the contemporary urban world.

With the notable exception of "Breaking Open" (*Pokai* 1995), the emotional tenor of many of Chen's stories is intensely melancholy. Struggling with aloneness and isolation, Chen's female protagonists do not find refuge in sexual relationships with men, in emotional relations with women, or in service to the state or to some other cause. "Breaking Open" not only represents a thematic departure from Chen's earlier, conflicted, and ambivalent stories on same-sex love but is more intensely self-reflexive and optimistic than most of her other fiction. Rather than mourning the loss of male father figures as in "A Toast to the Past," "Breaking Open" maps a future predicated on female intimacy grounded in close mother-daughter bonds. Accordingly, in China, the story was heralded as a manifesto for women, a characterization with which Chen herself concurred. At a moment of rapid social change, the story was understood not so much as an advocacy of lesbianism than as a viable alternative to the common narratives of (married) love and (single) loneliness.

While not opposed to being characterized either as an "avant-garde writer" (*xianfeng zuojia*) or "a writer of marginal psychological states" (*bianyuan xinli zuojia*), Chen herself self-consciously claims a place beyond any literary fashions and "isms." However, her self-proclaimed marginality notwithstanding, in the wake of the breakdown of the grand narratives of social commitment in the 1990s, her unrelenting dissection of the contemporary self has struck a chord with the reading public and major cultural critics alike. In as far as Chen does not belong to any identifiable literary circle, some critics have commended her integrity and seriousness of purpose in the face of other authors' pursuit of money and fame. Furthermore, rather than dismissing Chen's probing of the hidden recesses of the (female) mind as "narrow" and "trivial," as had been the case with intensely lyrical writings by earlier women writers such as Lu Yin and Zhang Ailing, Chen's writings have been read as a redemptive form of resistance to the totalizing obsession with China's national salvation. While occasionally pronounced "feminist," Chen's work, for all its emphasis on the female experience, has not been primarily regarded as that of a "woman writer," but as a literary embodiment of the intense sense of dislocation among an entire generation of educated men and women.

Chen Ran. *Chen Ran wenji.* 4 vols. Yangzhou: Jiangsu wenyi, 1997.

———. "Sunshine Between the Lips." In *Chairman Mao Would Not Be Amused: Fiction from Today's China*, edited by Howard Goldblatt and translated by Shelley Wing Chan, 112–129. New York: Grove Press, 1995.

Larson, Wendy. "Women and the Discourse of Desire in Postrevolutionary China: The Awkward Postmodernism of Chen Ran." *Boundary 2* 24, no. 3 (fall 1997): 201–223.

## CHEN XUE

Chen Xue was born in Taiwan in 1970. She graduated with a B.A. in Chinese Literature from Chung-yang University located outside of Taipei. After graduation she held a variety of odd jobs. At one point, she worked in her family's watch factory in Tai-chung. In 1994, after circulating in manuscript form for a number of years, the short story "In Search of the Lost Wings of the Angels" won one of Taiwan's most coveted literary prizes, the best short story award of the *China Times*. As in the case of other writers, the prize launched her career. In 1995, Crown Publishers, a major commercial house, issued "Lost Wings" and three other stories under the provocative title *The Book of Evil Women* (*E'nü shu*). The collection *Dream Journeys 1994* was published in 1996 and *Falling in Love with the Jazz Girl* (*Aishang jueshiyue nü'hai* 1997) a year later. With the support of the National Foundation of Culture and the Arts, Chen completed her first novel in 1999, *The Bewitching Girl* (*E'mo de nü'er*). A chronicle of a young woman's recovery from sexual abuse, the novel received attention through its serialization in the literary supplement of the *Taiwan Daily*.

Written in a plain and intimate style, Chen's fiction has consistently broached new thematic ground, especially in the domain of sexuality. Provocatively titled, *The Book of Evil Women* was among the first sustained Chinese explorations of sex between women. Hovering between irreducible facts and emotionally charged hallucinations, the stories sought to reimagine the female artist, female sexuality, and the Chinese family. Finely attuned to the undercurrents of sexual desire, *Dream Journeys 1994* explored complicated triangular relationships, including intimacy between brother and sister, older men and young women, and so forth. While some of her short fiction was loosely autobiographical, the main theme of her novel *The Bewitching Girl*, the psychological recalibration of a young woman who was sexually abused by her father, is not. As Chen notes in her postface, haunted by public intimations that she was incapable of writing genuine fiction and plagued by severe insomnia and despair, she began to read widely in the psychological literature. At the same time, as the thematics unexpectedly began to take shape, she gathered stories over e-mail from women in Taiwan and abroad. The resulting novel alternates between two first-person narratives, one an account of the twenty therapy sessions written from the point of view of the female therapist, the other twenty excerpts of the diary the young woman keeps in between the weekly encounters. As the novel ends on a note of optimism, it rewrites the seemingly obligatory death scenario so vividly represented in Qiu Miaojin's diaristic novels, *The Crocodile's Diary* (1994) and *Testament from Montmartre* (1996).

Amid a commercial appetite for lurid sex and a social conservatism, Chen's fiction defies both. Unlike some of her contemporaries, Chen is not given to literary experiments; instead, in a deceptively simple language, she seeks to get at the complicated emotional truths informing the lives of her female and male protagonists. At the same time, her willingness to write on sexual taboos has upset some critics. One of the judges on the *China Times* 1994 prize panels threatened to resign if Chen's story was awarded first prize. As a compromise solution, the daily awarded the prize but did not print the story. Similarly, *The Book of Evil Women* was shrink-wrapped and appointed with the kind of warning labels usually reserved for pornography, if the bookstores displayed it at all. However, despite—and, in some cases, perhaps because of—the notoriety, her work has gained her a following among critics and general readers alike.

Chen Xue. *E'nü shu* [The Book of Evil Women]. Taipei: Huangguan, 1995.

———. *Mengyou 1994* [Dream Journeys 1994]. Taipei: Yuanliu, 1996.

———. *Aishang jueshiyue nü'hai* [Falling in Love with the Jazz Girl]. Taipei: 1997.

———. *E'mo de nü'er* [The Bewitching Girl]. Taipei: Lianhe wenxue, 1999.

———. "Searching for the Lost Wings of the Angels," translated by Fran Martin. *Positions* 7 (1999), 51–69.

Ding Naifei. "Feichang tiejin yinfu yu enü—ruhe yuedu *Jin Ping Mei* (1695) he *E'nü shu* (1995)." *Zhongwai wenxue* 303 (1997), 48–67.

Martin, Fran."Hybrid Citations: Chen Xue's Queer Tactics." *Positions* 7 (1999), 70–94.

## HE AN

Born in 1964, He An grew up in Taipei. In her education, He pursued two passions, Chinese literature and childhood education. After obtaining a B.A. in Chinese literature from National Taiwan University, the premier institution of its kind, she pursued an M.A. in the same field. At the same time, she worked as an editor for children's books for a Taiwanese publishing house. Together with her husband and her two sons, He lived in the United States from 1990 through 1998. In 1996, she received an M.A. in education from Harvard University. After their return to Taiwan, she and her family settled in the southern part of Taiwan. Her current professional pursuits include translation work for an educational publishing company, educational outreach in primary schools, and private piano lessons for children. Having previously written and published children's stories, He is working on her first book of short fiction. Her fiction focuses on the diverse experiences of Taiwanese women during the period from 1920–1990. In particular, her writing seeks to record how her female protagonists cope with the rapid and often male-centered changes in their social, political, and cultural environments. The stories explore the means by which the characters manage to hold on to personal, interpersonal, or spiritual ideals despite societal pressures to the contrary.

He submitted the current story "Andante" in response to a public call for submissions. In order to encourage younger and unpublished authors to step forward, *Funü xinzhi*, the monthly publication of the Awakening Foundation, Taiwan's first and largest feminist organization, agreed to publicize a call for entries for the current anthology. Two submissions, including He's, were sent to the care of *Nüshudian* (Fembooks). He's story was significant for two reasons. First, hers was a love story between two Chinese women set outside China. Resorting to a foreign setting to imagine new romantic possibilities has a tradition among Chinese writers. For instance, the Republican era writer Lu Yin situated desirable, but unconventional, romantic denouements abroad. In He's story, the United States serves as a similarly ideal setting for unconventional love. To some degree, such targeted use of a Western location can be understood as part of a common Chinese practice of alternately invoking the United States or Europe as positive models for change or as a negative paragon of vice.

Second, as He's story was submitted in manuscript form, it was likely that the English-language publication would precede the potential appearance of the Chinese original. Such precedence of translation is not unprecedented in the domain of Chinese women's writing. For example, Yang Buwei's (1890–1981) autobiography appeared in English in 1947 before it came out in Chinese in 1967. Such reversal of customary publication practices raises interesting questions with regard to the global circulation of literature. Authors and editors of such translated texts run the risk of being accused of pandering to Western audiences, as they appear to construct a China that has no currency within Chinese-speaking cultural contexts. However, for all its differences, He's story resonates with other work in this anthology. At the same time, for all the dangers implicit in such preemptive translation, such literary texts might also circumvent particular literary, social, or political constraints in their original environments. Thus, translation might not only add to the body of literary work available in the target language but eventually expand the boundaries of Chinese literature.

He's choice of a foreign setting or of a translation as a first publication does not necessarily result from the social conservatism of Taiwan. Instead, it may be a function of the autobiographical imperative to which all women's writing, regardless of genre, is subjected, in Taiwan as elsewhere. Writers such as Chen Xue, Hong Ling, or Qiu Miaojin are presumed to write about their autobiographical experience, an assumption often reinforced by the choice of first-person narrative, by lyrical narrative forms such as diaries and letters, or by revelatory prefaces and afterwords. Autobiography seems to guarantee authenticity and veracity, thereby underscoring the perception that women writers record rather than create. Since in real life, He is the married mother of two sons, her fiction militates against restrictively biographical reading habits. English-language publication circumvents some of the unnecessary biographical scrutiny to which her life would be subject upon Chinese-language publication. Thus, He's narrative highlights the importance of the imaginative dimension in women's fiction.

## HONG LING

Hong Ling was born in 1971 in Taiwan. After a brief stint at National Taiwan University, she graduated with an M.A. in English from the University of Sussex in 1997. Her first publication was a creative translation-cum-adaptation of Jean Genet's *Diary of a Thief* (1994). Extraordinarily prolific and prodigious, Hong has since published numerous collections of stories, which run the gamut from *manga*, science fiction, cyberpunk, to vampire stories. Furthermore, as a highly visible proponent of a self-identified queer literary movement, she has coedited special issues and literary supplements of various Taiwanese newspapers and magazines, participated in numerous symposia organized by scholarly journals such as *Comparative Literature* (*Zhongwai wenxue*), by prominent Taiwanese scholars specializing in feminist and queer theory, and by new research centers such as the Center for the Study of Sexuality and Difference. She currently lives in Taiwan as a professional writer.

Hybridity best characterizes Hong Ling's work. From the beginning of the twentieth century, Chinese culture has adapted Japanese, European, and American linguistic, literary, and cultural elements. Many modern Chinese words, for example, were adopted from modern Japanese renderings of European terms. The syntactic structure of modern Chinese has been profoundly transformed by European languages. In its playful exuberance, Hong's writing not only includes English sentences and words but self-consciously stretches the limits of the Chinese language. At the end of the nineteenth century, Chinese writers adopted the genre of science fiction to imagine an alternate "China." Carrying on the tradition of recent generations of science fiction writers in Hong Kong and Taiwan, Hong imagines not a different political world, but seeks to deconstruct the pretensions of "human nature."

Perhaps emblematic of a generation who came of age during the rise of the Internet, Hong's work does not take essences for granted. Instead, it draws on various cultural registers—highbrow, lowbrow, literary, nonliterary, Japanese, European, American, and Chinese—to imagine an alternate world of empowered rebels. Situated at the confluence of Japanese *manga* culture, American pop music, the European literary tradition, and postmodern theory, Hong's fiction charts a fantastic terrain in order to challenge dominant discourses of gender and sexuality. In as far as science has come to be the bedrock of the biology and commonsense, science fiction provides an ideal medium with which to imagine alternate realities. In some cases, Hong parodies the authority of science by adopting its rhetorical apparatus—prefaces, epigraphs, abstracts, reams of footnotes, extended bibliographies—to tell stories of fantastic creatures. In other instances, she mixes science fiction with other popular genres such as crime, romance, and the perennially appealing knight-errant tradition to right the wrongs of a patriarchal society. Straddling Greek and Indian myth as well as the world of video arcades and computer games, Hong's fiction admixes past and future in a surreal present of simultaneity.

Hong's fiction often revels in a tongue-in-cheek exultation over the sheer inventiveness of it all. Yet while Hong's stories may celebrate the disappearance of the real, they also register a profound terror over the implosion of all categories of perception. In their insistent examination of impending states of annihilation, Hong's literary explorations, including "Fever," bespeak a profound sense of cultural displacement and alienation, which is, as some would have it, symptomatic of the postmodern predicament of having had to renounce all grand narratives without being able to resign oneself to the piecemeal state of being that such renunciation seems to entail. Despite its apocalyptic sensibility, Hong's story "Fever" also brings to life a strange new creature, a Chinese feminist vampire. The story vividly illustrates the spirited promiscuity of cultural categories in a globalized world.

Hong Ling. *Yiduan xixue gui liezhuan* [The Model Biographies of Deviant Vampires]. Taipei: Huangguan, 1995.

———. *Zhijie yishou* [Dismembered Creatures]. Taipei: Yuanliu, 1995.

———. *Mori qianmei yu* [The Rain of Roses in the Final Days]. Taipei: Yuanliu, 1996.

Liu Yangya. "Guaitai yinyang bian: Yang Zhao, Qi Dawei, Cheng Yingshu yu Hong Ling xiaoshuo li nan bian nüxingren xiangxiang." *Zhongwai wenxue* 312 (1998), 11–30.

## LIANG HANYI

Liang Hanyi was born in 1959 and grew up in Taiwan. Raised in a devoutly Buddhist family, she graduated from the Foreign Language Department of National Taiwan University. Her impulse for writing grew out of her participation in relief work in Vietnam and Cambodia. Widely read in European literature, most notably Greek mythology, she has also written about her travels in Europe and the Sichuan province in southwestern China. Her first collection of fiction appeared in 1989. Since then, she has published several collections of short stories, essays, and most recently a historical novel, *The Song of Infinity* (*Wuya ge* 1999). In 1989, one of her novellas was a runner-up for the *United Literature* (*Lianhe wenxue*) novella prize; in 1996, one of her short stories won the short fiction prize of the *Gate to Liberation* (*Pumen*) magazine. Since the late 1990s, she has been living in the mountainous outskirts of Taipei. In this state of contemplative reclusion, she devotes her time to writing and to Buddhist spiritual practices.

Liang's oeuvre falls into three broad categories. First, some of her fiction is experimental in nature, incorporating surreal and fantastic elements. Second, other stories take place outside the customary constraints of time and space, presenting historical, philosophical, political, and religious issues in the guise of dark parables or fairy tales with a view toward probing the spiritual essence of the world. Third, other fiction seeks to infuse contemporary literary forms with a serious exploration of Buddhist doctrine and practice. Given her range of styles and concerns, it is perhaps not surprising that Liang's works have attracted attention from prominent and vastly different figures in Taiwanese society. At the outset of Liang's career, Li Ang, the Taiwanese writer who came to prominence through her pointed portrayal of sexual relations in both urban and rural Taiwan, commended Liang's short fiction for its generic versatility, its narrative mastery and its linguistic inventiveness. More recently, the internationally known Taiwanese Buddhist master and scholar Shengyan lauded Liang's novel *Song of Infinity* for its ability to combine literary excellence and factual accuracy with the explication of Buddhist teachings.

In her novel *The Song of Infinity*, Liang offers a different solution for the tensions between innocence, purity, and sexual desire adumbrated in "Lips." As Liang notes in the preface, she had been struggling with how to reconcile the demands of Buddhist renunciation with the demands on the life of a layperson. After experiencing a momentary suspension of these conflicting impulses in an enlightenment experience in Sichuan, she proceeded to expand upon what had been a recurrent theme in her short fiction. In the resulting novel, she traces the careers of the two founding figures of Korean Huayan Buddhism, one of whom, Master Yuanxiao (Korean: Wenhyo, 617–686), had become notorious after he broke his vows of celibacy by falling in love with an ailing princess. In Liang's novel, Yuanxiao's decision to become erotically and emotionally involved is presented as the moment of profoundest spiritual realization. Furthermore, Yuanxiao makes his decision in full knowledge of the adverse social consequence. Thus where "Lips" signals an impasse between innocence, desire, and self-realization, *Song of Infinity* offers a reconciliation.

Liang Hanyi. *Heiye li buduan chouzhang gouchi* [The Dog Teeth That Ceaselessly Grew in the Dark Night]. Taipei: Lianhe wenxue, 1991.

———. *Nianqing de yige si* [Death at a Young Age]. Taipei: Huangguan, 1992.

———. *Jiang mingzi xie yu shui shang* [Writing One's Name on Water]. Taipei: Huangguan, 1995.

———. *Wuya ge* [The Song of Infinity] Taipei: Jiuge, 1999.

## WANG ANYI

Wang Anyi was born into a writer's family in 1954 in Nanjing. Wang grew up in Shanghai. During the Cultural Revolution (1966–1976) she was sent down to impoverished northern Anhui province, where she joined a local performing arts troupe as a cellist. The hardship and loneliness of her time in the countryside provided the impetus for becoming a writer. She returned to Shanghai in 1978, where she published her first short story and began working as an editor for a children's magazine. She won her first national literary prizes in 1983 and 1985. In 1983, together with her mother Ru Zhijuan, a writer who had come to prominence in the late 1950s, she spent five months at the Iowa International Writing workshop, prompting her to "write on China" after her return. In 1986/1987, three novellas on the taboo subject of extramarital sex brought her public fame and notoriety. Since then, she has remained at the forefront of literary innovation. While critics find fault with certain aspects of individual works, they also agree that Wang is not only one of the best modern writers in the language but has the potential to produce a definitive masterpiece. She resides in Shanghai, writing full time.

Unlike some writers who tend to focus on a narrow set of themes, Wang has boldly explored new literary terrain, and continues to expand the scope of Chinese fiction. Her work falls into several stages: in the late 1970s and early 1980s, her stories are more concerned with the psychic interior of her characters than with external plot. An example is her collection of stories *Gentle Rain* (*Yu shashasha* 1981). Subsequently, her stories begin to examine social issues; for instance, the novella *Baotown* (*Xiaobaozhuang* 1984) analyzes the ethical codes of a village in the context of actual and mythological history. In 1986/1987, Wang published three novellas on the theme of "love," which portray sex as a beautiful force in itself rather than as an allegorical device designed to expose social ills. In "Brothers" (1989), Wang harkened back to the introspective emotional exploration of her earlier work.

The 1990s have seen a marked change in the narrative styles and range in her work. Increasingly self-reflexive, her works not only find alternative ways to explore the individual's relation to history but begin to situate the People's Republic in relation to other Chinese communities. Critics agree that *Story of an Uncle* (*Shushu de gushi* 1990) represents a turning point. Introducing a sense of melancholia into her oeuvre, it also becomes a metanalysis of its own story about the collaboration of modern male Chinese intellectuals with the cultural apparatus to create literary myths of self-deception. Freed from the confines of realism, she has ventured into the artistic construction of surrealistic histories as in the novels *Paternal Myth—Grieving over the Pacific Ocean* (*Shangxin Taipingyan* 1992) and *Maternal Myth—Reality and Fiction* (*Jishi yu xugou* 1993), one of which imaginatively traces her father's migration from Singapore to the PRC and the other her maternal family's life in Hangzhou. Set in Shanghai, *Song of Eternal Regret* (*Changhen ge* 1995) chronicles the life and murder of legendary beauty Wang Qiyao, blending metaphorical and concrete description in its subtle and nuanced evocation of historical change. *Song of Eternal Regret* was one of four winners of the Mao Dun Prize for Literature in 2000, one of the most prestigious literary prizes in the PRC.


Wang Anyi. *Wang Anyi xiaoshuo xuan* [Selected Stories by Wang Anyi]. Beijing: Zhongguo wenxue, 1999.

———. *Lapse of Time*. San Francisco: China Books & Periodicals, 1988.

———. *Love in a Small Town*, translated by Eva Hung. Hong Kong: Chinese University of Hong Kong, 1988.

———. *Baotown*, translated by Martha Avery. London: Viking, 1989.

———. *Love on a Barren Mountain*, translated by Eva Hung. Hong Kong: Chinese University of Hong Kong, 1991.

———. *Brocade Valley*, translated by Bonnie S. McDougall and Chen Maiping. New York: New Directions, 1992.

Wang Zheng. "Three Interviews: Wang Anyi, Zhu Lin, Dai Qing." In *Gender Politics in Modern China*, edited by Tani E. Barlow, 159–208. Durham, N.C.: Duke University Press, 1993. (The interviews were conducted in 1988, roughly the time when Wang was writing "Brothers.")

Chen Sihe, ed. "Dangdai wenxue chuangzuo zhong qing yu zhong." (Roundtable discussion with Wang Anyi on her latest works.) *Dangdai zuojia pinglun*, 1993:5, 14–23.

Zhang Jingyuan. "Jiegou shenhua: ping Wang Anyi de 'Dixiong men.' " *Dangdai zuojia pinglun* 1992:2, 31–34.

Zhong Xueping. "Sisterhood? Representations of Women's Relationships in Two Contemporary Chinese Texts." In *Gender and Sexuality in Twentieth-Century Chinese Literature and Society*, edited by Tonglin Lü, 157–173. Albany: SUNY Press, 1993.

Chen, Helen H. "Gender, Subjectivity, Sexuality: Defining a Subversive Discourse in Wang Anyi's Four Tales of Sexual Transgression." In *China in a Poly-*

*centric World*, edited by Yingjin Zhang, 90–109. Stanford, Calif.: Stanford University Press, 1998.

Tang Xiaobing. "Melancholy against the Grain: Approaching Postmodernity in Wang Anyi's Tales of Sorrow." *Boundary 2* 24 (1997), 177–199.

## WONG BIKWAN (HUANG BIYUN)

Wong Bikwan was born in 1961 in Hong Kong. She spent her middle school years in Taiwan. She graduated from the Chinese University of Hong Kong in 1984 with a B.A. in journalism and communication. Thereafter, she worked as a television scriptwriter for a year. In 1987, she studied French and French literature in Paris. In 1988, she spent five months in New York. Between 1989 and 1995, she worked as a journalist in Chinese and English broadcast and print media in Hong Kong, covering—among other things—Vietnam and Cambodia. She also worked as a legislative assistant and managed a boutique. In 1995, she graduated from Hong Kong University with an M.A. thesis on the criminality of women in Hong Kong films, a topic and a medium that finds echoes in her fiction. After getting a law degree, she worked in a law firm in London. More recently, she has been writing fiction full time, at times with the support of the Hong Kong Arts Development Council, a cultural agency founded by the British in the last decade of their rule over Hong Kong.

She is the author of many books, some of which have won prestigious awards. Her oeuvre includes essays, travel writings, several short story collections, and a novel. Her short story collection *Tenderness and Violence* (*Wenrou yu baolie*, 1994) won the Hong Kong Urban Council Biannual Literary Award for Fiction. Her essay collection *We Are Quite Okay Like This* (*Women ruci hen hao* 1996) won the Hong Kong Urban Council Biannual Literary Award for Prose. In 1997, Wong won the Hong Kong Arts Development Council Prize for Young Writers. In 1999, her novel *The Picture of Female Virtue* (*Lienü tu* 1999) was recognized by the influential Taiwanese daily *China Times*. Infused with the sort of sex and crime scenes commonly found in popular fiction as well as given to experiments with narrative structure, Wong's work embodies something of the freewheeling admixture of highbrow and lowbrow elements characteristic of recent Hong Kong cultural production.

In many ways, Wong's fiction expands on the thematic and aesthetic concerns of the generation of Hong Kong writers preceding her. Wong's short fiction chronicles the progress of protagonists who, by historical accident or by personal choice, migrate between countries, cultures, and continents. Ranging from Asian immigrant experiences in European and American contexts to explorations of the impact of the political, social, and economic transformations in China, Hong Kong, and Southeast Asia since the 1960, Wong's short stories charter the dismantling of leftist political ideals as well as the disillusionment with love and sex among her peripatetic characters. Wong's dispassionate, journalistic recording of her characters' experiences with disappointment, dislocation, disease, domestic violence, mental illness, death, murder, and suicide allows for virtually no emotional interiority, the frequent use of first person perspective notwithstanding. Her protagonists are frequently enigmatic ciphers to themselves and to others, incapable of redeeming their wrenching experiences in political, personal, or philosophical terms. Drawing on reportage, oral history, and film, her novel *The Picture of Female Virtue* expands the chronological frame to encompass the entire twentieth century. The novel interweaves second and first person points of view to create a panoramic tableau of three generations of Hong Kong working women from the fall of the Qing dynasty to the handover of Hong Kong in 1997.

Wong's short fiction reflects the fragmentation of identity and moral meaning through various narrative strategies. Focusing on appalling graphic details of violence and sex, her short fiction presents such incidents in a matter-of-fact fashion, without investing either the violence or the sex with a grander ideological purpose. As if to underline the precarious randomness of existence, protagonists with identical names crop up in many of Wong's short stories, without necessarily being identical characters. For instance, Yip Saisai, the narrator of "She's a Young Woman and So Am I," reappears as a young woman in Paris who commits suicide and as a haplessly infatuated woman who wants to be disabused of love through sex. In her novel *The Picture of Female Virtue*, Wong synthesizes the fragmentation of unified self with the flexible kinship structure of the extended family to offer something of an antidote to the sense of pervasive restlessness and rootlessness among her young protagonists. Through its generational narrative structure of chapters on grandmothers, mothers, and self, the novel endows the contemporary female protagonist with multiple female ancestors, thereby emphasizing, even more insistently than "She's a Young Woman and So Am I" does, on the importance of memory to salvage female intimacy from disappearing between the cracks of self-hatred, indifference, sexual games, and social imperatives.

Wong Bikwan. *Qihou* [Thereafter]. Hong Kong: Cosmos, 1991.

———. *Wenrou yu baolie* [Tenderness and Violence]. Hong Kong: Cosmos, 1994.

———. *Women ruci hen hao* [We Are Quite Okay Like This]. Hong Kong: Qingwen, 1996.

———. *Lienü tu* [The Picture of Female Virtue]. Taipei: Titan, 1999.

———. "Losing the City." In *Hong Kong Collage: Contemporary Stories and Writing*, edited and translated by Martha P. Y. Cheung, 205–232. Hong Kong: Oxford University Press, 1998.

———. "She's a Woman, I'm a Woman." In *A Place of One's Own: Stories of Self in China, Taiwan, Hong Kong and Singapore*, edited by Kwok-kan Tam et al. and translated by Yuet May Ching, 287–300. Hong Kong and New York: Oxford University Press, 1999.

———. "Plenty and Sorrow." Translated by Janice Wickeri. *Renditions* 47 and 48 (1997), 53–72.

Joseph S. M. Lau. "The 'Little Woman' as Exorcist: Notes on the Fiction of Huang Biyun." *Journal of Modern Literature in Chinese* 2:2 (1999), 149–163.

## ZHANG MEI

Zhang Mei was born in Guangzhou (Canton) in 1958. After graduating from high school, she was sent down to the countryside as an "educated youth" for three years, a period she would come to recall in some of her prose essays and in her award-winning short story "Coach Wen." For seven years she worked as a factory worker. After stints as a basketball player and as a newspaper reporter respectively, she began her ten-year career as a professional editor for the Guangdong People's Press in 1985. In 1995, she became the editor-in-chief for a literary journal, *Guangzhou Literature*. Her own essays and stories began to be published in 1988. She published a collection of her essays entitled *A Thousand Aspects of Human Life* (*Baimian rensheng* 1993) as well as several collections of short stories, including *Who Can Understand Such a Feeling?* (*Cizhong fengqing shei jie* 1995) and *Perspective on Love after Wine* (*Jiuhou de aiqing guan* 1995). More recently, she published a novel, *The End of Enthusiasm* (*Posui de jiqing* 1999).

Most fiction of the women writers who emerged in the 1980s has focused on urban settings. However, Zhang Mei's fiction is unusual in two regards. First, she evinces a profound interest in all material aspects of her home city, the southern seaport of Guangzhou, a city of rising affluence and increasing ideological separation from the central government in Beijing. As can be observed in "A Record," her stories pay close attention to local material culture. They describe the particulars of teahouses and the snacks they offer, restaurants and the special dishes they are known for, flowers markets, boutiques and the designer clothes they sell, the buildings and streets of the old part of the city, nightclubs, bowling alleys, and saunas. Presenting local habits among older and younger generations, her stories feature the local both as a form of resistance to the pervasive commodification of everyone's life and as an enticement to embrace that very consumer culture with a vengeance.

Second, unlike other writers who evoke the nitty-gritty of urban life to highlight their protagonists' resolve to stay above the commercial or the sexual fray, Zhang's figures take advantage of all their city has to offer. Under the glittering lights of the commercial and cosmopolitan city, Zhang depicts young girls from all walks of life—including peasant girls coming to Guangzhou to seek a better life but ending up as hotel waitresses, parasitic women kept by wealthy married men, and trendy women intellectuals. Most of her protagonists are without regular jobs, living either off the wealth of their parents or off rich men. Without passing any overt moral judgments, Zhang describes their light-hearted frivolity, their lack of purpose in life, their promiscuous sexual relationships, and their bitingly cunning love games. Her characters represent a new generation of youth, freed from political and ideological indoctrination and living intensely on the edge in pursuit of money and pleasure. Yet their relentless pursuit of entertainment often results in ennui and boredom.

Zhang's novel *The End of Enthusiasm* combines a novella first published in 1989 and a much longer sequel written between 1997 and 1999. The novel explores the shift in mood and priorities among the generation who came of age in the 1980s. In a witty and unsentimental fashion, Zhang dissects the delusions and the dreams of a group of quirky educated youth in Guangzhou. With touches of wry humor as well as the imagistic hyperbole of an unobtrusive surrealism, Zhang portrays the inner workings of the utopian fervor of the 1980s and coolly explores the materialism of the 1990s. Informed by loving attention to material and historical detail, Zhang's narrative is also restlessly philosophical as it seeks to fathom the surfaces and the recesses of her protagonists' actions. To an even greater extent than "A Record," *The End of Enthusiasm* refuses the consolation of simple narratives of progress that posit absolute difference or similarity between different time periods.

Zhang Mei. *Baimian rensheng* [A Thousand Aspects of Human Life]. 1993.

———. *Cizhong fengqing shei jie* [Who Can Understand Such a Feeling?]. Shanghai: Shanghai renmin, 1995.

———. *Jiuhou de aiqing guan* [Perspective on Love after Wine]. Beijing: Zuojia, 1995.

———. *Posui de jiqing* [The End of Enthusiasm]. Shanghai: Shanghai wenyi, 1999.

Ji Hong. "Dushi yuwang zhong de fuchen yu zhengzha: Zhang Mei xiaoshuo zhong nüxing xingxiang de xinling tezheng." *Nanfang wentan* 1998: 62, 35–37.

# Glossary

| | |
|---|---|
| aiqing | 愛情 |
| Anchee Min | 閔安琪 |
| biantai | 變態 |
| bianyuan xinli wenxue | 邊緣心理文學 |
| boli quan | 玻璃圈 |
| buluojia | 不落家 |
| cai | 才 |
| Chen Kaige | 陳凱歌 |
| Chen Ran | 陳染 |
| Chen Shuibian | 陳水扁 |
| Chen Xue | 陳雪 |
| Chen Xuezhao | 陳學昭 |
| Chen Yu-shih | 陳幼石 |
| *Congjun riji* | 從軍日記 |
| Dai Jinhua | 戴錦華 |
| *Daoyu bianyuan* | 島嶼邊緣 |
| de | 德 |
| diandao | 顛倒 |
| Ding Ling | 丁玲 |

| | |
|---|---|
| *E'mo de nü'er* | 惡魔的女兒 |
| *E'nü shu* | 惡女書 |
| *E'yu riji* | 鱷魚日記 |
| *Fangzhou* | 方舟 |
| funü | 婦女 |
| Funü xinzhi | 婦女新知 |
| Funü rexian | 婦女熱線 |
| He An | 何安 |
| Hong Ling | 洪凌 |
| jiebai zimei | 結拜姊妹 |
| jiemei hui | 姊妹會 |
| jiemei qing | 姊妹情 |
| ku'er | 酷兒 |
| laotong | 老同 |
| Li Ang | 李昂 |
| Li Yinhe | 李銀河 |
| Li Xiaojiang | 李小江 |
| lian'ai | 戀愛 |
| Liang Hanyi | 梁寒衣 |
| liangmu | 良母 |
| *Lienütu* | 烈女圖 |
| Lin Yutang | 林語堂 |
| Ling Shuhua | 凌淑華 |
| Lu Jingqing | 陸晶清 |
| Lu Yin | 盧隱 |
| Lü Xiulian | 呂秀蓮 |
| manga | 漫畫 |
| Mao Zedong | 毛澤東 |
| *Mengmate yishu* | 蒙瑪特遺書 |
| *Mengyou 1994* | 夢遊1994 |
| nannan nünü | 男男女女 |
| nü | 女 |

| | |
|---|---|
| *Nüpantu* | 女叛徒 |
| nüpengyou | 女朋友 |
| nüquan | 女權 |
| nüren | 女人 |
| nüshu | 女書 |
| Nüshudian | 女書店 |
| nütongzhi | 女同志 |
| Nüwudian | 女巫店 |
| nüxing | 女性 |
| *Posui de jiqing* | 破碎的激情 |
| Qiu Jin | 秋瑾 |
| qipao | 旗袍 |
| quanzi | 圈子 |
| ren | 人 |
| Ru Zhijuan | 茹志鵑 |
| Shengyan | 聖嚴 |
| Shi Pingmei | 石評梅 |
| si xiaoshuo | 私小說 |
| Sun Yat-sen | 孫逸仙 |
| tongxing'ai | 同性愛 |
| tongxing'ai de jiufen | 同性愛的糾紛 |
| tongxing lian | 同性戀 |
| tongzhi | 同志 |
| Wang Anyi | 王安憶 |
| Wang Meng | 王蒙 |
| *Women zhi jian* | 我們之間 |
| Wong Bikwan | 黃碧雲 |
| *Wuya ge* | 無涯歌 |
| xianfeng wenxue | 先鋒文學 |
| xianfeng zuojia | 先鋒作家 |
| xianqi | 賢妻 |
| Xie Bingying | 謝冰瑩 |

| | |
|---|---|
| *Xin congjun riji* | 新從軍日記 |
| Xing/bie yanjiu shi | 性/別研究室 |
| xinxin renlei | 新新人類 |
| Yang Buwei | 楊步偉 |
| *Yu wangshi ganbei* | 與往事干杯 |
| Yuanxiao | 元曉 |
| Zhang Ailing | 張愛玲 |
| Zhang Jie | 張潔 |
| Zhang Mei | 張梅 |
| Zhang Yimou | 張藝謀 |
| *Zhongwai wenxue* | 中外文學 |
| zishunü | 自梳女 |
| zixu zhuan | 自敘傳 |

# ABOUT THE EDITOR

**Patricia Sieber** is assistant professor in the Department of East Asian Languages and Literatures at The Ohio State University. She was born in Japan and raised in Switzerland. After studying Chinese, Japanese, and German literature in Tokyo, Zurich, and Beijing, she received her M.A. and Ph.D. in Chinese from the University of California at Berkeley. For several years, she served as editor and translator for *Connexions: An International Women's Quarterly*. Her own literary essays and short stories in Chinese, English, and German have appeared in various literary journals and anthologies. Her scholarly articles on Chinese canon formation, literary thought, and East/West cultural relations have been published in *Contemporary Buddhism*, *Graven Images*, *Journal of Chinese Religions*, *Modern Chinese Literature and Culture*, and *Monumenta Serica*. She is completing a study on the reception of early Chinese drama entitled *Theaters of Desire: The Circulation of Yuan Drama, 1300–2000*.